Wide Acclaim

"I was bowled over by the exceptional quality of the writing and research in this book. No dreary recounting of the same old Resurrection Mary and Devil Baby of Hull House stories, but a skillful blend of history, legend, and contemporary stories . . . An absolutely first-rate book!"
Invisible Ink

". . .a must-read for anyone with an interest in the paranormal."
Midwest Book Review

"Bielski serves up a fascinating sampling of 160 years of her hometown's phantoms, ably dovetailing eerie legends with in-depth anecdotal testimony, parapsychological insights, and clear-eyed cultural-historical interpretation. Bielski's perceptiveness about collective memory and popular consciousness balance intellectual investigation with an open-minded respect for folklore and an obvious delight in her subject."
Cricket in the Corner

". . . the most up-to-date information on haunted sites in Chicago . . . filled with interesting stories."
FATE Magazine

". . . this book's a must read this October . . . Within the book, there is great reading—whether one believes or disbelieves . . . the first such book in Chicago history that combines historical fact with stories told by generations of residents."
The Star

Also seen and recommended in:
Chicago Tribune, *Chicago Sun-Times*, *New City*, Lerner Newspapers, Pioneer Press Newspapers, *Near North News*, *Inside*, *Barfly*, *Southwest News Herald*, *The New World*, *Berwyn/Cicero Life*, *Chicago Flame*, *Loyola Phoenix*, and more!

As seen on national TV:

- A&E's *More Haunted Houses*
- The History Channel's *Haunted Chicago*
- The Travel Channel's *Haunted History of Chicago*

As seen on Chicagoland TV:

- *Fox Thing In the Morning*
- *Fox Morning News*
- ABC News
- WLS's *Chicagoing* with Bill Campbell
- *Ben Loves Chicago*
- *Northside Neighbors*
- CLTV's *Front and Center*

As heard on Chicagoland radio:

- WGN's *The Sunday Papers* with Rick Kogan
- WGN's *The Joe Show*
- WGN with Spike O'Dell
- WBBM-FM's *Eddie & JoBo Morning Show*
- AM-1000's *Steve Cochran Morning Show*

. . . and dozens of other radio stations in the U.S. and Canada

Recommended online:

- www.historyuniverse.com
- www.prairieghosts.com
- www.ufostoday.com

Chicago Haunts

GHOSTLORE OF THE WINDY CITY

By Ursula Bielski

Revised Edition

4650 North Rockwell Street • Chicago, IL 60625
www.lakeclaremont.com

Chicago Haunts: Ghostlore of the Windy City
by Ursula Bielski

Published October, 1998 by:

LAKE CLAREMONT PRESS

4650 N. Rockwell St.
Chicago, IL 60625
773/583-7800; lcp@lakeclaremont.com
www.lakeclaremont.com

Publisher's Cataloging-in-Publication
(Provided by Quality Books, Inc.)

Bielski, Ursula.
 Chicago haunts : ghostlore of the Windy City / by
 Ursula Bielski. — Rev. ed.
  p. cm.
 Includes bibliographical references and index.
 Preassigned LCCN: 98-85569
 ISBN: 0-9642426-9-9

  1. Ghosts—Illinois—Chicago. 2. Haunted houses—
 Illinois—Chicago. 3. Chicago (Ill.)—Folklore. 4.
 Chicago (Ill.)—History. 5. Urban folklore—Illinois—
 Chicago. I. Title

 BF1472.U6B54 1998   133.1'09773'11
                                 QBI98-1151

 05 04 03   10 9 8

**Printed in the United States of America by United Graphics—
an employee-owned company based in Mattoon, Illinois.**

For Adalbert S. Bielski—
a charismatic father, but a very dull ghost

Fr. Jerry Kroeger, of Summit's St. Joseph Parish, stands at the gate of Resurrection Cemetery believed to bear traces of the ghostly handprint of a former parishoner, Resurrection Mary. (*Courtesy of Frank Andrejasich*)

FOREWORD

All religions, including Christianity, believe in some supernatural beings and experiences. Hence, beliefs in God, a Trinity, the lasting effects of Adam and Eve: damnation, redemption, and eternal life.

There is still another level of the supernatural when it comes into contact with our earthly lives—prophecies, visions, being touched by an angel, miracles, healings.

Most of the above are beyond our ordinary experience. But at some time each of us has had a paranatural experience. We are fascinated by this, and it is no wonder that we are strongly attracted to these happenings: they are unique personal experiences with another world. They are deeply personal and we crave to tell others about them.

It is often hard to tell which of the paranatural experiences are truly real and what their significance might be. But at least they indicate that we are more than flesh and blood ourselves. We want to believe in something beyond. Proceed with some care in believing too quickly such stories. But, on the other hand, don't be overly skeptical. Some things might have truly happened here, and they may have deep personal implications.

—Fr. Jerry Kroeger, O.P., Ph.D.

CONTENTS

III. A SECRET SOCIETY
The Lure and Lore of Archer Avenue
73

IV. AN ACTIVE SPIRITUAL LIFE
Lasting Legends and Fresh Miracles in Chicago's Religious Communities

V. AN INEXPLICABLE RESIDUE
The Endurance of Tragedy

VI. THE DEVIL HIMSELF
Chicagoans Encounter the Evil One

VII. THE INEVITABLE HAUNTED HOUSES

VIII. BELIEVING IN MARY WORTH
Myth, Imagination, and Chicago's School Spirits

IX. A DIFFERENT WORLD
The Native American Connection

X. A MILITARY PRESENCE

ACKNOWLEDGMENTS

When I began research for the first edition of this volume, I envisioned the finished product as a comprehensive catalog of Chicago ghostlore. Foolish me. I soon realized that for each Chicagoan there is at least a full handful of ghosts, and that consequently, my goal of documenting them all would turn out to be a pipe dream indeed. Nonetheless, I have done my best in the time allotted (and then some) to assemble those tales most evident in Chicago's collective self-awareness. Even in this, however, I have been only partially successful.

Some lone experiences have forced themselves onto these pages by merit of their own intrigue. The reader should take them as evidence of the common nature of paranormal experience: as tastes of that unfathomable stew of personal experience which I have been privileged to sample and which, I must add, was offered to me with equal hospitality by both strangers and friends.

As impossible to realize as my goal of collecting all of Chicago's haunting legends is the hope for acknowledgment of all of those who did share their stories towards the reconstruction of the legends included in this volume. Many of the stories upon which the manuscript relied were related to me over the course of years and taken, not from carefully-kept files, but from a vivid and carefully-maintained personal memory. To those nameless individuals who provided these, I am bound in gratitude, as I am to those who made such generous contributions of their time, knowledge, and experiences specifically toward the construction of this book. Though the latter are numerous, they each deserve acknowledgment:

For historical background and other information, I am grateful to a wide variety of individuals and institutions, notably, John Aranza for information on the history of Bridgeport; Janet Nelson of the Vliet Center for her knowledge of Lake Bluff history; Larry Rawn for his expertise regarding the real Mary Worth; David Cowan and Ken Little for their knowledge of Chicago Fire Department history; Norma Johnson of the Lemont Historical

Society; Hull House Director Mary Johnson; David K. Nelson of the Eastland Museum; The Chicago Public and Newberry Libraries; Janice Griffin, curator for the Prairie Avenue House Museum; Joseph Pinter of the Peabody Estate at Mayslake; Virginia H. Barber of the Mitchell Indian Museum; the staff of the Justice Public Library; Peter Manti of the Great Lakes Chapter of the American Society of Dowsers; John Van Drie of the Seven Continents Dowsers; Leah Axelrod and Paul Melichar for their information on Fort Sheridan; and Jim Stonecipher for his knowledge, both temporal and spiritual, of Great Lakes Naval Training Center. Further, I owe great debts to the Forest Preserve Districts of Cook and DuPage Counties; the administrations of both the independent and Archdiocesan cemeteries I've explored; the staffs of the schools and churches I've visited; and the owners and employees of the following establishments: Chet's Melody Lounge (especially the Prusinski family); the Country House Restaurant; the Red Lion Pub (especially Colin Cordwell); and St. Andrews Inn; all of whom greeted me with patience and hospitality as did the many families who welcomed me into their homes to share experiences of their own haunted houses, especially the Dunhams of Waukegan and Jack and Diane Bochar of Geneva.

Particularly generous with their own memories and second-hand stories were Marilyn Gulan, Diane Cozzi, Matt Allaway, Mary Lou Cullen, Kathy Cullen Rondonella, Frances Brousil, Frances Kathrein, Michelle Yarka, Matt Hucke and Henry Erbach (the latter of whom has furnished me with enough tales to fill a second volume). A special note of thanks and affection is extended to all those children who inadvertently introduced me to their richly spiritual worlds.

In the world of psi research, my thanks are both locally and internationally routed. Here in Illinois, I owe much of my knowledge of practical research to the investigators with whom I have worked over the past ten years, notably James and Shelley Houran (who introduced me to the science of parapsychology), Timothy Harte, Mike Hollinshead, Michael Komen, and Jonathan Murphy. I also thank Tom and Steve McNichols of the Chicago-based Office of Paranormal Investigations, the Ghost Research Society and Dale Kaczmarek, and folklorist Richard Crowe for sharing with me their knowledge and field notes.

In developing my interest in professional parapsychology, I continue to rely on the support and interest of a number of individuals, among them Stephen Braude, Nancy Zingrone, and Carlos Alvarado (all of the Parapsychological Association). I also remember the kindness of Andrew Greeley, who offered so much early encouragement of my own experimental work, of Greg Singleton, who first recognized and fostered my interest in the study of belief and culture. To Dennis O'Neill I extend my deepest gratitude for encouraging me to complete the first edition, despite my misgivings.

On a very practical level, I owe much of the success of the first edition of this volume to the faithful companionship of Jimmy Olson and Douglas Prine, and, especially, the indulgent accompaniment and encouragement of my brother, Adalbert, and my mother, Dolores, all of whom were pressed variously into service as drivers, photographers, and navigators.

Finally, I am delighted to offer every best wish to my former research assistant, David Wendell, who was of enormous assistance in my compilation of the first edition; and to Patrick Miller, for his kind concern for and attention to my own work, regardless of his own extensive obligations. I thank Tim Kocher for his striking cover designs which have received endless praise, and I am inexpressibly grateful for the patience and expertise of the many sharp eyes who lent their editorial assistance to both editions. Readers have well noted Matt Hucke's wonderful photography, and I thank him again now for sharing his work and for inadvertently reconnecting me with Michael Fassbender, who has been of tremendous inspiration to me throughout this revision. I am grateful to Michael for his own insights and stories, and for introducing me to Fr. Julian vonDuerbeck, who provided much-needed insight into a variety of topics. To my publisher, Sharon Woodhouse, I offer my most heartfelt thanks for her inexhaustible patience, diplomacy and rationality, as I do to all those family members and friends who showed so much faith in the worth of this project, especially my mother, who taught me by example to respect and explore the beliefs and cultures of others, and David Cowan, who echoes those teachings every day in his own support of my efforts. May this result of all our work and hope bring much joy and satisfaction.

In the first edition of *Chicago Haunts*, I stated that I had made every effort to treat the accounts entrusted to my care with the greatest reverence. Since its release, readers have overwhelmingly assured me of my success in this regard, and for this I am most humbly gratified. While collecting new accounts for this second edition, I have tried to maintain that respect and objectivity which I held so dear in preparing the first. It is my sincere hope that, with God's grace, I have succeeded.

—U.B.

PUBLISHER'S CREDITS

Cover design by Tim Kocher.

Cover photograph of Ona (Anna) Norkus on her First Communion Day courtesy of Frank Andrejasich. (See story on pp. 18-20.)

Interior design by Sharon Woodhouse.

Interior photographs by Ursula Bielski, Matt Hucke, David Cowan, Dale Kaczmarek, Dave Black, and Jason Nhyte.

Editing by Bruce Clorfene.

Proofreading by Brandon Zamora, John Keagy, Sandie Woodhouse, Susan McNulty, Sheryl Woodhouse-Keese, and Brian Keese.

Indexing by Sharon Woodhouse, John Keagy, Brandon Zamora, Susan McNulty, and Ken Woodhouse.

Layout by Sharon Woodhouse, Susan McNulty, and Sandie Woodhouse.

The text of *Chicago Haunts* was set in Times New Roman with the headers in Viner Hand ITC. The cover was set in Times New Roman with the headers in Compacta.

NOTICE

Between the finite limitations of the five senses
and the endless yearnings of man for the beyond
the people hold to the humdrum bidding of work
and food while reaching out when it comes their way
for lights beyond the prisms of the five senses,
for keepsakes lasting beyond any hunger or death.

This reaching is alive.

—CARL SANDBURG
"The People, Yes"

From up here, nothing . . . can be seen; some say,
'It's down there,' and we can only believe them.
. . . At night, putting your ear to the ground,
you can sometimes hear a door slam.

—ITALO CALVINO
"Invisible Cities"

One of the more intense photographs of anomalous mist at
Bachelors Grove Cemetery, quite possibly one of the Chicago
area's most haunted sites. *(Photo taken by Dave Black of
Supernatural Occurrence Studies)*

Introduction

The love I bear for the city of my birth
is inspired not by a material greatness . . .
but by a spirituality of whose existence
the world at large is still ignorant . . . .

—HOBART C. CHATFIELD TAYLOR
Chicago socialite, author, and patron of the fine arts, 1925.

---

*I*N RECENT YEARS, INCREASING NUMBERS OF HISTORIANS HAVE ALERTED US TO THE IMPORTANCE OF COLLECTIVE MEMORY AND POPULAR CONSCIOUSNESS, WHETHER EXPRESSED in the diverse ways of interpreting solid facts and figures or in the form of myths, legends, and stories. What Chicagoans have remembered collectively about their past goes a long way in telling us about their present.

This project grew out of two passions of mine. The first is the study of the paranormal—what has come to be known in research circles as *psi* phenomena. And, what better place to pursue such a passion than in the hometown of Resurrection Mary, to name the most famous of the Chicago region's haunts. Yet, while this volume is a collection of just such ghostlore, Chicago's elite status in the world of *psi* research has not relied on its ghosts alone.

Twenty-five years ago, the city once stereotyped as utterly grounded in workaday reality had emerged as a kind of Mecca for the spiritually-minded. As Brad Steiger observed in his 1976 volume, *Psychic City: Chicago: Doorway to Another Dimension:* "Regardless of where I may have set out on my psychic safaris, I always ended up in Chicago." Indeed, nurturing dozens of pre-New Age organizations, fertile crops of self-styled psychics, and countless alternative church leaders, the city found its name linked, for better or for worse, to oddities like the locally-grown but internationally-renowned *Fate* magazine and the antics of hard-drinking native Ted Serios, who, in the early 1960s, immortalized himself through his apparent ability to imprint mental images on rolls of ordinary black and white film. As the guardian of such wonders, Chicago served effectively, if briefly, as a motherly magnet for thousands of would-be followers, many of them young people spiritually-orphaned amidst the social and moral upheaval of the 1960s.

A magnet, indeed.

According to some, the pull of the city was quite literal. Frederic DeArehaga, of the Sabaean Religious Order of Amn, observed that "according to ancient texts, what makes a city sacred is not so much its religious influences as a peculiar magnetism which seems to be centered in the place." In the case of Chicago, he stated quite esoterically that "the North Magnetic Pole passes right through the city. This . . . is a peculiarity of zero degrees, which also passes through Cairo . . . ."

Also in the 1970s, at what would be the height of his popularity, Joseph DeLouise, doubtless the city's most famous psychic, expressed his fascination with the apparently heightened ability of Chicagoans to develop *psi* (or psychic) abilities. In DeLouise's opinion, it was most likely the combination of "clouds, the altitude of the city, the wake in the lake, which make the chemistry and the vibrations just right."

Anton LaVey, in his popular work, *The Devil's Notebook*, credited some of Chicago's paranormal openness to its architecture; namely, the trapezoidal John Hancock building, the shape of which has been traditionally known as a gateway for arcane forces. Curiously, LaVey himself was born on the site of the Hancock building, a seemingly innocent bundle of joy who would go on to found the Church of Satan.

Whatever the reason, Chicago's hospitality towards psychic phenomena in the 1970s was nothing new. In fact, for more than 100 years the city had hosted far more than its share of inexplicable events, meeting them with that mingling of respect and curiosity typical of its pious but progressive history.

It is the safekeeping of these events, as remembered by both their witnesses and inheritors, that enlivens my second passion. The place of these stories in the popular memory of Chicagoans, from before the turn of the century to the present, is my other, and admittedly greater, concern here. This book is a study of community and identity, of urban history, as well as of a larger popular consciousness. It speaks to the notion of neighborhood, both in the geographic and the conceptual sense, but it also engages larger issues of the human experience. Taken together, these accounts address the concerns of many modern historians of gender, class, religion, and ethnicity.

The model for my efforts can be found in the writings of another Chicagoan—Jane Addams. When, sometime around the turn of the century, Addams' Hull House was besieged by hundreds of women in search of the so-called "Devil Baby," the progressive leader faced the phenomenon head-on. Refusing to dismiss the tale as meaningless, Addams peered into the myth with a keenly interpretive eye and revealed it as a complex expression of cultural concerns. To a significant extent, it was Addams' careful investigation of the Devil Baby story that inspired my own methodology, one comprised almost exclusively of respectful and patient conversation. I hope that the reader will find hints of her sympathy and insight in my own accounts.

Finally, as an historian, I have been particularly aware of the diversity of sources upon which a book of this nature must inevitably draw. Whenever possible, I have noted that an account relies on professional parapsychology or the findings of so-called ghosthunters; on the testimonies of curiosity-seekers or of unwitting witnesses; on newspaper articles or formal interviews. In doing this, I have refrained from ranking the authority or credibility of my sources. Rather, I have tried to give readers a notion of how Chicago's haunting legends have come down to us through all of these channels, and to suggest that, in a study such as this, all sources are really equal.

◆

I

ROAD TRIPPING
Phantom Hitchers and "Hungry" Fences

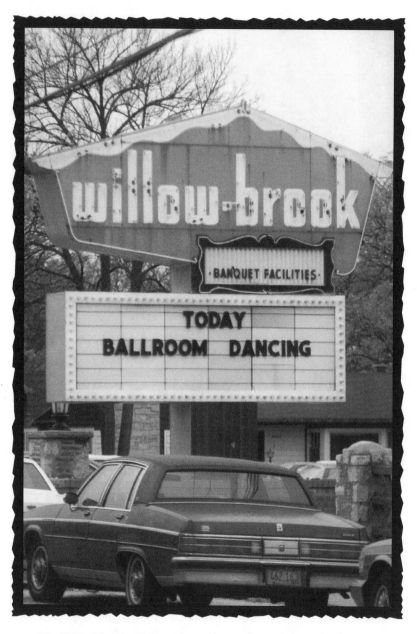

The Willowbrook Ballroom: haunt of haunts. (*Photo by D. Cowan*)

FOR CHICAGO DRIVERS, THEY SEEM TO WAIT EVERYWHERE: THE CITY'S SPRAWLING CEMETERIES. IN DAYLIGHT, THEY ARE THEMSELVES LITTLE CHICAGOS: URBAN BREWS of architecture and art, landscape planning and limestone, names great and small. Though they are, like the neighborhoods that have grown around them, crowded, jaded, and full of secrets, the burial grounds alone can, at sundown, close their gates against care. Then, between the light and life of urban intersections, the darkness blots out the distinguishing elements of monuments and trees, chapels and mausoleums, transforming them into vast stretches of blackness that run, like coastlines, along the roads.

The effect of these stretches on Chicago's collective psyche has perhaps been most evident in the city's ghostlore, notably in the accounts of phantom hitchhikers like St. Casimir's sneering stranger; a wayfaring young girl tied in legend to Evergreen Cemetery; an enchanting flapper seen on the road near Jewish Waldheim; and, of course, the compelling free spirit known as Resurrection Mary. Far from being indigenous to Chicago, phantom hitchhikers are, in fact, an international phenomenon, typically encountered along such stretches, and overwhelmingly by lone and disoriented travelers.

Married by local legend to the cemeteries or highways whose names they bear, these visions are best explained by their very contexts, but not necessarily as many might claim by the alleged death or burial of their earthly forms at these sites. Rather, it is more plausible that the hypnogogic effect of night travel along cemeteries may encourage the unwitting creation of phantoms to inhabit these curiously and suddenly empty lengths of highway. Startled by the contrast of darkened cemetery road with the brightness of city street, and reminded, to boot, of their own mortality, lonely drivers may have searched for the reassurance of life, and, finding none, ingeniously and albeit unconsciously created some of their own. Gently eased into the mildest of hypnotic states by the relaxing effect of blacked-out cemetery landscapes, drivers may find themselves expressing and easing feelings of disorientation or uncertainty by literally giving form to their fears. For example, a driver hits a person in the road, only to find that the "person" has disappeared on contact. Theoretically, the driver's fear of such an accident actually forces it to occur, if only in the imagination.

In a 1997 article for *Fortean Times*, a magazine devoted to the probing of baffling occurrences and related theories, Sean Tudor offered some further insights into the phenomenon of the so-called "road ghost" as he explored the phenomenon of the infamous phantom of Blue Bell Hill in Kent, England. As Tudor states at the outset of his analysis, "(I)t is to folklore that we must turn to gain any kind of understanding of what is really happening" in such cases. Indeed,

> (t)he same PHH (Phantom Hitch-Hiker) script is repeated around the country and indeed the world with an identical pattern of events being reported over and again by reliable witnesses: of figures rushing into the paths of vehicles, and/or of disappearing hitch-hikers . . . which suggests that it has less to do with any specific case and its accepted explanation . . . but, at the same time, more than purely 'human' factors such as imagination and hoaxing.

In the case of Blue Bell Hill, one of the spirit's manifestations is that of a young woman in white, who has been known to appear in front of moving cars, staring calmly at their drivers while she is run over. Like Chicago researchers who trace their Resurrection Mary to any of a half dozen 1920s and '30s accident victims fitting her description, residents of the Kent region almost always tie their road ghost to a 1965 incident in which three young women were killed in a car crash on Blue Bell Hill just hours before one of the girls was to be married. Highly skeptical of the connection, Tudor has his own theories concerning the "haunting" of Blue Bell Hill. One of the most intriguing is the relation of the story to that of the Cailleach of pre-Celtic mythology, an Earth mother or goddess who variously took the form of an old crone or a beautiful young woman. The Cailleach is known as a guardian of a particular sacred place, and it was Tudor's awareness of this mythology that allowed him to notice in his own research that great increases in road ghost sightings, including those at Blue Bell Hill, have occurred during times of environmental upheaval, especially during the construction of roads and highways. With this in mind, Chicagoans might ponder the fact that the building of Archer Avenue over an old Indian road, not to mention the digging of the Illinois and Michigan Canal which it preceded, seemed to coincide with the beginning of that road's extraordinary supernatural history, a history which features one of the most famous of all road ghosts, the blonde-haired and beautiful young woman known as Resurrection Mary.

Another of Tudor's compelling explanations for the sighting of road ghosts goes back to the subjectivity of the witness himself. Referring to Carl Jung's *Man and His Symbols*, Tudor reminds us of Jung's theory that the unconscious typically manifests itself in the dream state, and often symbolically, as a figure of a woman or man. The specific form taken depends on the gender of the dreamer. A woman's unconscious, then, usually resembles a man (animus); accordingly, in the dreams of men, the unconscious generally takes the shape of a woman or (anima). In light of the fact that the overwhelming majority of sightings of young and beautiful phantom females, including those of Resurrection Mary, are reported by men, it is almost easy to believe that the dreamlike state imposed by lonely late-night driving could be the culprit in so many of these cases.

Whether such an explanation for ghosts seen outside of cemeteries is a valid one is uncertain. If it is legitimate, however, it has certainly caused no great damage, either physically or psychologically. In recent decades however, a more problematic effect has been attributed to similar circumstances: our local phenomenon of the so-called "Hungry Fence."

According to unofficial accounts, the theory of the Hungry Fence was first forwarded by investigators puzzled over an inordinate number of traffic accidents at south suburban Mount Olivet Cemetery. Eventually, a consensus emerged that the headstones inside the cemetery were placed at such an angle that they reflected car headlights in rapid succession, creating an almost strobe-like effect. The result was a dangerously hypnotic influence on drivers, which may have caused more than one motorist to veer into the cemetery fence. Once applied exclusively to Mount Olivet Cemetery, the Hungry Fence theory has recently been extended to explain multiple traffic accidents at cemeteries like Bohemian National on Chicago's northwest side. There, the Hungry Fence phenomenon is reportedly created by headlights reflecting off the fence's wrought-iron bars.

Of course, it is impossible to blame either the reflection of high beams or the distracted reflections of weary drivers themselves for the images and the accidents reported on Chicago's cemetery roads. Nonetheless, however legitimate any of the proposed theories may prove, one certainty will surely remain: Chicago's cemeteries will continue to attract those who pass them by day and by night psychologically, if not physically.

♦

Chasing Our Favorite Phantom

SQUEEZING A LIFE OUT OF RESURRECTION MARY

(A)s I move though this river of young-woman life
I feel a wonder about where it is all going,
So many with a peach bloom of young years on them
And laughter of red lips and memories in their eyes
Of dances the night before.

—CARL SANDBURG
"Working Girls" from *Chicago Poems*

*C*het's Melody Lounge sits bravely across the road from Resurrection Cemetery, drawing in a steady stream of locals to shoot the breeze and have a few. For years, regulars pretty much disregarded the Bloody Mary eternally perched at the end of the bar and "The Ballad of Resurrection Mary" listed among the selections on the jukebox, just as they have adopted Chicago's most famous phantom as an accepted fact of life. Certainly, the impact of phantom-related folklore on Southwest-side culture, well captured in Kenan Heise's novel, *Resurrection Mary: A Ghost Story*, is indeed most obvious in the cultural prominence of this persistent legend.

But while Mary's legendary spirit has contented itself with the haunting of a tiny stretch of Archer Avenue in the village of south suburban Justice, the image of this elusive personality has thumbed itself into the hearts and history of all Chicago. From the old-timers' still-vibrant accounts of her to the young Chicago rap artists singing about "Rez Mary," this specter's appeal reaches every generation.

For more than 60 years, travelers along Archer Avenue have reported bizarre encounters with a single-minded young woman in a white dress and dancing shoes who seems as real as can be until she proves herself decidedly otherwise. Mary first appeared to unsuspecting Southwest-side drivers in 1939, when late-night revelers complained to the police that a woman had tried to jump on the running boards of their automobiles. A few years earlier, in 1936, the late Jerry Palus spent a whirlwind evening dancing with a lovely young woman at the now-demolished Liberty Grove Hall and Ballroom, on Chicago's Southwest Side. When Palus offered her a ride home, she accepted, directing him down Archer Avenue. In front of the gates of Resurrection Cemetery, the young woman said she had to leave him, and that he could not follow her. She left the car, disappearing at the main gate.

As dance hall encounters with this phantom partner multiplied, they seemed to move southwest, centering on the old Oh Henry Ballroom (now the Willowbrook Ballroom) on Archer Avenue, just south of the cemetery. It was here that Mary forged her reputation.

Time and again, young men would meet the moody young woman, share dances with her, and later describe her as "cold," both physically and emotionally. After these dances, the girl would accept rides home, giving vague directions to her escorts to drive north along Archer Avenue. As their cars passed the gates of Resurrection Cemetery, the girl would most often simply disappear from the car. At still other times, drivers have watched a woman in a flowing white dress walk along the roadside and then vanish, as if switched off like a light. In some of the most harrowing incidents of all, the woman has been struck while bolting in front of moving cars. Bleeding in the road after these crashes, she has been known to dematerialize before or during approaches by would-be rescuers.

Other Archer Avenue drivers have been surprised by a beautiful young woman who will simply open the car door and climb in, directing the driver to proceed up Archer Avenue, where she disappears in the usual way, at the cemetery gates. Some bewildered drivers have even watched as she runs right through the locked gates and into the darkness beyond.

Some researchers speculate that this mystery woman heads for one grave among thousands at the 475-acre burial ground known as Resurrection Cemetery: site number 9819, section MM, that of a young Polish woman, Mary Bregovy. Records indicate that Bregovy was killed in a car accident in 1934, allegedly on her way home from a dance at the Oh Henry. But attempts to link this Mary with the Resurrection legend have yielded far less than satisfactory results.

The evidence begins with the following report, which appeared in the *Chicago Tribune* on March 11, 1934:

> Girl Killed in Crash. Miss Marie [sic] Bregovy, 21 years old, 4611 S. Damen Avenue, was killed last night when the auto in which she was riding cracked up at [word missing] Street and Wacker Drive. John Reiker, 23, of 15 N. Knight Street, Park Ridge, suffered a possible skull fracture and is in the county hospital. John Thoel, 25, 5216 S. Loomis, driver of the car, and Miss Virginia Rozanski, 22, of 4849 S. Lincoln [now Wolcott] were shaken up and scratched. The scene of the accident is known to police as a danger spot. Thoel told police he did not see the El substructure.

A close friend of Bregovy's discovered in the mid-1980s that her late girlfriend's name was being connected with the famous phantom. She went on to describe the fateful day of the accident to an understandably eager reporter. According to Vern Rutkowski, who was interviewed by the *Southtown Economist* on January 22, 1984, the two young women had planned to go shopping on March 10th, 1934, near 47th Street and Ashland Avenue. The girls accepted a ride to the popular shopping district from two young men who Bregovy had met, but Rutkowski became irritated with the young men, who she remembered as "wild boys." The girls left the men's car while still some distance from their destination, but not before Bregovy made a date for that night. On their way home, Bregovy criticized Rutkowski's unfriendliness and her disapproval of Bregovy's taste in men.

Nonetheless, Rutkowski continued to express her dislike of their latest escorts and cautioned Bregovy about her plans for that night. Determined to keep her date, Bregovy left her girlfriend for the day and went home to 4611 S. Damen Avenue.

Rutkowski stayed home that Saturday night, and was awakened the next morning by her mother, who informed Rutkowski that Bregovy had been killed in a car accident in the Loop sometime during the evening. Bregovy's parents would learn that, although their daughter had been sitting in the back seat before the time of the accident, she was persuaded by her girlfriend to switch seats, since the latter was not getting along with the driver. Described by Rutkowski as an agreeable and personable young woman, Bregovy was happy to oblige. Because of that congeniality, she was thrown through the passenger window when their car struck one of the I-beams of the downtown elevated structure. Three days later, Mary's Polish and Czechoslovakian parents buried their daughter at Resurrection Cemetery.

Since Bregovy was killed in downtown Chicago, probably at Lake Street and Wacker Drive, it is highly doubtful that this Mary was on her way home from any Southwest-side ballroom and most definitely not on the road outside the legendary cemetery. This Mary, according to the records of the Satala Funeral Home from which Bregovy was buried, was a young factory worker who died in the ambulance on the way to Iroquois Hospital, then on North Wacker Drive.

According to Rutkowski, Bregovy loved to dance. But she also had short, dark hair, a far cry from the flaxen fantasy described through the years by Mary's various escorts. In addition, the late John Satala, the undertaker who prepared Bregovy's body, and once described Mary as "a hell of a nice girl," remembered that the eternal attire was, in fact, an orchid-colored dress, not a white one.

Old newspaper interviews with Satala suggest one obvious reason why Bregovy was pegged as the famous phantom, despite having the "wrong" hair color and style, the wrong clothes, and regardless of her dying in the wrong place. Nearly 50 years ago, a caretaker at Resurrection phoned Satala and told him about a "ghost" that had been walking the cemetery grounds. In the caretaker's opinion, the ghost was Bregovy's.

Ultimately, the musing of that one man may have been responsible for the permanent matching of the two Marys in local memory. Apparently, the social conditions of Bregovy's neighborhood were such that the pairing was instantly acceptable, the rumor was spread, and no one seemed to mind the dubious nature of the connection. Still, the transformation of the Bregovy ghost into a "vanishing hitchhiker" did not gain regional cultural prominence until much later. A general feeling exists that neighborhood old-timers knew of a phantom Bregovy long before the folklore of distant Archer Avenue popularized the story, presumably according to universal vanishing hitchhiker legends. It is probable that Mary's peers picked up adults' talk about the ghost of Bregovy in Resurrection Cemetery and began to elaborate upon the tale during their drives to and from the old Oh Henry Ballroom. Far more compelling is the connection solidified through the rigorous research of Frank Andrejasich of Summit, Illinois, which matches the legendary lady to a wholly different entity. In August 1994, Andrejasich's brother mailed him an article which mentioned the Southwest Side's most famous phantom. Already familiar with the story, Frank became swiftly smitten with the tale, finding that a number of his fellow parishioners at Summit's St. Joseph Catholic Church had more than a nodding acquaintance with the local legend.

In assembling his impressive dossier on the elusive Mary, Andrejasich accumulated many opinions on the phantom's earthly identity. Relying heavily on the recollections of his cousin, Mary Nagode, and the keen memory of John Poljack, Sr., a Slovenian emigrant, retired Prudential insurance manager and St. Joseph parishioner, Frank waded through a variety of first and second-hand accounts, newspaper articles, burial records and photographs. He was astounded by the prominence of the legend in local lore and fascinated by the ability of so many individuals, including a number of his fellow parishioners, to place Mary in their own experience.

One of these, Chester "Jake" Palus, turned out to be the younger brother of the now-famous Jerry Palus, who is supposed to have been Mary's first dance partner at the Liberty Grove Hall and Ballroom in Brighton Park in 1936. According to Jake, Jerry had been a passenger in his friend's car when the pair took "Mary" home that remarkable night, and she disappeared en route to the address she had given as her home. Though he recites the story with ease, Jake himself has no comment on his brother's tale, refusing to express either credulity or disbelief.

Claire and Mark Rudnicki—friends, neighbors, and former St. Joseph parishioners—told Andrejasich that Resurrection Mary could be traced to the 1940s, when a young Polish girl crashed near Resurrection Cemetery at around 1:20 a.m., after she took the family car to visit her boyfriend in Willow Springs. According to this version of the story, the girl was buried in a term grave at Resurrection. Appropriately, Andrejasich wonders why a couple that owned a car in the 1940s would need to bury their daughter in a term grave.

Adding to the explanations is another parishioner, Ray VanOrt, who tells how he and his bride-to-be were the first witnesses at the scene of an accident on Archer in 1936, when a black Model A sedan collided with a wide-bed farm truck at 1:30 a.m. According to VanOrt, of the two couples in the car, only one person survived, a girl who was badly hurt. Both men and another girl perished. Today, VanOrt is convinced that this was the accident that killed our would-be Resurrection Mary.

Still another parishioner, claims that the wayward wraith was, in life, Mary Miskowski of the southside Chicago neighborhood of Bridgeport. In this narrative, Miskowski was killed crossing the street in late October in the 1930s, on her way to a Halloween party.

After pondering the variety of accounts, combing early editions of the local papers, and checking with funeral directors and cemetery managers, Andrejasich came to believe that the ghost known as Resurrection Mary is the spiritual counterpart of the youngest of all the candidates: a 12-year-old girl named, surprisingly, Anna Norkus.

Born in Cicero, Illinois in 1914, Norkus was given the name of Ona, Lithuanian for Anne. In that era, it was not the custom to christen infants with two names. But after 1918, children were baptized with a Christian name and an historic name to further pride on their main country. As a young girl, Anna's devotion to the Blessed Mother led her to begin using the name Marija, Mary, as her middle name. By the time she neared her teenage years, Anna had grown into a vivacious girl. Blonde and slim, she loved to dance, and it was her relentless begging that convinced her father, August, Sr., to take her to a dancehall for her 13th birthday. On the evening of July 20, 1927, father and daughter set out from their Chicago home at 5421 S. Neva for the famous Oh Henry Ballroom, accompanied by August's friend, William Weisner, and Weisner's date. On their drive home, at approximately 1:30 a.m., the travelers passed Resurrection Cemetery via Archer Avenue, turning east on 71st Street and then north on Harlem to 67th Street. There, the car careened and dropped into an unseen, 25-foot-deep railroad cut.

Anna was killed instantly.

After the accident, her father, August Norkus was subject to devastating verbal abuse, even being told that Anna's death had been God's punishment for allowing the girl to go dancing at such a young age. In reality, the blame rested with the Chicago Streets Department, who had failed to post warning signs at the site of the cut. In fact, another death, that of Adam Levinsky, occurred at the same site the night after Anna's demise.

Between July 28th and September 29th, an inquest was held at Sobiesk's Mortuary in adjacent Argo. Heading up the five sessions was Deputy Coroner Dedrich, the case reviewed by six jurors. The *DesPlaines Valley News* carried the story of the inquest. Mary Nagode described the sad procession that left the Norkus home on a certain Friday morning.

First in line was Anna's older sister Sophie, followed by her older brother August, Jr. The pastor, altar boys, and a four-piece brass band preceded the casket, borne on a flatbed wagon with pallbearers on each side. Relatives and friends followed the grim parade for three blocks to the doors of St. Joseph's in Summit, where Anna had made her first communion only a year before. Between the band and the priest walked a terrified Mary Nagode, a friend of Anna's who had been pressed into service as a wreath-bearer. On summer vacation, Nagode was weeding on an asparagus farm in Willow Springs when she had a visitor. It was Gus Norkus, Anna's father or brother, asking her to participate in the funeral, since Mary had made her first communion with Anna and owned a white dress. When Mary returned home that evening, her mother informed her that she had accepted the request on her behalf. The girl was deeply dismayed at the proposition. Mrs. Nagode reminded her daughter that refusal of such a request would be a sin against Roman Catholic moral living, which dictates that one must attend to the burial of the dead.

Anna was scheduled for burial in one of three newly-purchased family lots at St. Casimir Cemetery, and it is here where Andrejasich found the "if" that may have led to an infamous afterlife for Anna as Resurrection Mary, or as Anna called herself, Marija.

Andrejasich discovered that at the time of Anna's death a man named Al Churas Jr., brother-in-law to Mary Nagode, lived across the road from the gates of Resurrection Cemetery, in a large brick bungalow that still stands today. Al's father was in charge of the gravediggers and was given the house to live in as part of his pay. In the mid-1920s, gravedigging was hard, manual labor, rewarded with low pay. Strikes were common. As Resurrection was one of the main Chicago cemeteries, the elder Churas was often sent to the cemeteries of striking gravediggers to secure the bodies of the unburied. Returning to Resurrection with a corpse in a wooden box, Churas' duty was to bury it temporarily until the strike ended and the body could be permanently interred in the proper lot. Because of poor coffin construction and the lack of refrigeration, a body could not be kept long, except in the ground. If the strike dragged on, identification at the time of relocation could be gruesomely difficult. Thus, reasons Andrejasich, if the workers at St. Casimir were striking on that July morning in 1927, it is quite possible that young Anna Norkus was silently whisked to a temporary interment at Resurrection, and that a rapid decomposition rendered her unidentifiable at the time of exhumation. The result? A mislaid corpse and a most restless eternity, if only one is willing to believe.

Those not quite convinced may be persuaded otherwise by a further bit of Frank's musing, this time connecting the otherworldly Anna to the sneering specter seen on the road outside of her alleged resting place.

The elder August Norkus followed his youngest child to St. Casimir 30 years after her death, a broken man besieged by alcohol and blamed to his grave for his daughter's demise. As Andrejasich reasons, it wouldn't take much else to make a ghost out of this ill-fated character. And yet, how much more there is (again, if only one believes in ghosts) if Anna was mistakenly buried away from her family.

For here, the stories merge, almost too easily. The resulting image is classically and completely appealing: Resurrection Marija combing the southwest suburbs for her kin, her father wandering the road outside her unknown destination, watching and waiting for his lost beloved. (See also "A Man in the Road," p.35)

Despite widespread belief in such scenarios and the untiring work of devoted researchers like Frank Andrejasich, specialists in modern folk tales have utterly disregarded local attempts to trace

Resurrection Mary to any earthly counterpart. Instead, many scholars explain Mary as merely a localized version of the widespread vanishing hitchhiker legends. These legends have passed from generation to generation throughout history, but the 20th-century versions always follow a strikingly similar pattern. A hitchhiker, usually a young woman, is either picked up along a dark road or met at a dance, from where she is given a ride home. In the latter situation, her would-be suitor may report having danced with the young woman, finding her somewhat cold. In both situations, she gives her escort vague directions to her house, but along the way she suddenly vanishes from the car. Sometimes, the driver will have procured her address and proceeds to the house to ask whether the girl has returned safely home. Upon his arrival, he is told that the girl, whom he recognizes in a photograph displayed in the home, was previously killed in a car accident on the road or near the dance hall where she met her unfortunate escort.

The Resurrection Mary stories bear an uncanny resemblance to these widespread tales. In fact, accounts of Mary by eyewitnesses have conformed to the universal model even more perfectly than do most second-hand legends. However, the existence of so many first-hand reports raises questions about the assertions that Mary is mere folklore.

Typical is the following incident: Many years ago, several young men, out for a night of dancing and drinking, met an aloof but gorgeous young woman, with whom they danced and tried to socialize. At the end of the evening, she asked for a ride home and squeezed into the front seat of the car with the driver and one of his friends. Sure enough, after directing the driver to head north along Archer Avenue, she vanished from the car at the cemetery gates. After some deliberation, the young men, having earlier coaxed the girl's address out of her, decided to drive to her home in Chicago's Back-of-the-Yards neighborhood and see if she had turned up all right. True to the classic tale, they were promptly informed that the girl was dead, having been killed in an automobile accident some time before. Weary but wiser, they resolved to forget the whole incident and go on their way.

Reports of Resurrection Mary increased significantly during renovations of the cemetery in the mid-1970s. It was also around this time that the phantom began to become more animated . . . and adventuresome.

In 1973, Mary is believed to have shown up at least twice in one month at a far Southwest-side dance club called Harlow's, 8058 S. Cicero Avenue, wearing a dress that looked like a faded wedding gown. A Harlow's manager described her as having "big spooly [sic] curls coming down from a high forehead. She was really pale, like she had powdered her face and body." Dancing alone in an off-the-wall fashion, she was as obvious as could be, yet, despite bouncers at the door who carded all guests, no one ever saw her come in or leave.

That same year, at Chet's Melody Lounge, an annoyed cab driver bounded in asking about his fare, a young blonde woman. The manager gave him the only answer he had: "A blonde woman never came in here."

A number of years later, a driver happened to be passing the cemetery when he glimpsed a young woman standing on the other side of the gates, clutching the bars. Worried that someone had been locked inside after closing, he hurried to report the incident to the local police, who hastened to rescue the reluctant prisoner. Upon their arrival, they found the cemetery deserted, but their inspection of the gates revealed a chilling spectacle: not only had two of the bars been pried apart, but the impressions of a pair of delicate hands remained, bearing witness to the feminine touch that had accomplished the task.

When cemetery management saw the state of the bars, they reportedly called in officials from the Archdiocese of Chicago, who allegedly removed the imprinted bars and whisked them away. Akin to stories of aliens in warehouses are local whisperings about the mysterious bars sitting today in some secret Archdiocesan storehouse. Not long after the removal of the damaged bars, embarrassed cemetery officials installed what they called "repaired" bars, insisting that the bent bars had been welded back to normal and not, as many asserted, replaced with new ones.

Still, some cemetery workers maintain that the bars were bent by a crew member's truck backing into the gate; the handprints were left by a worker's glove when he attempted to heat the bars with a blowtorch and bend them back into shape. In response to that claim, local believers say: Yes, the cemetery tried to blowtorch and restore the bars, to eradicate evidence of the spectral handprints, which witnesses continue to describe as the well-defined fingers of a frail female.

Whatever the claims, the tale's undeniable fascination lies in viewing the cemetery gates even to this day, as two strips of discolored metal remain in the exact spot which once bore the mysterious handprints. In fact, and there seems to be no reason to doubt the rumor, it is said that this part of the gate refuses to "take" either primer or paint. The result? An embarrassing but apparently ineradicable scar on the face of the cemetery and its management.

As if this carnival weren't enough for the cemetery to bear, it was also around this time that Mary began to experiment with new methods. Actually, folklorists have described a certain model of the phantom hitchhiker which is best termed the "spectral jaywalker," that is, the ghostly vision that walks or simply appears in front of a moving vehicle. One such story tells of a Justice police officer who called an ambulance after hitting a woman in a bloody white dress who was wandering the road in front of the cemetery. When the paramedics arrived on the scene, there was no trace of the distressed woman. According to some stories, the officer in question went on the nationally-syndicated television show, "That's Incredible!" and told of his experience. Before doing so, he was warned that he would be fired if he did. Notwithstanding the alleged threats, the officer told his story to network audiences and was at least by local accounts relieved of his duties.

After a bizarre decade that seemed to mark the climax of her restlessness, Mary was back to her old tricks. Yet she didn't seem quite her old self. In 1989, on a blustery January night, a cab driver picked up a desolate young woman outside the Old Willow Shopping Center. Despite the inclement weather, she wore a beautiful white party dress and patent leather dancing shoes. Climbing in the front seat, she made it clear that she needed to get home, motioning the driver up old Archer Avenue. But this time she behaved differently. She seemed confused, unable to give lucid answers to the cabby's polite questions. Finally, with all the clarity she could muster, the girl remarked, "The snow came early this year." Then, in front of a time-worn shack across the road from Resurrection, the disoriented passenger ordered, "Here!" disappearing without another sound.

Also in the late 1980s, two teen-aged boys were driving along Archer Avenue at Christmastime when they saw a strange woman dancing down the road outside the cemetery fence. They noted that other passers-by seemed totally unaware of her antics; in fact, they didn't seem to see her at all. The teens reported the bizarre scene to their parents, who at once related the famous tale of Resurrection Mary. Never having heard the story before, the boys must have questioned whether the off-the-wall vision they had seen was really the same as the legendary hitchhiker, whose aloof sophistication seemed wholly unbefitting the wacky wayfarer of their own experience.

What has happened to Mary in these last 25 years? A ghosthunter's classic summation would point to the disruption of the Bregovy grave during cemetery renovations. Investigators might theorize that this disruption could have caused Mary's apparent disorientation. Possibly. For, although the site of the grave was finally disclosed to the public after many years of secrecy, the plot turned out to be unmarked. Mary Bregovy's was a "term grave," a plot that was sold on 25-year terms during the '20s and '30s, in a section of Resurrection that was renovated during the '60s and '70s. It is therefore possible that the girl's family either did not repurchase the grave, resulting in the filling-in of the plot, or that they or the cemetery administration moved the grave to discourage the curious.

There is one other peculiarity worth noting. Resurrection Mary has traditionally been connected with the Oh Henry (Willowbrook) Ballroom, where she is alleged to have danced during her lifetime, and where she is guessed to have danced her last. Some accounts, however, specify that on the night of her death, Mary was at a dance for Christmas or even Advent, the Christian season preceding Christmas. The fact that so many Resurrection Mary encounters occur in December might seem to render this obscure lore somewhat more credible, although the timing would also undermine the connection to the Mary Bregovy who was killed on March 10th. Dealing only with conjecture about the behavior of ghosts, researchers continue to seek the Bregovy grave at Resurrection Cemetery in hopes of finding some end to a grueling but engaging search.

Whoever Resurrection Mary is, and whenever she may

materialize, the apparent changes in this legend's "personality" continue to present a nagging appeal to the folklorists who have denied that Mary has any psychic reality, and who have accordingly classified her with other bizarre by-products of the oral tradition.

With good reason. One "lost" haunting, which is supposed to have occurred in the late 19th century at St. James-Sag Cemetery at the southern end of Archer Avenue, curiously parallels the Resurrection Mary story. In fact, the two legends share a great number of specific elements, including the singular image of a woman in white waiting for a ride in front of a dance hall on Archer Avenue. (For details, see "A Secret Society," p.79.)

Ultimately, regardless of the temptation to give in to folkloric categorization of Mary, the primary difficulty remains: a good number of first-hand accounts of these encounters have been recorded. In the case of urban legends like that of the vanishing hitchhiker, the incidents are supposed to have occurred to "a friend of a friend" or someone's "boyfriend's mother's friend" and so on. If we accept the first-hand accounts of this hitchhiker at face value, the phenomenon of Resurrection Mary continues to challenge the most skeptical observers, and to lure the most hopeful believers to her stomping grounds.

Susan Stursberg was one of the latter who decided to try her luck at spotting the famed and filmy form. Her account is unique in this author's experience, and deserves retelling:

> I was out with a friend one night who had just bought a new car. I had not been to Archer Avenue and was itching to go, so we decided to take a drive. First we stopped to see her boyfriend who was playing in a band at a nearby suburban bar. We said hi, told him we were going for a drive but did not tell him where. So we proceeded to Chet's Melody Lounge, talked to the regulars, played "The Ballad of Resurrection Mary" on the jukebox and some pool. We left in a couple of hours when 2 a.m. rolled around, drove to the cemetery gates, parked and peered in, seeing the repaired gates and getting a good case of the creeps. On the way home we joked about giving Mary a ride in the new car. Later that night my friend, Kristin, dropped me off at my apartment and went home to hers.

As her boyfriend, Mike, heard the car pull up he peeked out the window, then not wanting to appear worried and waiting up he dropped the shade. Kristin let herself in and closed the door. Mike asked, "Where's Susan?" Kristen told him that she dropped me off first. He asked, "Well, who was in the car with you?" To this day he swears that when he looked out the window he saw a pale face look back at him from the passenger's side of the front seat.

Despite such compelling accounts as this and those others detailed in these pages, the doubters stand fast. Among them are those extreme locals like Gail Ziemba, who lives across the road from Resurrection Cemetery. Easily summing up her 20 years' experience with the legendary ghost, Ziemba maintains: "I've never seen anything." In response, believers would remind her that only men are privileged to see Resurrection Mary, although there have been cases in which a man and a woman traveling together have both reported a glimpse or two of something.

And while neighbors like Ziemba continue to shake their heads at the legend, other neighbors of the cemetery have been pushed to reconsider their doubt. Early one morning in late summer of 1996, Chet Prusinski himself, owner of Chet's Melody Lounge, was backing out of his driveway when a man came rushing across the road, yelling that he needed a phone. He had hit a woman on Archer Avenue and couldn't find the body. Attesting to his claim was a truck driver who had been driving behind him. He, too, had witnessed the grisly incident and remained at the scene to testify on the woman's behalf. Prusinski agreed to call the police, but hastened to disengage himself from the whole affair, fearing that he would be accused of staging a publicity stunt for his bar. The "accident" was quietly resolved and little was made of the event. However, those who always take note, took note. And, of course, those who always laugh, laughed.

Yet, even those Southwest-siders who discredit Resurrection Mary know that much of what makes their culture special is wrapped up in the folds of her legendary white dress. And because of this, she is, even to nonbelievers, a priceless treasure, just as she was to a fictionalized witness in Kenan Heise's novel, " . . . something precious, whoever or whatever she is. . . . To her, I say, 'God bless you.' "

♦

Mexico on the Calumet

A MIGRANT LEGEND FINDS A HOME

*G*ary, Indiana, is connected to south Chicago not only by the snaking Calumet River, but by an industrial culture built by generation after generation of hardworking families. It is not surprising that this gritty town should have come to share folklore with its Illinois neighbors, just west over the Indiana border. In fact, Gary folklore includes its own distinct version of Chicago's Resurrection Mary: a Woman in White said to haunt the intersection of Cline and Fifth Avenues near the Calumet River. The Woman in White is part of the folklore of the Anglo community of Cudahey, and, like her Chicago counterpart, she is known for hitchhiking. Hailing taxis from the Cline Avenue overpass, she usually requests rides to Calumet Harbor, but disappears from these vehicles within a half-mile. Though her similarity to other Anglo Women in White is obvious, there is an added flavor to this Hoosier haunt, owing to the influence of Mexican settlers of the Indiana harbor area. When those settlers came north to Indiana, they brought a whole culture with them, including a particularly vivid piece of folklore.

For nearly 450 years, a phantom called La Llorona ("the one who cries profusely") has chilled the blood of Mexico City residents with her wails of "Mis hijos, mis hijos (my children, my children)." Wringing her spectral hands, her blood-soaked dress trailing behind her, La Llorona, tradition asserts, is the spirit of a murderess, a woman damned for the brutal killing of her two illegitimate children.

The woman called La Llorona actually existed. She was Doña Luisa de Loveros, an Indian princess who fell in love with a Mexican noblemen, Don Nuño de Montesclaros, in 1550. Although Doña Luisa loved Montesclaros deeply and had two children with him, he refused to marry her, asserting that she was beneath him in social station. When he deserted her and married another woman, Doña Luisa went mad and stabbed her babies to death. She then took to the streets, her clothes covered with blood, sobbing for her lost children and her lost love. When the authorities discovered her despicable deed, they charged her with infanticide and sent her to the gallows, where her body hung for nearly six hours. Ever since, she is supposedly doomed to walk the Mexico City streets, in search of her dead children.

Apparently it is this Mexican legend, exported to Gary, Indiana, that has meshed with the Anglo tale of the phantom hitchhiker to create a rather unique manifestation. For, like La Llorona, Cline Avenue's Woman in White is searching for her own children, children whom, according to local legend, she drowned in the Calumet River.

◆

The Forest Park Flapper

ANOTHER RESURRECTION, ANOTHER MARY

Passers-by will identify Jewish Waldheim Cemetery by its eye-catching entry, comprised of several columns that were once part of the old Cook County Building demolished in 1908. But while this site is recognizable by its gates, it is known for its ghost.

Located at 1800 S. Harlem Avenue, the cemetery is home to hundreds of restful souls and apparently at least one restless young spirit. The pattern of her recurring escapades is a fondly familiar one, both to folklorists and to Chicago South-siders. This ghost, too, is a beautiful young hitchhiker, all dressed up for a night on the town. She has been known to beg rides to and from the local ballroom down the road. She sounds for all the world like her Archer Avenue sister, but she's different. For this girl is no blonde beauty, but a striking brunette with smoothly bobbed hair. Instead of long white lace, she sports a scandalously knee-skimming chemise. And when she thumbs a ride late at night, it's definitely not back to rest with her Polish-American kin. Rather, as her unwitting escorts have discovered, this girl is headed for Jewish Waldheim Cemetery.

A remarkable variant on the overwhelmingly Aryan stereotype of the vanishing hitchhiker, many drivers have claimed to have caught a glimpse of this phantom flapper, stealing silently into the cemetery's mausoleum just off Harlem Avenue in west suburban Forest Park. Such sightings of the engaging young woman occurred most frequently in 1933 and 1973. Worth noting is the fact that these sightings pre-date sightings of Resurrection Mary.

Although the enchanting young flapper tends to amuse herself by hanging out at the cemetery gates or wandering the road outside the fence, she is, like Mary, forever in search of life, music, and a dance partner. As legend has it, she finds these things at the once popular Melody Mill Ballroom, just a thumb's ride down DesPlaines Avenue, a road well-worn by her delicate heels, at least according to those who have borne witness to her exploits.

♦

Following in Their Footsteps

THE LITTLEST HITCHER

*T*he dance-loving, sophisticated ladies are not the only Chicago spirits doomed to an afterlife on the road. In the 1980s, motorists in the south and western suburbs began picking up a child at the side of one or another thoroughfare, asking for a lift to the city. Like her more famous big sister on Archer Avenue, this young wayfarer has alarmed her impromptu chauffeurs by disappearing from the car en route to their destination. Clearly another example of the "home"-seeking model of phantom hitchhikers, this young woman has been naturally called a ghost by those who know of her antics.

According to what tradition has developed about this legend, the child is the spirit of a girl buried in Evergreen Park's Evergreen Cemetery. Ghost or not, the mouths of babes may verify the apparition's connection to this curious locale. Like so many of Chicago's burial grounds, Evergreen Cemetery sprawls adjacent to another cemetery, St. Mary's. And it is here that a Palos Hills toddler witnessed a most unusual gathering.

Since the death of his great aunt, little Michael, a child bright beyond his years, had reported seeing a woman around their southwest suburban home, in the kitchen, watching them from other rooms, and even "standing in the dog cage." After a number of sightings, the family guessed that the apparition in their home must be that of the recently deceased aunt. During the time of the apparitions, Michael was taken by his family to St. Mary's to visit his aunt's grave. During the visit, the boy seemed utterly mesmerized by something nearby. Though his mother, Diane, frequently looked around expecting to see some other people or even a bird or other distraction, she found nothing that could so completely engage her son's attention. On the way home, however, her puzzlement at Michael's preoccupation became clear when he asked his mother, "Who were those ladies?"

Confused, Diane listened as her son described the scene he claimed to have been watching from his great aunt's gravesite. Some little distance away, a group of "ladies," when pressed, he put their ages at around 12 years old, had been gathering around a "witch," a woman in a black dress and "pointy hat." According to Michael, the "witch" seemed to speak with the younger "ladies" gathered around her. In the midst of this interplay, the family went on its way, leaving the bizarre and mostly unseen scene to continue among the tombstones.

This clue may lead some to speculate that our little hitcher may be one of the 12-year-old "ladies" bound to the St. Mary's/ Evergreen cemetery area and seen by Michael during that seemingly ordinary graveside visit. The account holds some additional intrigue for students of folklore, who will recall throughout international folklore the juxtaposition of lovely young women and witch-like figures. In areas all over the world, and across the years, witnesses have come upon enticing girls and terrifying "witches," "crones," or "hags" at the same site and at various times; however, these sightings usually occur according to the models set forth for Phantom Hitchhikers or so-called "spectral jaywalkers" (i.e. along a road at night, by a male driver traveling alone). Nevertheless, local culture's adamant categorization of our young girl as a hitchhiker, along with Michael's bizarre cemetery vision, may make us wonder about the connection of this tale to international folkloric models.

Wonder as we may about her existence in our minds or on our main streets, the endless journey of the littlest hitcher goes on. Though, as mentioned earlier, this Evergreen Park phantom behaves a lot like the famous Resurrection Mary, she has a few quirks of her own. Unlike Mary, for example, the petite wayfarer has not been wholly reliant on the goodwill of passing drivers. When unable to procure a free ride, she has been known to resort to Chicago Transit Authority buses. The brunette adolescent, however, has cleverly managed to avoid the payment of fares, though with varying degrees of ease.

On one occasion, after she nonchalantly breezed past a bus driver to take a seat, the driver left his seat and stormed down the aisle to demand her fare. Though the girl may have been startled by his unexpected reaction, she nonetheless knew exactly how to respond. Daunted but undefeated, she calmly vanished.

◆

A Man in the Road

SIGHTINGS AT ST. CASIMIR

*T*he Southwest-side burial ground of St. Casimir makes its home in a veritable land of cemeteries, along with the sprawling properties of Holy Sepulchre, Chapel Hill Gardens South, Oak Hill, Beverly, Mt. Hope, Mt. Olivet, and Mt. Greenwood. Yet there is no mistaking this striking Roman Catholic ossuary for any of its neighbors. Rising from flawlessly-maintained lots, renderings both Christian and secular are expressed on monuments of stainless and Cor-ten steel and fiberglass that dwarf those typical of other Chicago-area cemeteries. The result is nothing short of breathtaking.

The extraordinary visual appeal of this Lithuanian cemetery has provided an odd context for one of Chicago's few legitimately frightening phantoms, a wan and wandering thin man with a distinctive sneer. Mimicking the more harrowing shenanigans of his ghostly comrade, Resurrection Mary, the disheveled figure has been reported to appear in the headlights of cars as they pass the gates of this 111th Street landmark. His trademark, a hateful grimace expertly focused, is typically followed by his prompt disappearance and the natural bewilderment of motorists.

As the star of one of Chicago's more vague haunting legends, this unsettling stranger has not been connected with any historical event until recently, verified or dubious. In fact, local lore has ventured not even a tall tale to explain him. Accordingly, local ghost hunters have rarely attempted to locate his lot at St. Casimir's, largely because he does not seem to "belong" to the cemetery proper. In nearby backyards, a similarly rumpled wanderer is often seen by homeowners, even in the cheerful light of day. Staging the same vanishing act from ever-varying venues, he reportedly disappears amidst the yelping chorus of any nearby dogs.

Over the past several years, however, an intriguing theory has been formulated by Frank Andrejasich of Summit, Illinois, whose in-depth research into the world of Resurrection Mary has led him to connect that wildly famous legend to the nearly unknown and much less appealing haunt of St. Casimir. Andrejasich's investigation convinced him that Resurrection Mary was, in life, a 12-year-old girl named Ona Norkus, a girl who grew to call herself Anna Marija.

The buoyant Norkus was killed in a car accident in July of 1927, as she traveled home to Chicago with her father from a night of dancing at Willow Springs' Oh Henry Ballroom. Although she was, in the eyes of the times, too young for dancing, her devoted father, August, Sr., agreed to escort Anna to the dancehall as a gift for her upcoming 13th birthday. According to Andrejasich, the girl was to have been buried in a family lot at St. Casimir; however, since gravedigger strikes were common in the '20s, it is possible that her body was temporarily interred at Resurrection and then wrongly identified and mistakenly buried later on.

Anna's father died 10 years later, alcoholic and overcome with remorse for his daughter's early death. He was laid to rest at St. Casimir, some distance away from the family lots, as there weren't enough left to go around. Could the ragged wraith outside those gates be a pitiful Gus Norkus, wandering and watching for his displaced daughter, none other than Resurrection Mary?

If the curious are to believe St. Casimir's administration, the office has not been informed of any close encounters with the grimacing ghost rumored to roam its environs. In fact, the quietude of St. Casimir's is only very rarely disrupted by the sort of ghastly antics which, decades ago, began to lead the staff of Resurrection to frequent hand-wringing and rage. Of course, St. Casimir's has a significantly less lovable legend to offer. Given the choice, most motorists would opt for a glimpse of the glamorous Mary over a near collision with this confrontational corpse. However, if the theory of Frank Andrejasich is true and the kin keep up their quests future drivers may be blessed, or bombarded by an eyeful of both father and daughter, as they witness a most unusual family reunion.

♦

Steeped in Mystery
A DROWNING ON THE NORTH SHORE

*I*n its attempts to sort out various types of *psi* phenomena, popular parapsychologists have distinguished between recurrent spontaneous psychokinesis (RSPK) or *poltergeist* activity, haunting RSPK, and retrocognitive or residual hauntings. The latter are best described as "replays" of events, often tragic in nature, in which the victim of an accident or murder will seem to repeatedly live out the final moments of life at the location where the tragedy occurred. The phantoms featured in such hauntings do not interact with living agents, but simply go about their ghostly business, over and over. Actually, it is believed that this type of ghost is little more than a psychic videotape of past events, capable of being viewed only by certain psychically-sensitive observers.

Briefly during the 1970s, passers-by on Chicago's Lincoln Avenue reported a shadowy figure retreating down the alley several doors south of the old Biograph Theater, only to stumble and vanish from sight. Known as Dillinger's Alley, the site had gained instant notoriety when the infamous gangster, John Dillinger, met his bloody end there in 1934 after watching his last movie at the nearby theater. (See "Show of Shows," pp.127-135.)

Yet, while the spectral after-effects of the Dillinger tragedy are old news to most Chicagoans, a lesser-known and more definitely resolved retrocognitive or residual haunting is said to have occurred further north, just over the Chicago-Evanston border, between the oft-icy waters of Lake Michigan and the gates of the old Calvary Cemetery across Sheridan Road. Because of the nature of its apparent resolution, however, this phenomena has been reckoned not a "haunting" but rather what some parapsychologists term a true apparition or true ghost, a ghost in the classic sense.

According to witnesses and those who have passed along the tale, the phantom replay of events would begin with the vision of a man drowning just over the edge of the rocky shoreline. After a tortuous death, the shadowy figure would haul his saturated frame out of Lake Michigan and over the jagged boulders. Staggering between swerving cars, he would drag himself across Sheridan Road and through the gates of Calvary Cemetery. A legend among the rich and famous on Chicago's North Shore, his identity remains unknown. However, there have been some definite speculations regarding his origins.

He has been called "The Aviator." During World War II, ships were converted into aircraft carriers, and pilots were trained to land planes on their decks. Sometimes, an uncertain pilot would careen into the Lake Michigan waters. Attempts would be made to rescue the unfortunate airman, but occasionally, they were unsuccessful, and the pilot would be lost in the lake. According to the common tale, The Aviator was an unknown young pilot who met just such a fate and who was ultimately left to spend his eternity in a watery grave.

During the 20 years following his drowning, travelers along Sheridan Road reported sightings of a young man rising out of the lake and crossing the pavement to Calvary Cemetery, where he would pace back and forth in front of the closed gates. This sequence of events, or parts of it, were supposedly witnessed by thousands of

The view across Sheridan Road towards Lake Michigan, from inside Evanston's Calvary Cemetery. (*Photo by Ursula Bielski*)

passers-by, until the 1960s, when suddenly the phenomenon ceased.

Reports of the apparition seem to have ended abruptly after the Sheridan Road gates to Calvary were left open one night, causing locals to believe that The Aviator had at last found the drier rest he so desired. Indeed, according to local lore, The Aviator was never seen again, either inside or outside the confines of the cemetery. Thus, The Aviator's distinguished status in the spirit world rests on a peculiar characteristic. In traditional ghost stories, spirits generally walk until the living provide a proper burial for the deceased. In this unusual story, our victim seems to have sought, and ultimately found, his own resting place.

If, indeed, our Aviator did find rest at this site, his taste in eternal companionship turned out to be exquisite. This, Chicago's first Catholic Diocesan cemetery, is one of Chicago's loveliest but least-known treasures. Behind the massive limestone gates designed by noted architect James Eagan rest, among others, Charles Comiskey founder of both the Chicago White Sox and the American League itself, past Chicago Mayor Edward Kelly, local lumber giant Edward Hines, and furniture manufacturer John M. Smyth. Yet, to North Shore residents, perhaps no inhabitant continues to excite the imagination as much as the sopping stranger of local legend.

◆

II

DEAD AND BURIED
In a City of Cemeteries

*On fine afternoons the living population pays a visit to the dead,
and they decipher their own names on their stone slabs;
like the city of the living this other city communicates
a history of toil, anger, illusions, emotions,
only here all has become . . . set in order.
And to feel sure of itself, the living . . .
has to seek in the . . . dead the explanation of itself,
even at the risk of finding more there, or less . . .*

—ITALO CALVINO
"Invisible Cities"

The plaque at Julia Buccola's grave in Hillside's Mount Carmel Cemetery contains the picture taken six years after her death of her perfectly preserved corpse. (*Photo by Matt Hucke*)

Saints and Sinners

MOUNT CARMEL'S MOTLEY CREW

ALONG ROOSEVELT ROAD IN WEST SUBURBAN HILLSIDE, A CURIOUS CONGLOMERATION OF SOULS AWAITS JUDGMENT. HERE, IN ONE OF THE LARGEST POST-MORTEM GATHERINGS OF Chicago's Italian-Americans, some of the most notorious of Chicago's gangland players lie side by side with some of the most pious of the city's faithful, all nestled in a curious and cramped communion. While generally there is a fair balance between good and evil, now and then the strength of one or another seems to overpower its opposite force.

Mt. Carmel briefly captured international attention in 1996 when Joseph Cardinal Bernardin was entombed in its Bishop's Mausoleum after losing his grueling battle with pancreatic cancer. Pilgrims trudged to the site for weeks, toughing the cold to glimpse the interior of the otherwise closed tomb, everlasting home to the bodies of Chicago's past Archdiocesan leaders. But before the spectacle of that recent season, pilgrims had been traveling to Mt. Carmel for a peek and a prayer at the comparatively modest monument that marks the grave of a mysterious young woman named Julia.

Over the past seventy-five years, Julia Buccola Petta has been engaging the interest of thousands of Chicagoans, becoming no less than a martyr to many of Chicago's Italian-American women. Such status is partly due to the circumstances of her death, but is ultimately due to the circumstances that came after that death.

In 1921, the young bride died in childbirth and was buried at

Mt. Camel carrying her baby. When in 1927, Buccola's mother had recurring visions of Julia begging to be dug up, Julia's casket was opened. To the shock of witnesses, the girl's body, six years in its grave, had remained in unblemished condition. Astonished admirers hastened to display a photograph of the perfectly preserved corpse on Buccola's tombstone, where it remains today along with the Italian-English inscription:

Filumena Julia Buccola aged 29
Questa fotoraha presa dopo 6 anni morti.

As a further tribute, a life-sized statue of "The Italian Bride" serves as a beacon to the endless stream of curiosity seekers who come to pay homage to a powerful image, the instantaneous meeting of birth and death.

According to some of those visitors, not only Julia's flesh has endured the rigors of the grave. Buccola's spirit also seems to have survived, joining the handful of Women in White featured in Chicago ghostlore. The ghost of this dead mother, clad in the wedding gown she was buried in three-quarters of a century ago, wanders near her resting place, say witnesses. In fact, one story recounts the day a small boy was accidentally left behind in the cemetery by his family. The boy's shaken kin rushed back to the cemetery and spotted the child taking the hand of a white-gowned woman. Upon the family's arrival at the scene, however, the woman vanished.

Over the years, the ongoing search for the phantom Julia spread to all generations. Even local Proviso West high-schoolers would make ritual attempts to catch a glimpse of this fabled apparition, sometimes leaving school dances en masse to line up, eyes wide, along the Mt. Carmel fence.

In 1947, 20 years after the unearthing of the Buccola grave, Mt. Carmel's ground was broken once again, this time for the interment of Alphonse Capone. The family plot, gathering several of Al's siblings, his mother Theresa, and his father Gabriel, is nondescript by Mt. Carmel standards. In a burial ground filled with life-sized likenesses and family mausoleums, the Capones' humble flush stones would go unnoticed but for the force of the family name.

Visitors to the Capone grave find flowers, beer cans, coins, and other tokens of varying sentiment: the love and regret of family; the compassion or curses of strangers; the grotesque admiration of the anonymous. At least a few unknown visitors, perhaps heirs to his wrath, have made attempts to soothe Al's soul with peace offerings. Though few haunting-related stories exist to enforce the fear, the admonition to tread softly here is taken to heart by most.

The fear of being haunted was something to which Capone himself confessed. In his later years, he became convinced that he was being stalked by the vengeful spirit of James Clark, brother-in-law of Capone's arch rival, Bugs Moran, and a victim in Capone's cold-blooded coup, the St. Valentine's Day Massacre.

◆

Apparitions of Frances Pearce and her infant daughter have been seen by visitors to their Rosehill resting place. (*Photo by D. Cowan*)

The Restless Rich

ROSEHILL AND GRACELAND

*B*ehind a fortress-like facade at 5800 N. Ravenswood Avenue lies the 350 acres of Rosehill Cemetery. Here you'll find 16 Civil War generals, 14 Chicago mayors, scores of rags-to-riches millionaires, hundreds of local heroes and pioneers, about 200,000 other assorted personalities of varying note and notoriety, and at least five ghosts.

Adorning the place is the world's largest collection of secular Tiffany glass housed in the world's first communal mausoleum, a memorial chapel once named the most beautiful building in Chicago by the American Institute of Architects, and more than 5,000 pieces of funerary art, among them the exquisite Pearce monument hailed by Chicago Magazine as the city's best.

The city's oldest and largest cemetery lured cemetery historian, David Wendell, here in 1993. When Wendell first came to Rosehill, he brought with him a list of some 1500 notable but deceased Chicagoans, confident that a good number of those were buried at Rosehill. He was surprised to discover that no census had ever been taken to verify the particular prestige of the Rosehill population. Thus, the position of Rosehill Cemetery historian was simultaneously created and filled.

As he searched the cemetery records and their accompanying stones, Wendell found that, indeed, hundreds of notable Chicagoans had been resting largely unnoticed at Rosehill. He also found some notorious foreigners, among them Victor Frankenstein, M.D., whose tombstone affectionately refers to the deceased as "PAPA." Wendell refrained from including such misleading entries in his census; nonetheless, he regularly stopped by Dr. Frankenstein's grave with tour groups of school children, much to their delight.

Although Rosehill's "no ghost" policy prohibits the staff from alluding to the cemetery's more "active" residents, nosy ghost hunters can seek out some particularly spirited sites.

Among the more famous of those sites is the Hopkinson

Mausoleum. Charles Hopkinson was a real estate investor who made his fortune around the time of the Civil War. In his will, Hopkinson provided for the erection of a mausoleum to serve as a temple and burial space for his family. When he died in 1885, architect James Eagan designed a miniature Gothic cathedral to satisfy the wishes of the deceased. The property owners behind the Hopkinson lots, however, took both Charles' family and the cemetery to court, charging that the finished mausoleum would disrespectfully obstruct their site. The family pushed the case through to the Illinois Supreme Court, which ruled that the prosecuting families should have foreseen the possibility of such a project. Construction resumed.

Notwithstanding the fact that the Hopkinsons' initial turmoil met with a happy ending, it is said that on the anniversary of Hopkinson's death a faint but ghastly moaning rises from the crypt inside the mausoleum, accompanied by the unmistakable rattle of chains. Charles, it seems, continues to carry a grudge against the property owners who attempted to destroy his vision.

Backing up the eyewitness accounts of Rosehill employees, another source has testified to the genuine nature of the Hopkinson haunting. *The National Enquirer* printed a photograph of the Hopkinson Mausoleum in 1992 with an account of the site's alleged phenomena. Typical of a newspaper which routinely undermines its own already infamous credibility, the paper falsely stated that the mausoleum is situated in Chicago's Graceland Cemetery, several miles away.

Across the road from the Hopkinson family is the grave of Frances Willard, founder of the Woman's Christian Temperance Union. In testament to Willard's charisma and organizational talent, she persuaded three million people worldwide to sign a document swearing never to drink a drop of alcohol.

Although the progressive leader's willful personality might certainly have lived on after her death, there have been no reports of a phantom Frances. Her movement, however, seems to have received an inadvertent boost from her sister's ghost. For when Frances' closest friend and associate, Belle Milner, contracted a mild but persistent case of tuberculosis, doctors urged her to move from her North Shore home to a more hospitable climate. According to Frances, as her associate languished in her room one muggy afternoon, Frances' late sister, Mary, appeared to the sickly girl and pleaded with her to take the advice of friends and doctors and move west in the interest of her survival. As the apparition reasoned, Frances would not want her friend to die a martyr with so much work left to be done for the cause. And so Belle went west to Arizona, where she survived for two more years, establishing successful chapters of the WCTU in the challenging surroundings of the Wild West.

For her part, Frances insisted that upon her death she be buried in the casket of her mother, also named Mary. To this day, they rest together at Rosehill in a single grave, according to Frances' wishes.

Specifications for burial are not always spoken before death. Sometimes the deceased seem disappointed in postmortem arrangements. In October 1995, one of the groundskeepers at Rosehill came rushing into the administrative offices at around eight o'clock in the evening. He spoke excitedly about having seen a woman out on the grounds, standing next to a tree off the access road, near the Peterson Avenue wall. He went on to explain that after seeing this woman he left his car to confront her and find out her business. As he attempted to approach the figure, however, what he saw froze him in his tracks. The apparition, dressed in a long garment, seemed to be floating above the ground. Gradually, the vision dissolved into a mist, and the grounds keeper, freed from his paralysis, hurried to report the incident.

According to rumor, the next day an excited DesPlaines woman phoned Rosehill's office, "You're not going to believe this, but . . ." She went on to tell that her aunt had come to her as a spirit the preceding night, expressing her concern that after her death she had not been properly remembered. The woman, giving the surname of Kalbas, requested that a marker be ordered for her Aunt Karrie's previously unmarked grave, which was part of an old family plot. When the staff went out to the site to verify the lot and the type of stone that should be ordered, it was discovered that the grave with no stone was the same site where the apparition had been seen the night before.

With the stone ordered, Karrie Kalbas was never seen again, either by her niece or by anyone at Rosehill. Most appropriately, when the locally-based Ghost Research Society investigated the apparition sighting, no evidence was found to suggest the presence of paranormal activity. Karrie Kalbas wanted to be remembered. She seems well satisfied that she has been.

One of Rosehill's most interesting sites has no known haunting legends associated with it; yet, it is connected to one of the most intriguing and enduring of all Chicago mysteries. When the old City Cemetery was disbanded by the city council in 1837, it was foreseen that all of the interred bodies would be moved to other sites. One of those bodies belonged to Ira Couch.

Couch died young in 1856, but not before he had established himself as a successful haberdasher and one of Chicago's business pioneers. In tribute to his achievements, the Couch family built a mausoleum 16 feet wide by 30 feet long by 11 feet high, using stone imported all the way from New York. In 1863, when the city council ordered all remaining bodies removed from the cemetery, the Couch family fought for the mausoleum to stay where it was. The Couch family won that battle, and to this day the obstinate Couch Mausoleum holds its ground as a rather conspicuous oddity behind the Chicago Historical Society at the south end of Lincoln Park.

Ironically, the cemetery records maintain that Ira Couch rests in his family's plot at Rosehill Cemetery. However, because the tomb in Lincoln Park has been sealed, it would take an order by the Chicago City Council to have the mausoleum opened for investigation. The Couch family, well-schooled in court battles with the city council is working to do just that. Until their probable success, though, one of Chicago's favorite questions remains: Who is buried in Couch's tomb?

There is another artifact from the old City Cemetery with a curious story. Nearly lost among the thousands of beautiful sculptures at Rosehill, the marble images of Frances Pearce and her infant daughter command the attention of all who behold the monument's famed beauty.

When Horatio Stone married Frances Pearce in the mid-19th century, he looked forward to a bright future with his young bride. Tragedy struck early, however, not once, but twice. In 1854, Frances was dead at the age of 20; four months later, their infant daughter followed her.

In commemoration of his beloved ones, Stone commissioned Chauncey Ives to create a memorial statue for placement at the Lincoln Park graves of his wife and child. Later, the graves and the memorial were moved to Rosehill and a glass casing was added to protect the figures from the elements. According to legend, on the anniversaries of their deaths, a white haze fills the glass encasement, and, as visitors approach, mother and child rise to greet their guests. Believers say that Frances and her daughter, having died so young, return to bid farewell to the life and loved ones whom they never knew.

Such gravesite funerary art at Rosehill is arguably without peer in Chicago, but it is joined by another exceptional art collection of a different kind. It is the largest collection of secular glass ever created by Louis Comfort Tiffany and it is housed in Rosehill's Community Mausoleum where it is spread among the family rooms of some of Chicago's wealthiest and most influential personalities.

The Rosehill Cemetery Company proposed the erection of a community mausoleum around 1912, foreseeing the need for above-ground crypts that would serve Chicagoans longer. In their attempts to raise subscriptions for this project, the cemetery appealed to the city's elite businessmen, impressing upon them its revolutionary nature and comparing the concept to the burial customs of the Greco-Roman Empire. Their idea sold and by 1914 Rosehill had raised enough money to begin construction of the massive project.

One of the subscribers to the mausoleum was Mr. John G. Shedd, president of Marshall Field and Company from 1909-1926, who contributed three million dollars towards the establishment of Chicagoans' much-beloved Shedd Aquarium. Shedd's family room was to become the centerpiece of the structure, and indeed, this portion of the mausoleum testifies to Shedd's profound love of aquatic life. The chapel outside that room forms the apex of the building, and chairs in the chapel feature intricately-crafted backs depicting seahorses and sea shells. For the family room itself, Shedd commissioned Tiffany to create a unique window for his family alone—one which, at sunset, would bathe the room in a blue haze to mimic the underwater atmosphere to which he was so drawn in life. Shedd had Tiffany sign a contract specifying that no other such window could ever be created by Tiffany again. Shedd's insistence on the provision becomes understandable when one stands in this room at dusk. At every sunset since his death, Shedd's coveted blue haze has blessed his family's sleep.

Though no hauntings are associated with John Shedd, the same cannot be said of the mausoleum's two most famous residents, mail-order pioneer Aaron Montgomery Ward and Richard Warren Sears, a merchant king if ever there was one. Ward's death in 1913 was quickly followed by that of Sears, in 1914. Since they were bitter rivals in life, it is not surprising that the sole specter said to haunt Rosehill's Community Mausoleum should be one of these two competitors.

Long after the dreamy haze has fled from the Shedd chamber and the last footfalls have retreated from the clammy corridors of this massive tomb, the towering figure of Sears, in top hat and tails, has been seen through the private doors of his family room, leaving that chamber to walk the halls of the mausoleum, between his own crypt and that of Ward's. Perhaps Sears tries in vain to provoke Ward into late-night argumentation; perhaps he wants merely to discuss business or days gone by; perhaps he only wishes, after all, to make amends. But Ward has refused to stir. We know that Sears, restless in life, feared an eternity of compulsory rest. In fact, his family room is the only such room in the whole mausoleum that was designed with an outside entrance. Perhaps, somehow unaware of the handy provision, Sears is merely looking for a walk and, thus, a way outside.

♦

Much more popular than Rosehill, but also less haunted, is Chicago's Graceland Cemetery, bordered by Irving Park Road, Clark Street, Montrose Avenue, and the Howard elevated tracks on the city's north side. Like Rosehill, many of Graceland's early burials were transferred from the old City Cemetery, once located at the southern end of present-day Lincoln Park. Chock-full of breathtaking monuments built for famous and wealthy Chicago families of years past, fans of Graceland marvel at the names on these stones: Pullman, Palmer, Cyrus McCormick, Goodman, Ludwig Mies Van der Rohe, John Kinzie, Alan Pinkerton, Ruth

Page, Charles Wacker, John Altgeld, William Kimball, Holabird and Root, Marshall Field, and on and on. The still unimpressed will perhaps be won over by the cemetery's two prized monuments designed by Louis Sullivan, including the peerless Getty Tomb (listed on the National Register of Historic Places, or by lovely Lake Willowmere, with its footbridge leading to the island resting place of city planer Daniel Burnham and his family. For ghosthunters, the tour is much briefer.

Graceland's well-established haunts number a mere three in all, and even this is the high end as the "haunting" of sculptor Lorado Taft's foreboding monument, Eternal Silence, has now passed completely into legend. That eerie creation, a larger-than-life tower of bronze depicting a looming, hooded figure, was said to be unphotographable when it was erected over the grave of Ohio-born hotel owner, Dexter Graves. One of the most fascinating, and hence, most photographed, images in Chicago cemetery art, that tale is obviously untrue. Yet, some still insist that a look into the deep-set eyes of the so-called "Statue of Death" will give the beholder a glimpse of the afterlife to come.

Somewhat more substantiated are the stories concerning the grave of Ludwig Wolff, a seemingly claustrophobic Chicagoan who required an entire underground room, complete with ventilation system, for his eternal resting place. That room, dug out of a mildly sloping hill on the south end of the cemetery, is supposedly guarded by a green-eyed dog that howls at the full moon.

Yet, while the fantastic rumors of the Wolff hound still invite the raising of most eyebrows, there is one Graceland ghost that has won the loyalty of a surprising number of local believers: that of little Inez Clarke.

Struck down in her girlhood by either tuberculosis or a lightning bolt (the versions differ), Inez was buried in Graceland by her devastated parents, who proceeded to commission a statue of their lost angel for her gravesite. That monument, perhaps the most affecting of any Chicago child, depicts the tiny Clarke in her favorite dress, perched on a tiny stool, and holding a dainty parasol. Her hollow eyes hover above a whisper of a smile. Years ago, reports began to circulate that the statue had come up missing one night, only to be found in place the next morning. Apparently this happened on several occasions until, according to the story, a glass box was placed over the monument to prevent vandalism. When a security guard making his rounds discovered the empty box one night, he fled the cemetery at once, leaving the grounds unattended and the gates standing open.

Accounts differ as to whether Inez's statue began disappearing before or after her monument was encased in glass. Those who attest to her death by lightning say that she only disappears during violent storms, perhaps seeking shelter from the frightening weather, while those who credit her death to tuberculosis say that she runs off at random. Occasionally, a visitor will claim to have seen a child who wanders and disappears among the graves near the Clarke monument, but to this day no known formal investigation has been undertaken.

◆

In a Bad Place

THE PUZZLE OF BACHELORS GROVE

*B*achelors Grove Cemetery is nothing less than God's gift to Chicago ghost hunters—a one-acre plot bound on all sides with chain-link fence and topped by barbed wire. Part of the Rubio Woods Forest Preserve, the cemetery lurks in the forest across the road from the main preserve, set back from the road down a wooded dirt path a quarter of a mile off the Midlothian Turnpike near south suburban Midlothian. Dense woods border two opposing sides, a murky quarry pond the third, while the path into the cemetery completes the enclosure. The entrance to this path is "closed" off by a makeshift and worn chain fence weakly announcing this fact. Felled trees and branches have been placed by unknown hands to emphasize the warning, and often, construction crews working nearby piled their materials, equipment, and signs in front of the path

Can some of the vandalism and supernatural activity at Bachelors Grove Cemetery be attributed to the satanic practices rumored to occur there? (*Photo by Matt Hucke*)

as well. Still, for everyone who knows where Bachelors Grove Cemetery is, it is an easy task to step around the warnings onto the path behind. Once on it, however, even the hardiest of souls half regret the trespass.

Though not silent because of the whoosh of nearby throughways, the path, the preserve, and the cemetery are their own world. The path back seems to create itself as you walk, like a lonely road in a Hawthorne tale. There's a little black hole at the end that never entirely goes away, stretching it appears into eternity. Birds chirp and the trees rustle; it should be just a walk in the woods. Everyone on this path thinks of the sign blocking the entrance, though, and the wiser ones know the stories. So there is the looking behind and around, and the wondering, especially about the flesh-and-blood dangers of an isolated forest preserve. The mind becomes a mix of news flashes about found bodies, rumors of satanic sacrifice, memories of those urban folk legends associated with this place, and the fear of finding exactly what one is looking for: a place haunted, not by mere legend, but by inexplicable and notoriously disturbing phenomena. Somehow, one walks through the fear. Suddenly, the cemetery is there, and it's a long way back to the car.

To gain entrance, one must commit further trespass and step through one of the adequate holes in the padlocked gate.

Step inside.

On a sunlit day, the brilliance of light is almost blinding, white-washing the overgrown expanse of grass and wild flora, and tipping tree leaves with quick strokes of gold. Through another hole in the fence across the field, one may see the murky brown quarry pond, and in a far corner, the lush overgrowth of plant life. Squint and it's just a sad but peaceful place: a little cemetery abandoned by long-gone gardeners and uninterested or deceased relatives. But open your eyes. Beer cans and cases betray the recent visits by strangers, as they littered the path in. Rings of dirt and charred wood and ashes tell of impromptu bonfires of recent nights; a plastic doll's hand reaches up through a patch of grass, grasping a half-smoked cigarette. With the sun still shining and the wind still gently stirring the trees, the effect can be ghastly. Many have described a classic sense of the chills upon entering the cemetery's confines. Others insist that the peace of the place persists despite the profane scatterings. The difference of opinion is at least partially due to the ever-changing atmosphere of the site. Though the area is, uncannily, always deserted, on each successive visit, one is guaranteed to witness a different state of disarray, evidence that many have come and gone, with purpose and familiarity, but without respect. The place may be almost free of debris or it may be a mess of garbage. It may offer more macabre displays, like the aforementioned doll's hand reaching up from the grave for a smoke, or it may smell of extinguished fires and incense. Still, on rare days, Bachelors Grove looks for all the world like what it's supposed to be, at least according to historian and genealogist Brad L. Bettenhausen of the South Suburban Genealogical Society (SSGS): an abandoned cemetery in a placid suburban preserve.

Called one of the Chicago area's most haunted sites, there have been more than 100 reports of unusual phenomena at this, what local ghost hunter Norman Basile has claimed as "one of the most haunted cemeteries in Chicago, if not the world." Another author went even further, including Bachelors Grove on her list of "The 25 Scariest Places in the World," ranking it among such horrifying hangouts as England's Suicide Pool. In observing the site for inclusion in his 1978 volume, *Weird America*, Jim Brandon made the grand understatement that the place "has problems." Though the cemetery witnessed its last known burial in 1989, that of the ashes of a local resident, Robert Shields, the ground has hardly remained unbroken. Torn up for decades by both known and unknown hands, the grounds bear witness to a long history of desecration.

Bachelors Grove was first settled in the late 1820s, although larger numbers of immigrants arrived in the '30s and '40s. The first settlers, from New York, Vermont, and Connecticut, were of British descent, while the second wave were primarily Germanic and immigrated directly from Europe. According to Stephen H. Rexford, whose brother Norman was a founder of south suburban Blue Island, the Grove was named after he and three other single men settled the area around 1833, to perfect their titles to government land. Though the story has its charm, as Bettenhausen points out, it is also more folklore than fact, as a family named "Batchelder" had already settled in the area. In fact, many variations on the erroneous "Bachelor" name are still in use, including Bachelder, Batchel,

Bachellor, and even Berzel and Petzel, in addition to the more popular and proper designations of Batchelder and Batchelor. Whatever the origin of the place name, the cemetery here was first called Everdon's. Everdon's saw its first burial in 1844 when Eliza Scott was interred in the grove one November morning. As the years passed, the 82 lots began to fill with some of the earliest settlers of Bremen Township, and eventually, their children.

In a 1977 article, Clarence Fulton, a descendent of one of these founding families, remembered the park-like atmosphere of the "old" Bachelors Grove, where families would picnic near the graves of their relatives and where fishing the quarry pond presented a peaceful diversion for area residents. Today, a visit to the cemetery brings on a confounding mix of emotions. Surprisingly, that sense of peaceful leisure remains part of the experience, at least for most visitors. But for many others, that small sense is overwhelmed by a distinct conviction of trespass. Of course, part of this comes from the seemingly deliberate attempts by the Forest Preserve District of Cook County to keep the curiosity-seekers, as well as the uninformed nature-walkers, away from the very real dangers of this unattended and isolated site.

Local opinion suggests that the closing of the Midlothian Turnpike in the 1960s not only blocked automobile access but ushered in the site's era of decay and haunting. Yet, according to Bettenhausen, the cemetery had by then already begun to attract local youth "as a lovers lane and for drinking parties." Regardless of the cause, by the late 1960s reports of vandalism at Bachelors Grove began to spot local papers and eventually, even the *Chicago Tribune*. Characteristic of the mounting notoriety of the site was a September 1973 incident in which the local sheriff's police took seven teenagers into custody for digging up one of the cemetery's graves. Upon questioning, the vandals attested that they had been unearthing the site "as a lark."

By the early 1970s, the papers were rife with news of more unearthed graves, demolished tombstones, and what appeared to be evidence of satanic rituals. Brandon remarked that "the tombstones have been totally disarranged." Over the years, dozens of grave markers were dislodged from their places and thrown into the quarry pond or pilfered from the cemetery, only to show up in neighboring police stations in later years. Because of this and other elements of the cemetery's reputation, many of the bodies at Bachelors Grove were moved to other cemeteries.

Whether the vandalism that peaked in the 1970s was a cause or effect of the cemetery's notoriety remains a question for debate. Whether that damage was done for the sake of Satan or for the thrill of Saturday Night also remains a mystery. What is certain, however, is that the physical state of the site primed it as a perfect canvas for the legends to come. In the space of two decades, Bachelors Grove took a profound aesthetic and sociological plunge. By the close of the 1970s, the site had been permanently established as "haunted."

Although both the well-documented vandalism and the less verifiable practice of ritual activity seem to have peaked in the '70s, neither has completely stopped. Even recently, one couple hiking in the cemetery told of a dog that had been found hanged in a forest tree several weeks earlier, and of finding on a regular basis other animal remains back in the woods behind the cemetery. They agreed with local belief that "a lot of weird stuff goes on there."

Of course, because of the site's particular notoriety, it is impossible to ascertain how much of the phenomena connected with Bachelors Grove has actually been experienced, and how much has been "accumulated" or re-claimed by others over the years as their own. It is interesting, however, that most of the reported phenomena is relatively unusual, with rare exceptions. The area's most peculiar phenomena, and incidentally, the most credible, are wholly unrelated to humans or human events.

Certainly, if one inexplicable phenomenon can be said to "belong" to Bachelors Grove, it is that of the "vanishing house." This "floating house," "dream house," or "magic house," as it has been variously called, has been described by more than a few visitors to Bachelors Grove. One researcher has collected about a dozen drawings of the phantom house. Reportedly, all are nearly identical, though drawn by various people, of varying ages, and spanning several decades. These depictions portray a two-story Victorian home with a swing on a colonnaded porch. Through elaborate draperies, a trace of dim light seeps into the surrounding woods. There is no house on the property, nor anywhere near the site. No property records exist to suggest that there ever was.

Intense physical sensations experienced at Bachelors Grove
prompted researchers to randomly snap photographs that captured
this anomalous mist, undetectable by the human eye. (*Photo courtesy
of Jason Nhyte and Dave Black of Supernatural Occurrence Studies*)

Those who have seen this "house," however, claim that it is as real as can be. Some have approached it, only to watch it shrink, becoming smaller and smaller and eventually vanishing altogether. So real is the vision of the dream house that many never realize it is not a "real" house until much later, perhaps on a return visit, from a local newspaper story, or to their horror and the guide's delight, on a "ghost tour." Some remain convinced of the reality of the house against all opponents, as did one woman who claimed to have seen the house herself, several years ago. In response to protestations that "there never was a house here," she adamantly maintained that "there used to be." Further, most anyone familiar with the area will offer to show you the foundations of a house that they claim did exist, and earnestly add that much of the grove's satanic ritual goes on right there, upon the foundation of this mystery house.

Local youth typically speak with great animation of Bachelors Grove and particularly of their late weekend drives there to drink and look for this "disappearing house," as they call it. Although mischievous kids who have searched for the house have rarely caught even a glimpse of it, many of them have been privy to another anomalous occurrence for which Bachelors Grove is notorious.

Once, around midnight, sometime in the 1980s, high-schoolers gathered in the cemetery were startled by a flashing blue light through the trees and hurried to their cars, fleeing from what they naturally suspected to be the police. Though they heard no accompanying siren or car engine, and wondered at the likelihood of a squad car driving through dense woods, they left the area for the evening, disappointed at the breakup of their eerie vigil. Later, they learned of a mysterious flashing blue orb that had been reported by many visitors to Bachelors Grove. The 1970s were rife with accounts of this blue orb, which were joined by those of a red light that would streak across the sky over the wooded path, and of white lights flashing around the cemetery, both night and day.

At once compelling and inexplicable, the Bachelors Grove "lights" seen in recent years nonetheless seem quite different from the "ghost lights" or "spook lights" that were reported here during the 1970s, and which are fairly widespread phenomena. In fact, they are almost wholly uncharacteristic of the description offered by experts on the subject. "Traditional" ghost lights appear to be actual red or yellowish-white balls of light that suddenly appear, usually move toward the viewer, and just as suddenly "wink out." Overwhelmingly, they are quite visible to the photographer and her camera. Quite to the contrary, the recently reported Bachelors Grove "lights" only appear on film, after development, and usually question the very categorization of "lights." The "white lights" appear semi-opaque, almost as tangible objects; the blue orb has appeared as an arc of blue wash over part of a landscape. Interestingly, the red streaking lights were actually viewed, though not photographed, in recent years, as a sort of after-effect following an apparition of a yellow-hued human form.

Of course, Bachelors Grove has its share of "real" ghosts, too (i.e., aside from ghost lights). The cemetery has its version of a "White Lady," alternately named by storytellers as "Mrs. Rogers" or "The Madonna of Bachelors Grove," who is sometimes reported as walking through the woods with a baby in her arms. There have also been accounts of a two-headed man who rises out of the quarry pond, as well as of darkly-hooded figures who stand silently for a few moments and then vanish. One local resident claimed that a flurry of bats, completely invisible to his companions, flew into his face and disappeared. A Hammond, Indiana woman who grew up in nearby Posen reported having been startled by a figure in an overcoat that streaked past her on the wooded path and vanished. A phantom farmer with his plowhorse are reported to be the ghosts of a farmer and his animal who were plowing near the water in the late 19th century when the horse suddenly careened into the pond, drowning both of them.

Aside from Bachelors Grove's relatively unique phenomena, the "usual" occurrences are plentiful as well: cold spots that come and go, feelings of oppression or dread, the perception of negativity or "negative energy," the sensation of being stared at, and the occasional touch of unseen hands.

It has been suggested that the dumping of bodies in the pond during the gangster era may account for at least some of the inexplicable apparitions and activity at Bachelors Grove. Others have wondered if the satanic practices connected with the site are somehow responsible, particularly for the reported sightings of hooded figures on the property. Custom maintains that the site was once an Indian tribal ground. Perhaps the rituals enacted there, or the desecration of later years, might account for the remarkable psychic energy of this area.

Notwithstanding the bounty of theories, solutions to the puzzle of this place are sorely wanting, even by psychics. In the early '80s, a medium was brought to the site and communicated the vague message that at least some of those buried at Bachelors Grove had to remain within its confines for a specific amount of time.

Because of the tremendous appeal of this cryptic site, only Heaven and the cemetery itself know just how many photographs have been shot on this single acre and in the surrounding woods. For many, such efforts have been remarkably successful. In fact, it would be unusual to shoot a full roll of even the poorest drugstore film at Bachelors Grove and attain no anomalous imprints. Photographs such as those taken in late winter of 1998 by Dave Black and Jason Nhyte of Chicago-based Supernatural Occurrence Studies depict images reminiscent of the old spiritualist photos of ectoplasm, emanating from the tombstones, seeming to take on almost human form. Such photos were taken when Dave Black experienced strange sensations described as a tingling chill that creeps throughout the body. Some photos taken by Jason Nhyte actually depict the mist wrapped around Dave Black when these sensations were registered. Other interesting photographs have captured what seem to be faces, appearing briefly on the cemetery's tombstones. Such photos, however, have normally been explained as "simulacra"—images that are found by the eye in random patterns. Though "tricks of the eye," such images can be disconcerting and those who claim to see them are often hard to dissuade from the conviction that they are authentic images of the deceased, of demons, or of other unknowns. One of the most controversial photos of the Grove was taken by the Ghost Research Society's Dale Kaczmarek, and clearly shows the figure of a woman clad in a diaphanous dress, sitting on a tombstone, looking out over the landscape. Though lovely to look at and exciting to ponder, the photo has often been dismissed as a double exposure.

The sheer variety and volume of the Bachelors Grove phenomena would be enough to account for its high ranking in the annals of parapsychology, ghost-hunting, and curiosity seeking;

however, there are several elements involved in the "haunting" of Bachelors Grove that make it particularly engaging. One is the uniqueness of several of the phenomena involved, in particular, that of the "vanishing house" on the cemetery path. This phenomena, a rarity even among the paranormal, has intrigued local residents and researchers since the 1950s. Another highly unusual Grove phenomena is the reporting of "phantom vehicles," either moving or stationary, that have been sighted on the cemetery path or along the Midlothian Turnpike, only to vanish when they are passed by other drivers. One incidence occurred to a Mokena resident more than 11 years ago. According to Laura Cleveland's account,

> It was about 5:15 a.m. and it was snowing. I was driving to work . . . west on the Midlothian Turnpike, approaching Ridgeland Avenue. There was an old, black (big) car ahead of me. All of a sudden the car disappeared.

Not surprisingly, Cleveland admits that she "didn't take that way again for a long time."

Added to such unusual phenomena, a second interesting aspect of the incidents at Bachelors Grove is that, with few exceptions, local lore does not connect them with verifiable historical events such as accidents, murders, or other past occurrences, although at least one legend does seem to be an attempt to rationalize the phenomenon of the vanishing house, and another, to explain both the haunting of the Grove and the origin of the misspelled place name "Bachelors Grove."

According to the first tale, the house in question did at one time exist. It was owned and occupied by the groundskeeper of the cemetery and his family and stood in the woods beyond the burial ground. Unfortunately, some evil intervention spoiled their happy arrangement, when "voices from the cemetery" began urging the groundskeeper to kill his family. Dutifully, he sharpened his ax, did the deed, and then hanged himself in a nearby tree. In other versions, the caretaker is a hunter living in the house, who goes berserk one day and shoots and guts a number of visitors to the Grove, hanging them like animal carcasses from the surrounding trees. Local kids will swear to these unwarranted stories and show skeptics the alleged foundation of the old house, back in the woods, where they claim satanic rituals still go on. Once again, although traces of such a foundation do seem to remain, there is no legal documentation of a home ever existing there.

The second of these tales is even less "historically" based, as it melts into other urban legends and exhibits motifs internationally common to vanishing hitchhiker stories. Jaime, a 14-year-old Midlothian resident, tells it well:

> (T)he legend goes that a very beautiful woman who liked to dance and was relatively young was killed by decapitation, and her body was disposed of in Bachelor's Grove. After about two years' time, she began to rise from her grave and go to local dances, since her passion for dancing was so great. She always wore the same long white dress. At each auspicious occasion, she would meet some young man and stay with him for the entire event. At the end of the gala, she would always promise the young man that if he stuck with her, he would have a 'good time' (if you know what I mean). They would drive on into Bachelor's Grove, then a nameless grove of trees, and she would gruesomely murder the young man by decapitation. In doing this, she is trying to find the young man who killed her, and give him his feedback. For all the young men killed and never found again, the spot was named Bachelor's Grove.

As if an ax-murdering groundskeeper and a violently vengeful young woman weren't enough, local culture has gone on to further "prove" the haunting of the cemetery by associating the site with several localized versions of American urban folk legends. As is usual with such legends, local youth are convinced that certain of these tales do have an historical basis originating at Bachelors Grove.

Jan Harold Brunvand has written extensively about the endurance of folk legend even in our time. In the first volume of his series on urban folk legends, *The Vanishing Hitchhiker*, he recounts several versions of two very popular legends, those of "The Hook" and of "The Boyfriend's Death." Although we find many local versions of each of these legends throughout current folklore, the kids of south suburban Chicago have managed to attribute both of them specifically to Bachelors Grove.

The legend of "The Hook" goes something like this: A young couple is parked off the road late at night, presumably holding hands. The music on the radio is interrupted for an urgent announcement: A maniac with a hooked hand has escaped from the local asylum and is on the loose and dangerous. Listeners are warned to keep inside and are notified that the maniac may be identified by the hook he wears in place of a missing hand. Frightened, the girl in the car convinces her boyfriend to take her home at once. Reluctantly, he agrees. Once at the girl's house, the boyfriend exits the car to open the girl's door for her. On the handle of the car is a bloodied hook. The couple had managed to drive away in the nick of time.

The second legend, that of "The Boyfriend's Death," occurs in an identical environment. A couple is parked off a road, but is definitely not just holding hands. The girl becomes resistant and forces her boyfriend away, demanding to be taken home at once. Again, he reluctantly agrees, but the car won't start. He tells the girl to remain in the car while he goes to try and flag down help on the road. The girl assents, begging him to hurry back. After he has been gone awhile, a rainstorm starts up. Her fear mounts as the wind starts blowing and tree branches scrape across the car roof. At last, the girl sees a police car pull up behind the car. Thinking her boyfriend has flagged down the police and asked them for a ride home, she eagerly gets out of the car and heads towards the squad car. One of the officers inside speedily jumps out and says, "Now, miss, just walk towards us, and whatever you do, don't look back." Of course, she immediately turns around, only to see her boyfriend hanging upside down from a tree, his throat slit from ear to ear, with his fingernails scraping the car roof.

These gruesome tales, bad enough if they happened in some distant place are made downright devastating through localization. Such has been the case with Bachelors Grove. Both events supposedly occurred on the path outside the cemetery "awhile ago" according to local youth. Although the Bachelors Grove versions are classic, local culture has attempted to partially explain the haunting of the cemetery by expanding the role of the hooked maniac. Not only did the horrible event occur there "awhile ago," but ever since, the cemetery has been haunted by the maniac's "Hooked Spirit."

It is difficult to date the origins of either the paranormal phenomena of Bachelors Grove or of the legends. The earliest recorded accounts of "The Hook" legend dates to 1960s Indiana, around the same time the tale of "The Boyfriend's Death" first circulated. Both legends, then, began a full decade after the "dream house" was first glimpsed among the trees off the Midlothian Turnpike. It was also by the 1950s, as one former Bridgeport resident recalls, that "no one would go out there because it was haunted,"a reputation based largely on reports of "lights dancing around . . . blue lights and white lights." By the time the Indiana rumors made it to southwest Chicago, there must have been enough of a stigma about this deteriorating graveyard and its attendant visions to make it a good home for wandering folk legends. It should at least be considered that local youth was—and is generally still, according to teenagers like Jaime—unfamiliar with the history of the place name of the cemetery and perhaps felt obliged to create or circulate "bachelor," or courtship-related urban legends with respect to the site.

Much later, after reports of other unusual phenomena began to circulate, and years after the urban legends had lost their initial spark, it would certainly have been an easy task for local culture to resurrect the old shock tales to account for some of the newly-alleged occurrences. One might also wonder if local authorities intentionally perpetrate such tales, playing to local youth's enduring fascination with the Grove. Moreover, historians like Bettenhausen believe that a number of the supernatural tales associated with Bachelors Grove were merely fabricated by local ghosthunters eager to excite and impress audiences with their expertise regarding a lavishly haunted yet local site.

Today, Bachelors Grove Cemetery no longer draws the crowds it once did. On fine days, amateur ghosthunters come to snap Polaroids in hopes of capturing a frame or two of something unusual; autumn afternoons bring the casually curious, directed by Halloween newspaper features listing legendary haunted locations. And on summer nights, a few local kids still duck back into the woods to drink and talk and give each other the creeps. But as authorities and historians have coolly observed in recent years, this helpless little wasteland has little left to offer. The damage has been thoroughly done.

♦

Echoes Up North

WHITE CEMETERY AND ST. MARY'S

*D*ating back to the mid-to-early 1800s, each of these north suburban spots shares various of Bachelors Grove's curious visual phenomena. Over the years, Barrington's White Cemetery has sent many witnesses to the local police with claims of rather unbelievable experiences, many uncannily paralleling those said to occur at the Grove. In fact, along with luminescent balls of light, phantom vehicles, and other visions, visitors to the cemetery and along Cuba Road have reported nothing less than—yes—a vanishing house. But while there are no historical records of a real Bachelors

The gates of St. Mary's Cemetery in Buffalo Grove. (*Photo by Ursula Bielski*)

Grove house, there actually was a house that once stood down the road from the old White Cemetery, a house that burnt to the ground a good number of years ago. Notwithstanding its demise, local culture insists that the house has occasionally shimmered into sight, much like its south suburban cousin, only to vanish just as mystically.

Not far from Barrington is the village of Buffalo Grove, home of St. Mary's Cemetery. Passers-by along Buffalo Grove Road report stories similar to those of visitors to Bachelors Grove and White cemeteries—shapeless forms floating near the fence, phantom cars cruising the cemetery paths. Local police have made a practice of good-naturedly shrugging off the reports of excited eyewitnesses. In the early '80s, the Buffalo Grove police chief shared his own personal tactic with one *Chicago Sun-Times* reporter: 'If we get a guy who really thinks he has seen a UFO or a ghost, we refer him to one of the doctors at Northwestern.'

♦

III

A SECRET SOCIETY
The Lure and Lore of Archer Avenue

The Kean Road gates of southwest suburban
Archer Woods Cemetery. (*Photo by Ursula Bielski*)

S OUTHWEST OF THE CITY'S BORDER, ALONG KEAN ROAD, ARCHER WOODS CEMETERY WAITS WITH INDRAWN BREATH. A CHICAGO GHOSTHUNTER TYPICALLY COMES TO THIS PLACE AS AN afterhought, following a tour of Archer Avenue's more notorious sites. Locals, however, may dread this spot more than any other. Archer Woods, dilapidated and claustrophobic, seems even more ruinous when juxtaposed with nearby cemeteries like the pruned and pristine Resurrection. But beyond appearances, there is no doubt that Archer Woods Cemetery is in itself expressly unsettling.

In fact, the alleged haunting of Archer Woods prompts some of the more fearful responses by area residents who consider this cemetery the most foreboding of Archer Avenue's four burial grounds. Those who grew up near Archer Woods remember night treks to the desolate site in search of the supernatural. Back then, the area, dotted with horse stables and some honky tonk bars, was the place to go to hear the Sobbing Woman, a filmy form said to wander among the trees.

The very real discomfort with Archer Woods Cemetery, however, seems to have grown, not from this story, but rather from the fear of a lonely run-in with Archer's most transient, and perhaps most terrifying, specter: a driverless old-fashioned hearse headed by a team of mad horses.

While Southwest-siders rarely shrink from the prospect of an inadvertent encounter with the Sobbing Woman, Resurrection Mary, or any of the avenue's other elusive phantoms, they seem significantly less indifferent about meeting up with the specter that is said to bound out of the woods near this desolate place. As former *Tribune* columnist Kenan Heise has observed: "The terror of the hearse rips a hole in the frightened soul of anyone who has ever encountered it." That fear, nurtured by the infectious horror of eyewitnesses, has effectively spread to vast numbers of unseeing-but-believing.

Residents of these parts have been testifying to this disturbing apparition for years, reporting that it is seen along Archer Avenue between Resurrection and St. James-Sag Cemeteries, a stretch where one may leave the road and wander through the trees to the Archer Woods burial ground. According to descriptions, the vehicle is built of black oak and glass through which the unsuspecting viewer might glimpse its ghastly cargo: the luminous casket of a child. Driverless, its horses hurl the carriage through the darkness "with the panting of creatures trying to escape hell itself."

Although suggestions are rarely offered as to the origins of this vision, the hearse has occasionally been linked to Resurrection Mary. This theory supposes that, upon the death of the young girl fated to become Resurrection Mary, the girl's parents, being from the old country and opposed to modern ways, refused to allow Mary's body to be taken to the cemetery in an elevated train car, the typical mode of casket transport for poorer Chicagoans in the 1930s. Thus, Mary's coffin was placed in a black horse-driven hearse for carriage to the burial site.

Those who associate the phantom hearse legend with that of the famous hitchhiker speak from a culture informed by a complex folk tradition, a tradition intensely focused on the enigma of Archer Avenue. That old Indian road, built up by Irish workers on the Illinois and Michigan Canal in the 1830s and '40s, has established itself as the magnetic center of Chicago's supernatural forces.

The strength of Archer Avenue's preternatural notoriety rests largely on local belief in the psychic activity of a wildly sloping cemetery in south suburban Lemont, the oldest in the county. This point seems to mark the southern end of the "haunted" portion of Archer Avenue. While the image of the unassuming country churchyard prevails in Lemont, locals have perceived that this particular site clearly occupies a more prominent place in the realm of the sacred.

Like Archer Avenue itself, St. James Church and its surrounding cemetery date to the 1830s, when Irish canalers, most of them from Chicago's Bridgeport neighborhood, put down this road along the route of the Illinois and Michigan Canal under the direction of Colonel William B. Archer. Construction of the canal, financially cursed from the outset, resulted in frequent periods of unemployment for the would-be workers. Nonetheless, they built the road and they built the canal. And many of them moved southwest of the city, to live and die along their Archer Avenue and ultimately to be buried in the bluffside burial ground that grew up there: a churchyard called St. James of the Sag, or, simply St. James-Sag.

Supernatural events have been reported at St. James-Sag since at least 1847 when phantom monks were first seen gliding up this bluff along Archer near the intersection of the Sanitary and Ship Canal, the Illinois and Michigan Canal, and the Cal-Sag Channel. One hundred and thirty years later, in November 1977, a Cook County sheriff was passing the grounds late one night and reportedly saw eight hooded figures floating from the adjacent woods towards the rectory. As he pursued what he assumed to be pranksters, the figures moved towards the top of the hill and vanished.

Another legend tells of a late pastor who claimed to regularly witness the cemetery ground rising and falling as if the entire landscape were one great body of water. Additionally, the unmistakable sound of Gregorian chant has been heard in the vicinity, and a ghost light has been reported, bobbing among the tombstones.

A wholly unrelated haunting at St. James-Sag was first reported by eyewitnesses some years after the first sightings of the churchyard's phantom monks, and it is this obscure and forgotten event that may shed some light on various of the Southwest Side's more well-known legends. The bizarre experience of two young Chicago musicians was detailed in both the *Chicago Tribune* and the local Lemont Observer of September 30, 1897, but has rarely been alluded to in descriptions of the haunting of St. James-Sag. Nevertheless, the motifs present in this singular account suggest that this very haunting might have provided some basis for the development of two other prominent Southwest-side ghost legends,

Much of Archer Avenue's remarkable ghostlore can be traced to the solemn churchyard of St. James of the Sag. (*Photo by D. Cowan*)

namely those of Resurrection Mary and the Phantom Hearse of Archer Avenue.

Late in September 1897, St. James's Fr. Bollman decided to hold a fundraising fair for the church and chose for the fair site a dance hall then situated at the base of the bluff on Archer. In order to attract the younger parishioners, Fr. Bollman hired two Chicago musicians, William Looney and John Kelly, to provide harp and flute music. Exhausted from the long night of playing to a good crowd, the two musicians decided to bed down in the upper floor of the dance hall rather than risk the late drive back to the city. Settling in on cots sometime after one o'clock in the morning, the two looked forward to a sound sleep. For Looney, however, sleep wouldn't come.

The chilly night and the bright moonlight kept the musician tossing and turning, until he was alerted to a commotion outside: the unmistakable galloping and rumbling of a horse and carriage. Curious about the frantic nature of the sound, Looney ran to the window to observe the scene. But although the sound from the road continued with increasing strength, no horse or carriage could be seen. Perplexed and quite shaken, Looney awakened his partner and told him of the incident. As he told his tale, the sound began again, growing in strength as before. This time, both men stood at the window, searching the landscape for a sign of the carriage. What they finally saw was something quite unexpected. In the middle of the road stood a tall, young woman in white. Her hands were raised and moving above her head of tangled dark hair. The two men would later comment that she seemed filled with despair.

Sensing something amiss, the men were on the verge of calling out to her when to their shock she floated through the cemetery fence and began wandering around the tombstones. Soon, the sound of the carriage began again.

At last the sound produced a visual counterpart, as the musicians watched the approach of galloping horses which were, in their words "snow white and covered with fine netting. A light of electric brilliance shone from the forehead of each." The animals preceded a "carriage . . . a dark vehicle of solemn outline. No driver could be seen." As the transport approached the dance hall, the woman returned to the road. Then, as the carriage whipped past her, a shadow enveloped her and "she began sinking into the center . . . until she was swallowed up . . . ."

Silenced by the spectacle, Looney and Kelly froze as the sound of the horses returned yet again and the woman reappeared. Finally, when the horses and carriage materialized for the second time, the woman called, "Come on," waved her hand once more, and "disappeared into the ground." Badly shaken, the two men left their window post for their cots, where they waited in fear through the night. In the morning, they took their story to the local police.

In response to their testimonies, Marshall Coen of the Sanitary Police admitted that both of the witnesses

> obviously saw something which . . . impressed them greatly. I do not believe there is anything of a practical joke in the affair. That would be dangerous in this locality. Everyone out here carries weapons since the rough characters have been brought in for the building of the canal. It would be tempting death to try such a thing, for any person so foolish would be likely to receive a bullet. Both men are sober fellows. There was no liquor at the dance. I believe these boys are telling the truth.

Some legends maintain that the haunting scene witnessed by Looney and Kelly in 1897 was the result of an elopement attempt gone awry. According to lore, a young man who came to St. James in the 1880s to serve as assistant to the pastor, shortly won the affections of one of the pastor's housekeepers. Unable to fight their feelings for one another, the couple decided to run away and be married. Late one night, the young man hitched up the team of horses and advised his fiancée to await him halfway down the hill. As the young man stepped down to help her board the carriage, however, the animals suddenly bolted. Tragically, the carriage overturned on top of the couple. They were both crushed by the weight and buried together on an unmarked plot at St. James-Sag. Those who believed in this tale and the ensuing haunting assumed that the couple was forever doomed to re-enact their elopement as punishment for disregarding social convention.

It is curious that this particular story has gone largely unremembered in the folklore of Archer Avenue. St. James-Sag's well-established reputation as haunted is almost always attributed to the sighting of the phantom monks, previously described, that have been seen there since the 1840s.

Nonetheless, certain elements of the elopement story seem to have provided the substance, or, at very least, support for later important legends that grew up along Archer.

In particular, the essential failure of local lore to account for the origin of the phantom carriage phenomenon, discussed earlier, suggests that, during the temporary "loss" of the elopement legend, local culture may have been forced to create explanations for the famous haunting (e.g., claims that the carriage is Resurrection Mary's). The similar descriptions of the carriage as ominously dark and driverless suggest some connection between the stories. Likewise, the witnesses' description of the elopement horses as 'high strung and came on with fantastic speed' parallel those of the Archer Woods accounts, described in recent years as galloping "with the panting of creatures trying to escape hell itself."

Even more engagingly, the tremendous popularity of Resurrection Mary may be partially attributable to the possibility that it was based on a locally familiar image: that of a Woman in White stranded on Archer Avenue. For if the elopement legend was still playing a part in area folklore in the 1930s, when the legend of Mary began, then local culture may have been thoroughly warmed to the tale's central motif, easily carrying it on through the newer story. Certainly, a phantom escort with his horse and carriage are efficiently updated by a spectral escort with an automobile.

St. James-Sag and Resurrection cemeteries mark the southern and northern tips of what seems to be the supernatural stretch of Highway 171. Almost absurdly, the lost legend of St. James-Sag seems to have migrated up the avenue to settle in the northern post of this otherworld. For as one continues to connect the tale with that of Resurrection Mary, the two accounts begin to seem like different stages in some inexplicable evolution.

The modernized legend of Resurrection Mary simply accounts for too many of the elements of the elopement legend of St. James-Sag: the Woman in White waiting in the road for a ride, the exclusively-male sighting of the ghost at some unspecified time after one o'clock in the morning, the witnesses' realization that the woman is not real after she passes through the fence of a cemetery, and perhaps most compelling of all, the haunting's location near a dance hall on Archer Avenue. Some old accounts of Resurrection Mary claim that the dance attended by this young woman was, in fact, a church dance, perhaps the folkloric version of the dance hall church fair where Looney and Kelly were playing.

Still, despite the temptation to dismiss the complex paranormality of Archer Avenue as simply a jumble of various renditions of some ancient ghost story, the continuing reports of eyewitnesses defy attempts to dismantle this road's reputation. And so, some, trusting in more than a century of experiential accounts, have tried to find an explanation for the seeming concentration of paranormal activity along Route 171.

Once again, theories abound, most based on the area's geography. Archer Avenue was originally one of a number of the Chicago area's old Indian trails; accordingly, many local and national geomancers and folklorists have suggested that the road may be one American example of a ley line.

The concept of ley lines originated in Britain, when Alfred Watkins, a retired brewer, noticed that the English countryside was covered by long tracks, which he termed leys ("lea" meaning "meadow"), which intersected at various points. Watkins' 1925 book on ley lines, *The Old Straight Track*, drew quite a following upon its release, creating a breed of researchers ("ley hunters") who began to locate and map these leys.

The points at which two or more ley lines meet were later termed nodal points. Observation of these nodal points led some researchers to believe that such crossroads were, in fact, ancient sacred sites. Many ley hunters came to assert that these nodal points/sacred sites often host extraordinary phenomena and that equally mystifying events also can occur along the lines that connect them.

Later, Guy Underwood, a dowser, claimed to have discovered that these points contained underground springs, which seemed to create patterns of spiral lines of "force" around them. He also found straight lines of this same force, which he termed holy lines, passing through these sites. Occult investigator Stephen Jenkins speculated that poltergeist activity and other haunting phenomena may actually take its energy from nodal points. Like-minded observers have wondered if ancient cultures harbored an awareness of these energies and utilized them as sacred paths and sites for their ritual activity.

Covering similar ground is E.T. Stringer's concept of Tellurianism, set forth in his 1974 volume, *Secrets of the Gods.* According to Stringer's philosophy, there is a Telluric or "earth" force that exists and "holds people together in a particular place..." Besides encouraging tight-knit communities, such places are often hotbeds of purported paranormal activity.

Author Joe Cooper, who studied Stringer's philosophy, speculated that Cottingley, an English settlement noted for unusual apparitional phenomena, especially so-called "fairy sightings," was one such place. Incidentally, ley hunters have pointed out that in many English areas ley lines are called "fairy paths" by locals, suggesting that there may actually be some sort of energy running along these paths which, magnified at their intersections, promotes the occurrence of unusual events, especially apparitional sightings.

One final theory that may explain the Archer Avenue phenomena holds that running water nurtures psychic activity. It is worth noting that St. James-Sag is nearly surrounded by waterways, bounded by the Cal-Sag Channel to the south and the DesPlaines River, the Illinois and Michigan Canal, and the Chicago Sanitary and Shipping Canal, which all run parallel to each other along Archer Avenue. These waterways follow Archer all the way southwest to Joliet and northeast to Summit, just north of Resurrection Cemetery. This whole area is also covered with lakes, sloughs, and other minor bodies of water. Nearby Maple Lake, not surprisingly, has been the site of dozens of ghost light sightings over the years. If paranormal activity really does feed off of water, the dank passage of Archer Avenue would certainly provide plenty of nourishment.

From these descriptions of ley systems and Tellurianism, one is tempted to peg Archer Avenue as a ley line, or the area it covers as some center of Telluric force. Working from such premises, we might appropriately credit the sighting of the road's phantom hearse and other specters to the "magic" of an ancient sacred path, just as we might credit the complex folklore of the Archer Avenue area to a kind of "force" that keeps its populace utterly enmeshed in the physical and cultural worlds of Chicago's far Southwest Side.

Whatever the explanation, the stretch of road mapped as Route 171 has long been associated with many unseen forces— forces which create inexplicable lights and eerily frequent car crashes, spectral chants, and full-fledged apparitions. The nature of these events—recurrent, sobering, ever-elusive—has long convinced South-siders that Archer Avenue is the one place in Chicago, if any there be, where life and death meet in the road, behold each other a moment, then pass on their own dark ways.

♦

IV

AN ACTIVE SPIRITUAL LIFE

Lasting Legends and Fresh Miracles in Chicago's Religious Communities

In Chicago our God lurks everywhere.
In the elevated train's husky roar.
Beside the blinking lights of intensive care.
In the clamor of the soybean trading floor,
with those who suffer poverty and fright.

—FR. ANDREW GREELEY

One of two statues at Holy Family Church that commemorate one of the
parish's many mysteries. (*Photo by Matt Hucke*)

A Saint Among Us

CHICAGO'S MIRACLE CHILD

STRETCHING FROM 111TH STREET TO 115TH, JUST WEST OF CICERO AVENUE, THE GROUNDS OF HOLY SEPULCHRE CEMETERY ARE SAID TO BE MORE SACRED THAN MOST, FOR THE SITE numbers among its graves the final resting place of Mary Alice Quinn. Reserved and religious in life, Mary Alice was believed by those who knew her to have been gifted with the power of healing, a gift which many believe continues even now, more than 60 years after her death at 14 years in 1935. Because of her professed abilities, Mary Alice Quinn has earned the nickname of "Chicago's Miracle Child." Soon after her death, she evidently appeared to Chicagoans on several occasions during the '30s and '40s. Some claim there have even been sightings of her around the world.

Upon her tragically young death, Quinn was buried in a lot marked "Reilly," in the hope that the false marker would keep the curious from disturbing her grave. Nonetheless, pilgrims flocked to the cemetery to pray for Quinn's intercession in the healing of various maladies, lighting candles and even taking handfuls of soil from her grave. At this writing, the faithful still maintain their vigilance and, as proof of the worth of their efforts, they point out a curious reality. On even the dreariest of January days, the Reilly gravesite exhibits a robust scent of roses. In fact, many visitors are astounded by the strength of the beautiful smell, some becoming nearly overwhelmed by the almost suffocative aroma.

During her short life, Mary Alice was devoted to St. Theresa of Liseux, the pious young woman known to Roman Catholics as "The Little Flower." Accounts of Theresa's life say that she expressed before her death a profound desire to spend her time in Heaven doing good on Earth. She hoped to petition God with the prayers offered to her after her death and promised to send "a shower of roses" to assure those in need that their prayers had been heard. Ever since Theresa's death, thousands of Catholics have turned to the young saint for intercession. Many of those who believe that Theresa has pleaded with God on their behalf attest that they have always received a rose, either the bloom itself, a picture of the flower, or sometimes even a whiff of its unmistakable scent, on the ninth day of their recitation of prayers requesting Theresa's assistance.

Theresa's way of life has been emulated by a large number of Catholics, from the most common parishioner to the Church's great 20th-century philosophers, who have sought to mimic her "little way," an unofficial rule of life based on humble and everyday expressions of loving kindness. Mary Alice Quinn was just one such follower of St. Theresa. Before her early death, Mary Alice, like Theresa, expressed her heartfelt wish to help other people after her death. For more than half a century, in her own little corner of Chicago, she seems to have been doing just that.

♦

Brother to Brother

A VERY HOLY FAMILY

Extending skyward from the corner of Roosevelt Road and May Street on the city's south side is the impressive spire of Holy Family Church, the centerpiece of one of Chicago's oldest Catholic parishes and a seemingly indestructible monument to the unmoving faith of its ever-changing congregation.

Erected in 1857 as the core of a Jesuit-guided parish, Holy Family Church was, according to folklorist Richard Crowe, built over the site of an Indian battlefield, and, incidentally, over the running waters of the Red Creek. When the Chicago Fire failed to destroy the church just 14 years after its completion, the parishioners attributed the apparent miracle to the intervention of Our Lady of Perpetual Help. Before a major renovation in the 1980s, generations of parishioners pointed out another piece of evidence to support their belief that Holy Family is divinely protected—the very endurance of the massive structure despite a fault running from floor to ceiling.

In accordance with their faith in their patron, a statue of the Blessed Virgin was placed in the front of the church. The statue had been in that same place for more than 100 years when a woman snapped a slide of it that turned out some startling results. When the photograph was developed, inexplicable faces appeared on the wall behind the statue. Upon further investigation, it was discovered that, in fact, these visages appeared through places where the paper had peeled off the plaster.

In the Jesuits' meticulous documentation of the building's architectural history, however, no records could be found to suggest that any such images were ever part of the design. Yet again we might speculate on the relationship between parapsychology and amateur photography.

A curious addition to Holy Family's decor is a pair of wooden statues depicting two altar boys in old-fashioned cassocks. The statues immortalize two youngsters who have played leading roles in the mysterious history of this spiritual community. Indelibly etched in parish memory is the story of the tragedy that befell the two brothers when they were drowned together in 1874 and of their subsequent appearances to fellow parishioners.

In 1890, Holy Family's founder, Fr. Arnold Damen, was awakened by what was later believed to be the deceased brothers. Dressed in cassocks and bearing lighted candles, the children led the priest to the dying mother of the departed boys, then promptly vanished. Along with this original account, later parish legends developed around the story. Some reports hold that even several years before their deaths, phantasms of the boys appeared to would-be victims of the Chicago Fire to warn these parishioners of their imminent danger. But while the presence of the boys has faded in recent generations, that of Fr. Damen has been infused with greater energy than ever.

Throughout the 20th century, clergy and staff have reported a figure, clad in clerical dress, passing through the church or patrolling the halls of adjacent St. Ignatius College Preparatory High School. In fact, while Holy Family was undergoing its renovation, St. Ignatius was receiving its own facelift next door. Knowing the tendency of paranormal phenomena to "act up" during building renovations, it is not difficult to imagine that Fr. Damen would have been troubled by the tremendous upheaval at his old home.

And so he was.

Late one evening in 1985, a St. Ignatius student was working in the library on a school fundraising drive when he took a break in the hall outside and glimpsed a figure, dressed in clerical garb, turning into a classroom. When he wondered to his co-workers what priest would be in the building so late, they answered that none were. After hearing the student tell of what he had seen in the corridor, they laughed.

For those who knew the stories, it was obvious that their weary classmate was only the latest in a long line of witnesses to the loving rounds of Arnold Damen.

◆

A Terribly Tangled Web
UNRAVELING THE PEABODY LEGEND

*T*he engraving on the single front step of the little Portiuncula Chapel at Mayslake, in west suburban Oak Brook, bluntly professes a truth to which thousands of visitors have testified:

Hic Locus Sanctum Est
This place is holy.

Sadly, a peculiar kind of fame has for decades overshadowed the sanctity of this paradise, where for generations, pure myth has run utterly amok. When in 1922, Francis Stuyvesant Peabody was thrown from his horse during a fatal heart attack, he initiated one of the most unfounded, yet enduring, of all Chicago haunting legends.

Born in Chicago on July 24, 1859, Peabody settled in his hometown after receiving a solid education from Phillips Academy and Yale University. Thereafter, he became a messenger in the Merchants Loan and Trust Company and, after a mere two years, quit that job and formed a company of his own. Entering the coal industry at a crucial time in its development, Peabody soon bought out his partner and formed his own firm, Peabody and Company. Following his break to financial independence, he married Mae Henderson, a Utica, New York native.

With eyes fixed on the future of the industry, Peabody incorporated in Illinois, forming wholesale and retail operations. Desperate to secure his own resources, he affiliated with Samuel Insull, who had served as secretary to Thomas Edison. Not long after, Peabody became president of Chicago Edison and went on to found and control a network of utilities, including Commonwealth Edison. Peabody and Insull formed a partnership and established the Illinois Midland Coal Company, after which Peabody secured holdings in Indiana, Ohio, Kentucky, Virginia, and Wyoming.

Continually in residence in Chicago, Peabody left the city in 1911 after the death of his wife. He remarried and moved his family to a towering Queen Anne house in Hinsdale. Settling into small town life, Peabody served as president of the Hinsdale Golf Club and founded the Chicago District Golf Association.

Earlier, Peabody, who was politically active in the Democratic Party at both the state and national levels, had worked toward the 1908 nomination of Adlai Stevenson for governor of Illinois. In 1912, Peabody himself was held up for the Democratic vice-presidential nomination, but declined owing to business demands. In 1916, however, Woodrow Wilson appointed Peabody to oversee Democratic campaign financing in the western states and to set up headquarters in Chicago. The mogul gladly accepted this position. His success led him to chair the Council of National Defenses Coal Production Committee during the 1917 coal crisis. Later, by appointment, he assisted the director of the Bureau of Mines.

By 1919, Peabody had moved into the chair of the board of Peabody Coal Company and his son Stuyvesant (Jack) Peabody took over as president. An overwhelming financial success, the elder Peabody was taking in 10 million dollars a year by his 35th birthday.

Acclimated to the western suburbs, Peabody decided to begin work on a dream house in which he might live out his retirement years in peace and relative isolation. Selecting a tract of over 800 acres. Francis Peabody retired from Peabody Coal just as his son assumed the company's presidential duties. Choosing Benjamin Marshall as his architect, Peabody commenced building his envisioned mansion. Three years and more than a million dollars later, the 39-room Tudor Gothic home was complete. Mayslake, named for Peabody's first wife and daughter, became the family's permanent home in 1921.

Life at Mayslake seemed to only intensify the good fortune of Francis Peabody. Throughout the 1920s he received numerous awards recognizing his lifetime achievements: an honorary doctoral degree in Human Letters from Temple University, for his World War I work with the Salvation Army; decorations by the King of Italy, for his work as a Knight Commander of the Crown of Italy; and induction into the National Mining Hall of Fame. No less intoxicating was day-to-day life at Mayslake, where 1920s opulence played out on the lawns of the sprawling estate. Indulging his guests in horse shows and fox hunts, Peabody himself enjoyed his galas immensely until the fatal afternoon of Sunday, August 22, 1922, when the coal baron was stricken with a heart attack while riding during a fox hunt. In a few moments, a remarkable life had ended. What remained was a $35 million personal fortune, a $75 million business, his carefully-planned paradise, and the family and friends that had made it all worthwhile.

The legend surrounding Francis Peabody began with his death in 1922 and his subsequent burial on the cherished grounds of Mayslake. For although the mogul's remains were interred on the hillside where he died, misunderstandings arose as to the exact whereabouts of the deceased. Questions were first raised when the property was sold to the Franciscan Order of St. Louis for the establishment of a retreat house. As a tribute to her late husband, Peabody's widow had a chapel erected over Francis' grave.

After its completion, local teenagers mistook the chapel for a mausoleum, falsely believing that Francis Peabody had been entombed within the chapel altar. Rumors that "Peabody's Tomb" was haunted spread thickly over the western suburbs. Why? According to accompanying and utterly contrived tales, Francis Peabody's interment was rather unique. Reportedly, his body was suspended in a glass box filled with oil in order to prevent its decomposition.

Stoking their storytelling engines with the fuel of such fantasies, local youth succeeded in establishing the Peabody legend as one of the most widely circulated, and baseless, of any in Chicago lore. Because of the tremendous popularity of the story, Mayslake seemed hopelessly doomed to endure the destructive drive of generations of teenagers, who tore up the Franciscan cemetery, defaced and ultimately destroyed a monument to the Blessed Mother, and who repeatedly broke into the Portiuncula Chapel. In the end their thoughtless pranks caused tens of thousands of dollars worth of damage to the grounds and immeasurable sorrow to those who to this day guard Mayslake as a sacred place.

For decades, the Franciscans struggled to keep the estate free of vandals and ghosthunters. Ironically, their efforts won the place even greater status among teenagers, owing to more rumors both false, that the monks patrolled the grounds with attack dogs, and true, that trespassers apprehended by them were sent to the chapel and forced to pray the whole night. While the unceasing attempts to despoil the estate did at times succeed, the Franciscans managed to maintain its essential peace.

Unfortunately, by 1990, financial concerns forced the Franciscan Order to place the entire estate up for sale. Peabody's remains were moved to a local Catholic cemetery and the graves of the Franciscan cemetery relocated. The Portiuncula Chapel was repositioned at the old cemetery site, where it stands today facing the dream house of the man whose grave it once marked. The 90 acres known as Mayslake were purchased for approximately $18 million by the Forest Preserve District of DuPage County and transformed into an interpretive center, with its forested hills and waterside trails opened to the public. For a brief period, the Portiuncula Chapel seemed destined for removal from Mayslake, as various churches vied for the right to purchase it. Fortunately, the Forest Preserve District's claim that the chapel was an integral part of the estate and should remain held sway.

Today, massive efforts are underway to restore the Peabody mansion to its former condition as the Mayslake Landmark Conservancy works towards opening the building to the public. Such formal efforts have drawn a remarkably diverse following of supporters, comprised of Mayslake fishermen; couples who have been married in the Portiuncula Chapel; past guests of the old St. Francis Retreat House; businesspeople and housewives; priests; sisters and brothers; actors, writers, poets, and singers; the dispirited and the spiritual; the lost and the found. Despite the efforts of some, namely, local developers and politicians, to foil their efforts, the loving determination of Mayslake's supporters will surely bring Peabody's vision out of legend and back to life again.

♦

The Queen of Heaven Apparitions

*A*lthough incarnate in a brusque and burly city, the spirit of Chicago is clearly pious. As the seat of the Archbishop of the second largest Archdiocese in America, Chicago has long sheltered a varied and dynamic Roman Catholic community. And while each of the Archdiocese's parishes, inspired by local culture, may practice its own version of the ancient rites, their common threads bind them together, and in turn, to the larger Catholic world.

Throughout the Archdiocese, Catholics have shared with each other and that larger world the mysterious and impassioned dedication to the Blessed Virgin Mary. From the whispered rosaries of elderly European immigrants after early morning mass, to the glorious feast days celebrated by Chicago's Mexican communities, to the silent pleas of attorneys and bankers at St. Peter's in the Loop, fidelity to the Blessed Mother animates the devout with a particular passion that has often confounded both nonbelievers and believers alike. Still, faith in the unique intercessive powers of the Virgin Mary have maintained this passion against all opposition.

Most encouraging to believers have been the intriguing and ongoing reports of Marian phenomena throughout the centuries. Even here in the Chicago area, Marian phenomena have become almost common. Witness the wooden statue of Mary at St. John of God Church on the Southwest Side, which was reported to have shed tears in 1984; the painting of the Blessed Virgin at St. Nicholas Albanian Orthodox Church, 2701 N. Narragansett, which started its own weeping on December 6, 1986; or the tearful icon at St. George Antiochian Orthodox Church, 1220 S. 60th Court in Cicero. After church authorities proclaimed the phenomenon to be miraculous, St. George's was renamed Our Lady of Cicero. With joy, Roman Catholics and Orthodox relate these and other events which parallel on a personal level the apparitions and miracles experienced by visionaries at Lourdes, Fatima, and dozens of other sites. Hundreds of thousands of pilgrims have traveled to these destinations and more continue to do so. Hopeful for blessings, cures, or the satisfaction of curiosity, most have sought a little bit of each.

Early in 1987, Joseph Reinholtz of Hillside harbored little hope for relief from his frustrating bouts with blindness. Despite this disability, Reinholtz made every attempt to lead an active and involved life. As a devout Catholic, Reinholtz had joined the faithful of Chicago and around the world in their fascination with the events reported in recent years at Medjugorje, Bosnia Herzogovina. Taking advantage of his retirement freedom, Reinholtz embarked on a pilgrimage to Medjugorje to experience for himself the tremendous spiritual graces reported at this site, where several claim to have experienced apparitions of the Blessed Virgin Mary. Reinholtz was privileged to pray with Vicka, one such visionary, whose friendship he would maintain in subsequent years. Upon his return to the United States, Reinholtz was overjoyed by the slow but definite restoration of his eyesight. According to his testimony, Reinholtz's first clear view was of a small statue of the Blessed Mother which he had purchase long before. The statue was weeping.

During a return trip to Medjugorje in 1989, Reinholtz received instructions from Vicka to return home and search for a large crucifix next to a tri-branched tree. There, he was to commence praying. Reinholtz's search led him to Queen of Heaven Cemetery in his own hometown. True to the instructions given by Vicka, Joseph began to pray at this trinity tree and continued praying there daily for well over a year.

On August 15, 1990, while he attended to his daily prayer at the site, Reinholtz experienced a vision of the Blessed Mother. Interpreting the apparition as a great but onetime gift, Reinholtz rejoiced in this sign of grace and persisted with his daily prayer schedule at the crucifix. Then, on November 1st, Reinholtz experienced a second vision, that of the Blessed Mother flanked by St. Michael and three other angels. After these initial visions, the apparitions began to occur daily, except Tuesdays. Chicago-area pilgrims, awestruck by the proximity of the reports, began to join Reinholtz in increasing numbers.

In response to the inevitable fervor growing in the diocese, the Archdiocese of Chicago placed a restriction of obedience on Joseph, requiring him to avoid the cemetery on Tuesdays, a restriction which Joseph readily met. On every other day of the week, however, Reinholtz devoutly minded the commission given him in Medjugorje. For his efforts, he was rewarded with continuing apparitions of the Blessed Mother, always accompanied by St. Michael and, occasionally, by St. Joseph. On church feast days, Reinholtz would report visions of Christ Himself.

Apart from the subjective phenomena held dear by Reinholtz, pilgrims to the Queen of Heaven site also began claiming a variety of marvelous experiences: enjoying the scent of unseen roses; participating in mystical conversations; and receiving widespread renewals of zeal in faith and love. In addition, many pilgrims began to trade apparent evidence of the visions in photographs depicting all manner of intriguing phenomena, from images of the Blessed Mother and other supernatural figures, to unusual light effects, to the apparent bleeding of the figure of Jesus on the cross. Other visitors returning home from the site discovered that their rosary beads had turned a vivid golden color.

During Joseph's interludes at the site, he led pilgrims in the recital of the prayers of the rosary while contemplating the blissful events in the life of Christ. Offering these prayers for a variety of intentions, including the peace of the terminally ill, the unity of churches and families, and the administrative officials of the Church, Reinholtz and the faithful focused special attention on the request of the Blessed Mother for prayers on behalf of the souls in purgatory. The crucial nature of this plea was expressly emphasized one August morning in 1993, when Reinholtz reported either an apparition or dream in his own home, during which he was escorted by the Blessed Mother to this dreaded place of suffering.

Joseph's stirring description of his nighttime journey into purgatory deserves quotation. He beheld an "endless area . . . dark like ashes," where souls of the dead are hidden from all sight, but who respond to their intuition of others with a ". . . begging and twitching for help." A place of suffering and punishment, Joseph saw purgatory as a trial that must be endured. According to the Queen of Heaven message, the daily collection and delivery of prayers and the release of purgatorial souls in exchange is a very real and effective process.

On the 25th of each month, a special message was given Reinholtz to share with the gathered penitents. These messages typically echoed messages offered at earlier sightings in Fatima,

Portugal. They stressed the importance of attendance at mass, the reception of the sacraments, and the meditation on the mysteries of the rosary on five consecutive first Saturdays, all important practices in the traditional teachings of the Roman Catholic Church. In gratitude for this vigilance, the Blessed Mother offered a very personal distinction—her own attendance at the faithful's moment of death.

In February 1995, a stroke left Reinholtz with impaired speech and paralysis of his left side. He nonetheless continued to report daily visitations from the Blessed Mother while hospitalized. Meanwhile, at Queen of Heaven, the prayers of the rosary continued by those with a profound faith in his heavenly messages.

Throughout the course of the Queen of Heaven apparitions, the Archdiocese of Chicago offered rare responses to those eager for an official affirmation or condemnation of Reinholtz's remarkable claims. In late July 1991, the Archdiocese issued a statement of neutrality to the general public, and in April 1995 offered one Chicagoan this personal response:

> I write at the request of Cardinal Bernardin in response to your letter of March 8, 1995. Concerning Mr. Joseph Reinholtz there has been no further statement or judgment than that issued in July, 1991. . . . Mr. Reinholtz continues to visit Queen of Heaven as his health permits.
>
> With cordial good wishes, I am
> Sincerely yours,
>
> Reverend Michael Place, S.T.D.
> Consul for Policy Development
> Research Theologian to the Archdiocesan Curia

◆

That Day at St. Rita's

While ostensibly haunted churches abound in the history of paranormal experience, Chicago church ghosts have been rare and fleeting, with the exceptions of those already mentioned at Holy Family and the occasional shadowy spirit at the altar of St. Turibius, 56th Street and Karlov Avenue. While most of the church-centered apparitional sightings in Chicago are brushed off without a second thought, others have an exceptionally terrifying quality that allows them to haunt both those who remember them and those who have, with intermingling dread and delight, heard them recounted.

Old Town residents are still talking, or, more accurately, not talking, about the run-in of an erstwhile parish priest with an unshakable vision. (See "Memories of St. Michael's," p.161.) An even more breathtaking and well-known incident however, is said to have occurred more than 35 years ago for just less than a minute. The key, then, to the tale's endurance? The insistence that the bizarre event was witnessed by no less than 15 people.

One All Souls Day, November 2, in the early 1960s, those 15, all faithful parishioners of St. Rita Church, were gathered for a prayer service there to benefit the souls of the dead. In the midst of their efforts, the organ began to play on its own, unleashing a chaotic string of shrill tones. The hands of the church clock began to spin wildly in opposite directions. As the organ churned out its ghastly offerings, the congregation beheld six monk-like figures, three draped in white and three in black, poised on either side of the instrument. Shocked but mobilized, the petitioners rushed to flee by the doors, which refused to open. They watched in horror as the figures began to glide down to the main floor, floating through pews above ground and towards the front of the church. In the organ's final shriek of discord, an unseen voice implored, "Pray for us." At that point the doors blew open, allowing the congregation to escape the dreadful scene.

News of the afternoon's events spread like fire through the close-knit neighborhood. In fact, for months few could refrain from discussing the chilling details of this singular piece of ghostlore, as related by the ample number of eyewitnesses. For a brief period of time, an already cozy community huddled even closer together in mutual wonderment.

These days, the supporters are split who once rallied around the tale of St. Rita's with unified insistence on its supernatural reality. Responding to still vibrant accounts of the bizarre event are those who explain its unusual magnitude, and consequent impact, by declaring the whole episode a post-Halloween adolescent prank. More sophisticated discountings talk of a mass hallucination, probably induced by the fervent and focused prayers of the witnesses.

Many local believers, however, deny these dismissals. For the faithful, doubt has failed to consume the memory of that day.

♦

V

AN INEXPLICABLE RESIDUE

The Endurance of Tragedy

Where there is sorrow there is holy ground.

—OSCAR WILDE
"De Profundis"

Facing the Biograph Theater on North Lincoln Avenue from
"Dillinger's Alley"—a location of past apparitional sightings.
(*Photo by Ursula Bielski*)

In the Beginning
A MASSACRE AT FORT DEARBORN

*I*T WAS AUGUST 15, 1812, WHEN CHICAGO WAS INITIATED INTO WHAT WOULD BE A HISTORY CHARACTERIZED BY DESTRUCTION AND RENEWAL. ON THAT DATE, THE CITY'S MYTHICAL cycle of birth and resurrection began with the slaughter of nearly two-thirds of the settlers at Fort Dearborn by Native Americans allied with the British. Four years after the destruction of the fort and its inhabitants, American soldiers and settlers would return to re-establish settlement at the mouth of the Chicago River. Little more than half a century later, in spite of tremendous growth, the still-struggling settlement would crumble again in the face of the Chicago Fire of 1871.

In the summer of 1812, the settlement at Fort Dearborn was young, diverse, and fatally unstable, comprised, in the words of Nelson Algren, of "Yankee and voyageur, the Irish and the Dutch, Indian traders and Indian agents, half breed and quarter breed and no breed at all." By 1800, the competition for hunting areas and trade routes had ruined much of the independence natural to the Great Lakes tribes. The native element of the emergent pan-Indian culture could not avoid engaging in trade-based subsistence and became largely dependent on trade goods. Their pottery making had become extremely rare by 1780, and the cultivation of maize, once a unifying tribal activity, had devolved into a means of supporting white populations. Soon, the inevitable depletion of wild game forced the Potawatomi to repurchase their own harvests from white traders.

The toppling of the Chicago area's native equilibrium was effected in the blink of an eye. Jean Baptiste Point DuSable, a mixed-race fur trader from Santo Domingo, had been the area's first settler, living at the river for 20 years before the turn of the 19th century. During his residence there, the wilderness had remained literally unbroken, as evoked in Algren's eloquent description:

> To the east were moving waters as far as the eye could
> follow. To the west a sea of grass as far as wind might
> reach.

After living peaceably in a modest home for nearly two decades, DuSable sold his land to a man named John Lalime, who aimed to take up indefinite residence in DuSable's quiet cabin at the mouth of the river. That intention was abruptly halted, however, when John Kinzie arrived in Chicago and seized the property in 1803.

Although the Kinzie title has still not been found, most historians agreed that the house, on the bank of the Chicago River opposite the fort, was the same lot that DuSable sold to Lalime in 1800. Records in Detroit, however, show the sale of that same land to Kinzie by Pierre Menard, who passed the parcel to Kinzie for fifty dollars, claiming to have purchased it from an Indian named Bonhomme. When Kinzie arrived in Chicago, he haughtily assumed the right to the disputed title, at the same time beginning a rivalry with Lalime that would end in the murder of the latter at the hands of his foe.

Only with Kinzie's whirlwind arrival, less than a decade before the fort's destruction, did the settlement at the river begin to come alive. Preceded by his reputation as a quick-witted Indian trader, Kinzie, a British subject born in Detroit's Grosse Point area, immediately settled his family in the safe shadow of Fort Dearborn. For nearly ten years, he ruled the realm of settlers and "savages" that together began to suggest civilization, at least when Kinzie himself wasn't sparring with his fellows. For Kinzie was a melding of opportunism and temerity, and when he came to Chicago, aiming to position himself between the portage fur trappers and the Detroit market, he brought along his whole collection of brash personality traits to help him along:

> . . . whatever the aspirations of local residents, guile, intimidation, and the soporific effects of British rum were devices Kinzie used to ensure that renegade trappers thought twice before embarking for Detroit to strike a separate bargain for their beaver pelts.

Kinzie's attitude set the standard for the business relationships that affected every aspect of life at Fort Dearborn. Doubtless, that attitude took its life from the shared distaste of each for all others. At the same time, the demands of settlement might have encouraged reciprocal goodwill had the ambition of personalities like Kinzie's not rendered it impossible:

> The multiracial settlement of the early 1800s at Chicago was no Utopian paradise . . . . Slander, theft, moral outrage, extravagant competition, hints of petty squabbling, and even murder marked the social lives of the old settlers. But those lives were also marked by the security of clan; a tenuous kind of racial harmony; an easy enveloping spirit that gathered in the entire village; and a peaceful, irreverent disdain for 'progress.'

"Slander, theft, moral outrage, extravagant competition, petty squabbling"—Kinzie was the model for all who aspired to master these activities. As for "racial harmony" and "the security of clan," Kinzie probably had little sense of either. His sense of harmonious security most likely derived from the sure sense of his family's superiority over his French Creole and Indian neighbors.

Regardless of its source, Kinzie's self-assuredness certainly served to comfort and encourage those who sensed in him a certain quality of leadership. And it was this self-styled security enjoyed by Kinzie and his comrades that left them ill-prepared for the events to come. Eventually, the resentment of the native population became too strong for even a charmer like Kinzie to dismiss.

The inevitable slap of reality came in 1812 when fighting erupted along the northwestern frontier. The fate of more than the fort was sealed when a pair of decisions was delivered. General

Hull's order of the evacuation of the fort was quickly followed by Captain Nathan Heald's own demand that the settlers and soldiers destroy all whiskey and gunpowder. Predictably, as the grim procession of soldiers and settlers crossed into the open landscape headed toward Fort Wayne, Indiana, Indian allies of the British beheld them with bitter eyes. When the line reached the vicinity of what is today 16th Street and Indiana Avenue, a group of Potawatomi pounced.

Of the 148 members of the exodus, 86 adults and 12 children were butchered. The survivors were taken as prisoners. Some of these died soon after, while others were enslaved and later sold to the British and into freedom. Appealing to the Potawatomi on the strength of the business relationships that John had forged, John Kinzie and his family were spared. The fort was burned down. The scalped corpses of victims remained unburied where they fell, splayed across the Lake Michigan dunes.

When troops began arriving four years later, they were met by a ghastly host of images: the pitiful skeleton of the erstwhile fort; the abandoned Kinzie cabin; the decaying bodies of settlers and soldiers, all returned to the prairie, all victims of the wilderness and of war.

By the time John Kinzie returned to his property a year later, troops erecting the new Fort Dearborn had buried Kinzie's neighbors on the banks of Lake Michigan. Never looking back, Kinzie sought in vain to climb again to his old seat at the peak of the portage fur trade. When his bitter efforts went unsatisfied, he stooped to employment with the new king, the American Fur Company.

The gruesome events that occurred on the Chicago dunes that summer day in 1812 seem to demand commemoration via haunting legends. Indeed, the site of the fort itself is reported to be well-protected by marching troops of massacred soldiers who stand guard over the phantom fort, now the south end of the Michigan Avenue bridge. Yet the site of the actual massacre remained placid until many decades later, after the physical formation of the city of Chicago. Only then, during routine roadwork near the site, did workers uncover remains dating to the early 1800s which were probably massacre victims.

Whatever the identity of the remains, after the accidental

excavation, apparitions described as "settlers" began to present themselves to passers-by. Classically, the disruption of burial sites has been a prime motivation for ghostly manifestations; the Fort Dearborn legacy certainly recalls that tradition. After being forced to accept an abominable fate, the victims of this massacre may have been irritated by later interferences with their respective eternities. In sharp contrast, John Kinzie took his place at the top where he always liked to place himself. He nestles with the great names buried miles north at Chicago's Graceland Cemetery.

For many years, Kinzie was left to the quiet of his grave. Lauded by the histories penned by his own kin and taught for years as part of the Chicago public schools' curriculum, Kinzie became the city's first hero. This entitlement went largely undisputed until the turn of the century, when historian Joseph Kirkland began to focus a more critical eye on the figure of Kinzie.

As the century progressed, Chicagoans began to learn more about the city's mythical founding. Summing up the new research was the sentiment expressed in Nelson Algren's commentary of early settlement in his classic, *Chicago, City on the Make.* There, he described the city's early white settlers as simply the first in a long line of hustlers, as those who would

> do anything under the sun except work for a living, and we remember them reverently . . . . . . under such subtitles as "Founding Fathers" or "Far-Visioned Conquerors," meaning merely they were out to make a fast buck off whoever was standing nearest.

With the publication of Alan Eckert's *Gateway to Empire* in the 1980s, the erroneous history of Chicago's settlement was finally overhauled. After various 20th-century jabs at his character, Kinzie became a victim himself, not of war, but of painstaking research. On visiting John Kinzie's grave today, one may be stricken by its placement at the outer edges of Graceland Cemetery. Symbolic of his own ultimate place in Chicago's history, Kinzie has found himself on the outside, looking in on all he imagined himself to have been: courageous, enterprising, strong, and faithful. Far from the wild shores where his fellow settlers found an earlier, though more honest rest, Kinzie may now wish for the violent but valiant death he once fled, a death to which some massacre victims may still be calling him . . . from a vacant lot at 16th and Indiana.

◆

Dem Bones

THE QUESTIONABLE END OF JOHN LALIME

*I*n addition to the embittered dead of the Fort Dearborn Massacre, another otherworldly critic of John Kinzie may continue to seek revenge upon the ambitious settler: John Lalime. Recall that Lalime's own life had come to a violent end at the hands of the ruthless trader.

These two, among the first to settle at the future site of Chicago, had been the worst of enemies from the moment Kinzie set foot in Chicago in 1804 claiming title to Lalime's riverside property, the land and cabin where John Baptiste Point DuSable had lived until the turn of the century. Kinzie and Lalime spent their relationship bitterly brawling, until according to surgeon John Cooper of the first garrison at Fort Dearborn, Kinzie ended the feud by killing the object of his hatred. It is supposed that Kinzie's brutal actions gushed from a boiling jealousy: Lalime had been the area's first white settler, a claim which Kinzie sorely coveted.

After Lalime's murder threatened to bring public scorn upon his killer, the hypocritical Kinzie attempted to appease the angry citizenry by offering to bury the corpse in question in his own front yard, that is, on the very property from which Lalime, in life, had been unjustly evicted. The bizarre burial ensued and there Lalime remained temporarily.

Many years later, after development of the north side of the river began, the bones of John Lalime were brought into the collections of the Chicago Historical Society, then housed in the organization's first headquarters at 632 N. Dearborn. Unfortunately, the brand new building and its contents was destroyed only three years later during the course of the Great Fire. A new structure was later erected on the site and occupied by the Society until its 1931 move to Lincoln Park. That gloomy Dearborn Street structure still stands today.

Ruling the nightlife of the surrounding area, the looming mansion is now home to one of Chicago's most enduring dance clubs, Excalibur, and its attendant bar, The Dome Room, where, according to employees, more than the dancers go bump in the night. In addition to poltergeist-style phenomena that have left the Dome Room a mess of liquor bottles and beer glasses, one of the club's staff has reported bluish-white forms running up and down the stairs at Excalibur.

While John Lalime would seem to be the obvious source of the bizarre occurrences at Excalibur, he has never been targeted as such. Rather, the phenomena focused on the old Chicago Historical Society have often been traced to the suicide of a lawyer who once lived in the building and, most often and erroneously, to the building's alleged use as a temporary morgue following the capsizing of the *Eastland* steamer on the Chicago River in 1915. In fact, the only buildings employed in such service were the Reid Murdoch Building (now City Traffic Court), the Second Regimental Armory at Washington and Custis streets (now Oprah Winfrey's Harpo Studios), and the J.P. Gavin Funeral Home at 642 N. Clark Street. The site of the last address, only a block away from the original Historical Society, may help to explain the past tendency of researchers to mistakenly connect the haunting of Excalibur with the victims of the *Eastland*.

♦

Buried Alive?

A SECRET IN THE CLOES BRICKYARD

*M*ore than houses can be haunted, and the ghosts of non-residential sites may in fact keep better, without storytellers to spill their secrets and spoil their sting. Certainly, it has only been in very recent years that one aging North Shore haunt has come into light, wrapped in a legend without a hint of romance and without a house to call home. While another story of dubious legitimacy, the legend of the Cloes Brickyard is nonetheless compelling.

Catherine Cloes and her husband John were the first settlers of what is now Lake Bluff, perhaps the most picturesque of the North Shore's placid lakeside villages. The couple had been married in Germany in 1824, but the substance of their lives between that event and their 1836 arrival in Lake Bluff remains unknown. For them, Lake Bluff was forest, cut through by deep ravines, the sound of the waves on the beach, and the occasional sighting of a ship on Lake Michigan, traveling between Fort Dearborn and Little Fort, now the city of Waukegan. John was a blacksmith, gunsmith, and locksmith by trade, and it was all he could do to build a cabin and a shop and to clear ten acres for subsistence farming.

Though life was lonely and tough, John and Catherine remained on the land they'd chosen. Eventually, though, their perseverance paid off. The area's Native Americans joined the Anglos seeking John Cloes' smithing services. By maintaining access paths to both the lake and to Green Bay Road, a well-traveled highway that ran north and south, John and Catherine's family name became well-known to residents and travelers. John eventually built a large frame house for his ever-growing family and his business and reputation continued to prosper. In the spring of 1850, however, John Cloes, like so many others, threw it all away.

Gripped by gold fever, he joined Abraham Frank and an associate named Kreutzer on the road westward to California. In late summer of that year, John wrote Catherine a lengthy letter in German. Separated from his companions along the way, John had lost many supplies and equipment and had abandoned his quest for ore. To survive, he had borrowed $85 for three months at 60 percent interest to start a blacksmith shop. Catherine never heard from him again.

In the 1850s, as industry moved through the North Shore, a brickmaker named Crawford set up small kilns where the clay was good. In the summer, he spent some time at each kiln making a modest batch of bricks. One of Crawford's kilns was on the Cloes property, and in 1855, Catherine Cloes took over the kiln and expanded it with a native of the county, Henry Ostrander, who had some experience with brickmaking. Together they built a large brickyard on Lake Bluff's Birch Road, and two of Catherine's children, Henry and Hiram, pitched in to run the business until their early deaths in 1858 and 1859 at the ages of 28 and 22. After Ostrander left the county in 1866, Ben, the youngest of the Cloes children, took over the brickyard's management and kept it running until around 1895, more than 20 years after Catherine's death.

According to local rumor, it was during the expansion of the Cloes Brickyard that a gruesome event occurred, an event that was hidden from local knowledge with great success until very recently. With the brickyard expanding to produce more inventory, the construction of a factory was begun soon after Catherine Cloes and Henry Ostrander took over its operation. During construction, a worker was allegedly killed accidentally during a row with a colleague. Terrified of retribution, the killer walled up the body in a nearly-completed portion of the factory. His deed was never discovered and the factory began operation as scheduled, complete with its chilling insulation. Fellow workers assumed that their comrade had simply deserted the job.

Legend says that for several decades after the incident Catherine was puzzled by despairing sobs that seemed to surround her as she made her inspections of the factory. Engrossed in the everyday problems of business operations, Catherine ignored the phenomenon. If she ever shared her experiences with anyone, they too kept the brickyard's secret, at least for the most part.

Only in recent years has the story of the murdered worker been circulated along the North Shore, most often during storytelling sessions at Halloween festivals. Whether the tale is true is for history alone to know. The Cloes Brickyard, long since demolished, will never tell.

♦

The Chicago River is said to remember the *Eastland* disaster of 1915, when the steamer capsized taking over 800 lives. (*Photo by D. Cowan*)

Shadows on The Chicago

THE *EASTLAND* REMEMBERS

B y 7:30 a.m. on Saturday, July 24, 1915, more than 2,500 passengers had boarded the *Eastland* steamer, docked between the Clark and LaSalle Street Bridges. The ship was bound for Michigan City, Indiana, where a picnic was to be held for Western Electric employees and their families. Five vessels had been chartered to take the excursion parties on the journey across the lake. The *Eastland* was the first of these to fill with cheering passengers eager to partake of one of the largest lake excursion parties ever assembled in Chicago. Just after the gangplank had been pulled in, the mooring lines loosed, and the anchor posts pulled, there followed one of the most horrific of all the city's disasters and the worst of all Chicago maritime tragedies.

Though there would be much speculation regarding circumstances of the event, the following account was eventually established as true. As the *Eastland* prepared to make its way towards the lake, a passing ship caused a sudden interest on one side of the ship's deck, creating a massive rush of bodies toward the diversion. Because the crew had emptied the ballast compartments to allow for more passengers, the result was a sudden and significant imbalance of weight. As the festive crowd waved from the Eastland's deck, the ship simply toppled over. The *Chicago Daily News* surveyed the scene:

> The river seemed covered with struggling forms. Life preservers were thrown from other boats, lines from shore, boxes and everything movable that would float by frantic spectators on shore, but dozens of those in the water disappeared under the waves or were dragged down by others.

Yet, the true horror of the moment was at first unseen. The weather had turned foreboding and many hundreds of passengers had already settled inside for the trip across the lake. When the

Eastland capsized, they were thrown together into a nearly solid mass which was immediately covered by the inrushing waters of the Chicago River. A few of these struggled to escape their ghastly prison, fighting to reach the upturned side of the vessel. Chicago firefighters and workers from the Commonwealth Edison Company rushed to the scene to chop away the woodworking above the waterline and to burn escape holes through the steel plates of the hull. Initially, bodies were pulled out and resuscitated. All too soon, however, no more life-saving was possible. The corpses of the drowned were wrapped in sheets and carried to the *Roosevelt*, another of the excursion vessels docked across the street, to await identification.

By five o'clock that afternoon, nearly 200 bodies were laid out on the floor of the 2nd Regiment Armory at 1054 W. Washington Boulevard. Less than an hour later, a diver who had been recovering bodies since mid-morning went out of his mind and had to be subdued by four policemen. City workers were dragging the river as far south as West Adams Street, having stretched a net across the waterway at West 12th Street to stop the drift of bodies.

At the end of the count, more than 800 passengers had been pronounced dead, among them 22 whole families.

The *Chicago Daily News* listed the "Dead, Injured and Missing" in its afternoon edition, offering what identification could be given to panicked friends and family dreading news of the worst. Too often, the descriptions of the deceased were maddeningly meager, such as "GIRL, blue dress" or "MAN, dark suit and white shirt." Others, however, were appallingly familiar, as one which read "WOMAN, about 21 years old; wore three rings, and another marked 'From D.L. to M.F.,' and a locket marked M.F."

The wreckage was eventually cleared, the legalities relatively settled, the living as comforted as they could be by their families, friends, and even the strangers who pitied their losses. But for years thereafter, passers-by on the Clark Street Bridge reported hearing cries of horror emanating from the river and its banks. Many assumed these screams to be those of the vanquished passengers of the ill-fated *Eastland* or of the hundreds of helpless bystanders who watched them perish.

In recent years, Chicago personality Oprah Winfrey

established Harpo Studios in the old 2nd Regiment Armory, which had served as a temporary morgue for the *Eastland's* victims. According to the experiences of employees, and of Winfrey herself, that grim moment in Chicago history seems to have imbedded itself in the very heart of the building. Winfrey and her staff have apparently reported unusual occurrences and sensations during their time there, which some have attributed to the victims of the *Eastland*.

Today, wanderers along Wacker Drive may pause a moment at the Clark Street Bridge to cast their eyes down upon the river and to study a plaque commemorating the *Eastland* dead, the casualties that comprised the worst disaster in Great Lakes history in terms of lives lost. Yet while these words carved in metal are at best silent reminders of that tragic excursion, the cries said to ring across the river are hardly as hushed, and, according to those who have heard them, infinitely more imperious.

◆

A tragic accident is memorialized by the stone elephants of Showmens Rest—a burial site for circus performers at suburban Woodlawn Cemetery. (*Photo by Ursula Bielski*)

A Case Solved

THE PHANTOM CIRCUS LEAVES TOWN

The day in 1918 when the Hagenbeck-Wallace Circus passed through the Chicago area turned out to be quite a grim one. By day's end, more than 50 of the circus' staff and performers lay dead, victims of a massive train wreck. Sometime around four o'clock that morning, the H-W Circus train was headed for Hammond, Indiana, carrying some 400 personnel. Near Ivanhoe, Illinois, the crew was forced to make a stop to tend to an overheated wheel bearing box. Unfortunately, following behind the halting cars was an empty troop train whose engineer, Alonzo Sargent, had been fired from a previous job for falling asleep while operating the engine. Although the circus train's crew had switched on red warning lights to indicate its stoppage on the tracks, Sargent ran his cars full speed into the obstacle. The impact destroyed three of the Hagenback-Wallace cars before coming to a halt. Immediately, a deadly fire broke out.

Many of the passengers and crew members were killed on impact; many more survived the initial blow only to die in flames while trapped in the wreckage. In all, 86 performers and crew hands lost their lives. Sadder still, most were never identified because of the nature of their profession. The majority of the victims were buried later that week on a substantial lot in Forest Park's Woodlawn Cemetery, which had been purchased previously by the Showmen's League of America and reserved for the burial of circus performers. Many graves were marked only with nicknames; still others, with the designation "Unknown Male." Years after the accident, five stone elephants were added to mark off the lot's boundaries which are about 100 feet west of the cemetery's entrance. These startling monuments with trunks lowered as in a gesture of mourning, inspired a legend to grow up around the tragedy.

Oral history maintains that some of the circus' elephants were killed in the train wreck, or even that they died trying to rescue performers from the ensuing fire by dislodging bits of flaming debris to free the entrapped victims. Keepers of these details report that the elephants were buried here at Woodlawn, with those they could not save. It was only after the erection of the monuments and the spread of the legends that neighbors began reporting the sounds of wild animals emanating from the cemetery. The belief quickly emerged that such sounds were audio apparitions of the animal victims of the 1918 tragedy. In actuality, not only are no elephants buried at Woodlawn, neither were there any elephants on that fated Hammond-bound train.

In spite of the lack of a factual basis, the legend of the martyred elephants, their burial at Woodlawn, and their haunting of the site lingered, becoming firmly entrenched in the folklore of the surrounding suburbs of North Riverside, Cicero, and Berwyn. Meanwhile, neighboring police departments and the cemetery management shared a mounting befuddlement. As remarkable as it seemed, many level-headed listeners admitted that these rumored sounds seemed real. Then, a local police officer made an ingenious, but retrospectively obvious, connection. The sounds were animal voices carried on the wind from the Brookfield Zoo, less than a mile away.

◆

Making His Mark
A HERO'S HANDPRINT

*T*he legend surrounding the cause of the Great Chicago Fire is arguably the best known in all of Chicago folklore. Certainly, a piece of the city's self-image rests on Chicagoans' stunning ability to rebuild the wasteland after Mrs. O'Leary's infamous cow kicked over a lantern which ultimately sent the entire city up in flames. The devastating conflagration of 1871, without a doubt necessitated a target for blame, a target that could withstand the burden of a city's grief. O'Leary's unsuspecting bovine proved to be the handiest of scapegoats.

Apart from this tale, however, folklorists note with puzzlement the glaring absence of legends—especially supernatural ones—associated with the Great Chicago Fire, aside from the rumor that the image of a hanged man has been spotted in an upper window of the old Water Tower, one of the few buildings to survive the fire. However, several other conflagrations have created some of the most poignant of Chicago's haunting legends. Among them is the eerie tale told by firefighters themselves. This is the story of the ineradicable handprint of Francis X. Leavy.

On the morning of Good Friday, April 18, 1924, Frank Leavy was stationed at 13th and Oakley—Engine Company 107 and Truck Company 12. As the naturally good-spirited firefighter half-heartedly performed his chores, Leavy was approached by a concerned colleague, Edward McKevitt, who sensed that Leavy was disturbed about something melancholy, over the grim holy day, or disappointed at the prospect of working that coming Easter Sunday. Yet, in response to McKevitt's inquiries, Leavy admitted to neither of these. Pausing in his window washing and resting his hand on one of the glass panes of the firehouse door, Leavy instead stated with utter bluntness, "This is my last day with the fire department." The prognostication came without any warning, as did the alarm bell that rang through the house at just that moment.

What did Leavy know? Over in the Union Stockyards, a huge blaze was underway, and as more and more companies were called to the scene, the men of 13th and Oakley had begun to worry about the potential lack of backup help should another fire erupt. In the midst of this concern, a call did come in from alarm box 372 summoning Engine Company 107 and Truck Company 12 to a blaze at Curran Hall, an office building just southwest of the Loop, almost two miles away.

As part of a detailed account of the Leavy legend, reporter Alex Burkholder envisioned for *Firehouse* magazine readers that fateful trip from the firehouse to the fire site. Imagining the scene, a busy spring afternoon in 1924, Burkholder imagines the ride as

> ...a perilous one. The street offered a veritable obstacle course of motorized cars and trucks, horse-drawn vehicles and red streetcars. Defensive driving in the fire department was still decades off and the haste to reach that plume of smoke to the east resulted in near disaster at every major intersection, where traffic signals were still a rarity. The fire companies . . . left behind a trail of frightened horses and angry, cursing owners tangling with their animals.

Arriving at the fire was, nonetheless, the easy part. Only then would the real challenge begin.

Frank Leavy was among the men who were ordered to the second floor of the blazing building where they began to quench the fire. But though the team fought to control the flames, supervisors soon began screaming to them to flee the building. The outside wall had begun to crumble. Though the firefighters immediately made for the fire escapes, most met their deaths on the way down, crushed by the tumbling edifice. Many hours later, after the fire was contained, Frank Leavy was pulled from the debris, along with his comrades of Engine 107. Legend has it that his was the only face distinguishable after the disfiguring force of bricks had taken its toll.

The following day, McKevitt was recalling to a group of firefighters Leavy's baffling premonition of the previous morning when he glanced at the firehouse doors. What he saw there in the glass was the image of a man's handprint, exactly where Leavy had rested his soapy hand while predicting his own demise.

After McKevitt's suggestion that the print might be Leavy's, a furious campaign ensued with everyone present attempting to wipe the handprint off of the pane. Nonetheless, after repeated scrubbing with both soap and ammonia and even attempts to scrape off the image with a razor blade, the handprint remained. In response to this dilemma, the Pittsburgh Plate Glass Company was called in to remove the stain from the window which they had manufactured. But this stain resisted even their most trusted chemical compounds.

As further attempts to remove it continued and failed, the handprint became famous, drawing newspaper reporters, other firefighters, and the merely curious, all baffled by the mystery of the ineradicable print. Finally, a city official obtained a copy of Leavy's thumbprint and compared it with the thumbprint of the window's stain. Though some were shocked by the news that they matched, many were hardly surprised.

For 20 years, the handprint remained. The firefighters at 13th and Oakley came and went. In the course of their duties, many attempted to wash the window, but no one ever quite succeeded. Then, on April 18, 1944, the twentieth anniversary of Leavy's death, a newspaper boy accidentally threw the morning paper through the window, shattering any hope of solving its mystery. Yet, there has been no lack of speculation regarding the legendary handprint.

Aside from the widely-shared belief in the print's supernatural origin, some have theorized that Leavy's fear of an impending crisis may have caused the production of some bodily chemical that left a permanent stain through his perspiration.

At 13th and Oakley, the tale of Frank Leavy's window was still told by the older firefighters to the new until the firehouse was torn down in 1971. The whispery memory surrounding his name has helped, as so many tragic events have, to forge a common bond between all Chicago firefighters. Ultimately, although Frank Leavy's window was destroyed along with the "evidence" it may have offered future researchers, there has been little erosion of the legend surrounding its creation.

◆

Dave Black of Supernatural Occurrence Studies captured
this rare photo of anomalous mist at the Lincoln Park site of
the St. Valentine's Day Massacre—on February 14, 1998.
(*Photo courtesy of Supernatural Occurrence Studies*)

To Bugs, With Love

THE ST. VALENTINE'S DAY MASSACRE

I will live and let live.

—AL CAPONE

---

*C*rime buffs eager for a tour of Chicago's gangland attractions are often disappointed by the city's lack of preserved locations. Many of the most notorious sites in the history of Chicago organized crime no longer exist, leaving no evidence but memories of the madness with which they were connected. Gone, for example, is Big Jim Colosimo's restaurant at 2128 South Wabash Avenue where the owner prided himself both on his smoothly-run empire of vice and the "500,000 yards of Spaghetti Always on Hand." Also gone is Sharbaro and Co. Mortuary, 708 N. Wells Street, which hosted two of the biggest funerals in gangland history: one in November 1924, when Dion O'Bannion was carried out the front door in a $10,000 casket; the other in October 1926, after Hymie Weiss was gunned down on the sidewalk across from Holy Name Cathedral.

The Four Deuces Saloon, now a vacant lot at 2222 S. Wabash, long ago welcomed Al Brown from Brooklyn to his first Chicago job as the bouncer who would become Alphonse Capone. Later, the Lexington Hotel at 2135 S. Michigan Avenue would serve as the seat of Capone's crime kingdom. Alas, that palace, along with Capone's own fifth floor suite, has also been demolished in recent years.

For organized crime enthusiasts, however, more missed than any of these is the warehouse which stood at 2122 N. Clark Street, where on Valentine's Day 1929, one of the most gruesome multiple homicides in gangland history was committed.

The building nearly eluded description: a one-story red brick structure, 60 feet wide and 120 feet long, tucked between two four-story buildings that in 1929 somewhat towered over the S-M-C Cartage Company garage between them. On the morning of February

14, a sordid group was gathered inside in retreat from a typical snowy Chicago morning. Ex-safecraker Johnny May, having been hired as an auto mechanic by the notorious gangleader, George "Bugs" Moran, was stretched out under a truck fixing a wheel. Living out of a slipshod apartment, May was grateful for the 50 bucks a week he got from Moran to support his wife, six children, and a dog named Highball, who happened to be at work with him that morning, tied to the axle of the truck.

Huddled around a percolating coffee pot on an electric hot plate, shivering in their overcoats and hats, were another half-dozen assorted characters, including Frank and Pete Gusenberg, who were, per Moran's orders, awaiting a truck-full of hijacked whiskey from Detroit. Moran himself was late for the 10:30 a.m. rendezvous. It was a little after the appointed time when he finally ventured out into the 15 below zero cold with Ted Newberry, a gambling concessionaire, headed towards the garage. The Gusenbergs were antsy, anxious to get started on their own part of the scheme, driving two empty trucks back to Detroit to meet a haul of smuggled Canadian whiskey. Their companions, however, were carefree, having been summoned by Moran merely to help unload the trucks when they arrived. Among the harder hearts—Moran's brother-in-law, James Clark; financial whiz, Adam Heyer; and newcomer Al Weinshank—was Reinhardt Schwimmer, a wanna-be of sorts and a young optometrist who had glommed onto Moran after befriending the gangleader at their mutual home, the Parkway Hotel. After that meeting, Schwimmer frequented the North Side warehouse hangout for the thrill of illicit companionship.

None of the group suspected that a police car had pulled up outside the building or knew that Moran, spotting the car upon his approach, had hightailed it back to the Parkway. While Moran's men whiled away the time under the light of a single naked bulb, four men emerged from the car outside, two in police uniforms and two in civilian clothes. The landlady of a neighboring rooming house watched as the men entered the building, then gasped at the clattering explosion of sound that followed a few moments later.

Soon after, four figures emerged, two marched at gunpoint by the two policemen, amid the clamor of a barking dog. After the car pulled away from the curb and headed down Clark Street, neighbors concerned over of the still-howling dog, sent a man in to check on the animal. He remained inside only a few moments before reappearing to report on the scene inside.

Moran's men had been lined up against the rear wall of the garage and sprayed by machine guns in careful swoops of fire which targeted first their heads, then their chests, and finally their stomachs. Despite the shower of death, May and Clark had lived, but with their faces nearly blown off by close-range shotgun blasts. Remarkably, Frank Gusenberg had also survived. When Detective Sweeney arrived at the massacre scene, he recognized the face of his boyhood friend on the body of the bullet-riddled Gusenberg. With 14 bullets in his body, Frank had crawled 20 feet from the blood-soaked rear wall, from where he was taken to Alexian Brothers Hospital. There, upon Gusenberg's revival, Sweeney would repeat the question he'd first posed in the garage: "Frank, in God's name what happened? Who shot you?" only to receive Gusenberg's famously hard-boiled response, "Nobody shot me." Still urged by Sweeney to reveal the killers, Gusenberg instead spat out his last words: "I ain't no copper."

But while the law was temporarily baffled as to the source of such brutality, Bugs Moran immediately named its orchestrator. Upon hearing the news of the gruesome deed, he flatly proclaimed, "Only Capone kills like that."

In fact, Al Capone was at that moment in Florida, playing host at a lavish Miami resort. When questioned by one of his guests about his involvement in the Chicago tragedy, Capone curiously but firmly responded that "the only man who kills like that is Bugs Moran." Of the two testimonies, Moran's was right on. Capone had been the brains behind the bloodbath. While some later stories differed on the names of the gunmen, the core team was comprised of Capone's standard slate of executioners.

In 1945, the front of the S-M-C garage was turned into an antique shop by a couple oblivious to the property's infamy. Unfortunately, their doorway was visited more often by crime buffs than by antiquers, the former of which came to the garage in droves from all over the world and eventually forced the disgusted couple to abandon their venture. Later, in the late 1960s, the building was demolished and the 417 rear wall bricks hauled away by George

Patey, a Canadian businessman who first built them into a wall of his nightclub, then envisioned them as wonderfully lurid souvenirs, which he promptly sold off to crime buffs. According to rumors, however, anyone who purchased one of the S-M-C bricks was besieged by bad luck, in the form of illness, financial or family ruin, or any of a variety of other maladies. The very structure seemed to have been infused with the powerful negativity of that Valentine's Day.

As did the site.

Five trees dot the otherwise nondescript space, the middle one marking the spot where the rear wall once stood. To this day, an occasional stroller along Clark Street will report hearing violent screams ringing off the fenced-off lot once occupied by the garage that is now part of a nursing home's front lawn. Jason Nhyte and Dave Black of Supernatural Occurrence Studies repeatedly visited the site to investigate well-known allegations of its haunting. On Valentine's Day of 1998 Dave Black finally captured a photograph of an anomalous ring of mist, the only known photograph of its kind from the site.

Moreover, those walking dogs are often puzzled by their pets' curious reaction to this stretch of sidewalk, as their animals either growl or bark furiously at the apparent nothingness or whimper as they crouch away from the iron fence.

Perhaps dogs, known to be more psychically sensitive than most of their masters, are reacting to something unknown to their human companions, a massive surge of energy produced and sustained at the site by the impact of the massacre; a vision of Highball, forever snapping his leash in the aftermath of the bloodbath; or the ringing in their painfully acute ears of the rat-a-tat of Capone's heartless love song, hand-delivered long ago to an unwilling gathering of wallflowers.

♦

Show of Shows

CURTAINS FOR A VERY DIRTY RAT

*A*s an important stop in the national touring circuits of smash Broadway productions as well as independent entertainers, Chicago has done its share of oohing and ahhing over the performers that continually sweep in and out of town, dazzling a city that despite its sophistication, still greets the famous with the eagerness of Wichita.

Hardly lacking in local talent, Chicago itself, especially in recent decades, has swept international theater critics off their feet by wooing culture vultures with the increasingly acclaimed productions of local theater companies, the continuing contributions of home-grown musical styles, and the pioneering comedic methods of the Second City troupe. Over and above the endless parade of entertainment, local and otherwise, that crosses their stages, however, some Chicago theater buildings have managed to produce rather unusual shows of their own, thanks to a handful of spirits that reportedly call them home.

Joliet's Rialto Square Theater and the Woodstock Opera House are both said to host famous female spirits. Woodstock's infamous Elvira takes center stage not only at the Opera House but in all of McHenry County ghost lore. This turn of the century suicide victim is believed to encourage contemporary actresses to relive her own self-destruction: throwing herself six stories from the theater's belfry to the sidewalk below. When not engaged in such efforts, she is said to comment on rehearsals from seat number 113.

In west suburban Downers Grove, the Tivoli movie theater remembers a tragic fire that occurred some years ago and the pathetic pyromaniac who is believed to have set it. According to local legend, the culprit found himself trapped in a backstage room after setting the fire, with no means of escape. Strangely enough, no remains were ever found, nor was the worker ever heard from again. Some theater-goers and employees, however, will tell of an eerie mist that seeps from behind the stage curtains each night after the screening of the last movie. Proof positive, they say, of the death of that incompetent arsonist.

In the city proper, stories are typically less detailed, but no less fascinating. One of the most recently discovered of the city's hauntings centers on the old Buena Park Hotel, a 1929 building which now houses a local acting company, The National Pastime Theater. When the ensemble moved into its performance space on north Broadway (the hotel's ballroom), the company's leader, Larry Bryan, thought he had stumbled on a forgotten fantasyland. Although the sumptuous space behind an unassuming storefront would make for dreamy drama, producers and performers soon discovered that the site was hardly their secret. After the theater was set up, Bryan began to feel "the magic of the place, an energy that perhaps stayed locked in all those years" when the ballroom was closed up. That magic has sometimes been attributed to carefree prohibition-era spirits thought to continue their revelry at this former speakeasy.

According to Bryan, the hijinks of the haunters are most obvious upon the return of the living after several hours of absence. For example, one night when Bryan was working alone, he went out for a while after locking up and turning off all the lights. He returned later to find the stage fully lit once again. On another occasion, while a group of workers were moving rows of seats into new positions, the group broke for dinner and came back after a long repast. A row of seats which had taken four men to move had been relocated to its original position. Physical evidence aside, Bryan, at least, feels the real evidence is intangible. It is rather the atmosphere that convinces company members and audiences that the theater's past is very much alive. As Bryan maintains, "It has the smell of notorious about it."

Without question, those acquainted with Chicago history would guess that the city's most haunted theater would be the site of the Iroquois Theater, now the Ford Center for the Performing Arts, and formerly the Oriental Theater. On December 30, 1903, a fire broke out in the Iroquois during a matinee performance of "Mr. Bluebeard," starring famed comedian Eddie Foy. Before the day was over, 572 people, including many children on Christmas holiday, had died. Thirty more would succumb to their injuries, bringing the death toll to over 600. The narrow passageway behind the theater was dubbed "Death Alley" after 125 victims were found stacked there.

Some had fallen to their deaths or attempted to leap to safety from an unfinished fire escape; others had been removed from the theater and piled there by firefighters. Amazingly, this event, the deadliest fire in Chicago history and the worst theater disaster in American history, failed to produce any known *psi* phenomena.

In fact, the city's most paranormally prestigious theater is actually not haunted at all, but has been reckoned as such nonetheless. With good reason. As the focal point in the thrilling tale that created one of the city's most famous and favorite ghosts, the Biograph Theater on north Lincoln Avenue welcomed a very special guest on a hot July night in 1934 to his last picture show: John Dillinger, christened by his pursuers as Public Enemy Number One.

That evening, Dillinger left the theater accompanied by Ann Sage, the legendary "Lady in Red" and his girlfriend, Polly Hamilton, with whom he had been holed up at her 2420 N. Halsted Street apartment. At that point, the infamous criminal met his long-avoided end in a narrow alleyway just steps from the theater doors. The bullet fired through the back of his neck by FBI Agent Charles Winstead had been a long time coming. Congratulations poured into the Chicago Police Department and U.S. government agencies from around the world. For while Dillinger's international renown had been quickly won, he made it unforgettable by being impossibly hard to nab.

For four months, Melvin Purvis, the soft spoken head of Chicago's FBI agents, had lived and breathed the chase for the Indiana-born gangster, desperate to snag him before Purvis' critics could oust him in favor of "a more experienced man." In hot pursuit of his prey, Purvis had lived from tip to tip, leading his agents in a foiled attempt to surround the scoundrel at a State Street and Austin cafe, an impressive but ill-fated attack on Dillinger's North Woods hideout at Sault St. Marie, and the infamous confrontation at Wisconsin's Little Bohemia Lodge, in which FBI agents recklessly injured two civilians and killed a third. It was here, too, that George "Baby Face" Nelson reportedly killed Special Agent W. Carter Baum, prompting FBI Chief J. Edgar Hoover to call Nelson a "rat." Yet these near misses with the FBI were only the last stretch of a sensational, though short, career.

A summary of the "High Points in Life of John Dillinger"

was provided by the *Chicago Tribune* on the morning after his fatal shooting. What follows the headline is a catalog of arrests, sentencings, shootouts, and escapes. At the age of 20, Dillinger held up his hometown grocery store in Mooresville, Indiana. Pleading guilty, he was sentenced to serve 10 to 20 years in prison, while his accomplice, pleading not guilty, received a sentence of little more than two years. Bitterly reflecting on this joke of justice, Dillinger spent a quiet eight and a half years planning his revenge on the law. On May 22, 1933, the then-unknown Dillinger was paroled and proceeded to rob three banks in as many months, making off with $40,000. He was incarcerated at Lima, Ohio in September of that same year. When, barely three weeks later, three former fellow inmates invaded the prison and sprung Dillinger, they ushered the convict into a brief but stellar stint as an internationally notorious gangster. His gang would be described after his death as "the most notorious band of outlaws in America, probably the world." Eluding a police trap in November, the gang pulled off a bank robbery later that month. To celebrate the new year, an unrepentant Dillinger shot and killed police officer William O'Malley in another bank robbery in East Chicago, for which he was arrested in Arizona and sent to Crown Point, Indiana to stand trial. Predictably, he escaped a month later by carving a gun out of soap and blackening it with shoe polish and eluded pursuers for another month. Finding himself at that point in another jam, he shot his way out of a St. Paul police trap on March 31st and made a similar escape from the FBI trap near Mercer, Wisconsin, where he killed two people in the process. Two months later, police found a Ford V-8 at Roscoe and Leavitt streets treated with a fingerprint-dissolving chemical and with one of the windows smashed out to facilitate shotgunning. Inside the car were a half dozen pop bottles, a baby stroller used to tote tommy guns during getaways, and a matchbook from the Little Bohemia Lodge. There was no doubt about it. Dillinger was in Chicago.

In late June, Dillinger was home again, his gang robbing a South Bend, Indiana bank, wounding four civilians and slaying police officer William P. O'Malley, a close friend of East Chicago's then-police chief, Martin Zarkovich.

In little more than a year, Dillinger had led six major bank robberies, killed two police officers, a civilian, and two FBI agents, escaped imprisonment twice, and eluded or shot his way out of a half-dozen cleverly-laid traps.

Prior to his death, the hardened gangster had been well aware of his streak of fortune and was none too secure about its future continuance. In May 1934, a skittish Dillinger had called his lawyer to discuss the prospect of plastic surgery. On the run from nearly every law enforcement agent in the country, the outlaw yet dared to hope for a new freedom, freedom which might be realized through the alteration of his well-known countenance and the obliteration of his infamous fingerprints. Accustomed to relying on none but himself and his gang for salvation, Dillinger was nonetheless prepared to put his money on one man, a surgeon by the name of Loeser. The gangster felt his trust was well placed, for he and his would-be doctor were birds of a feather: the latter had done time in Leavenworth on a narcotics charge. Sprung from his cage, Loeser was in dire need of funds. In payment for the surgeon's services, Dillinger opened his billfold to the tune of five grand.

On May 27th, the optimistic hood arrived on schedule for the promised procedure, met by his lawyer. In a derelict northside flat, owned by an ex-speakeasy operator, the two passed the night in expectation of the doctor's arrival the next day. When Loeser showed, however, the gangster and his counsel were disturbed to find him accompanied by a pallid and nerve-wracked young assistant. Soothed by the doctor's reassurances, the patient recited his wish list to the attentive Loeser: remove three moles and his giveaway scar; fill in his cleft chin and the bridge of his nose; and, most importantly, nix the damning fingerprints. Agreeing to the changes, Loeser showed Dillinger to a cot, instructed his assistant to administer a general anesthetic, and left the room to prepare for the operation. Placing an ether-soaked towel over Dillinger's nose and mouth, the assistant advised his charge to take some deep breaths. The patient obliged, with dire results. The flustered accomplice had given the gangster a dangerous dosage and his face proceeded to turn blue. Then, to the young man's horror, Dillinger swallowed his tongue.

Summoned by his assistant's screams, Loeser grabbed his forceps and pulled Dillinger's tongue from his throat. The patient was not breathing. In a ramshackle flat on a quiet Chicago morning, the world's most wanted criminal was dead.

Thoroughly alarmed to action, Loeser worked furiously to restore respiration. After a few moments on the other side, Dillinger was revived, reassured, and re-anaesthetized. The surgery was resumed and completed to the gangster's satisfaction. Ironically, a mere 25 days later, Dillinger's new lease on life was bluntly terminated by a well-placed bullet from the frantic FBI.

At approximately 8:30 in the evening on July 22nd, the surgically-altered outlaw strolled into a screening of "Manhattan Melodrama" at the Biograph Theater on north Lincoln Avenue, observed by no less than 16 police officers and FBI agents, including Melvin Purvis himself. For two hours and four minutes, the watchers waited, one or another occasionally entering the theater to walk the aisles in search of their prey. When Dillinger finally emerged onto the sidewalk, his would-be captors were more than ready, but a little bit wary.

Public Enemy Number One he was, but he looked nothing like the romantic trench-coated antagonist *noir* that popular culture imagined. Instead, agents beheld a weary moviegoer on a hot summer night, clad in a straw hat, a gray-and-black flecked tie knotted onto a white silk shirt, canvas shoes, and gray summer trousers. Coatless, he appeared unarmed as well and must have undermined the resolve of more than a few of his stalkers, especially in light of his altered features. To Purvis, however, he was unmistakable: 'I knew him the minute I saw him. You couldn't miss if you had studied that face as much as I have.'

As the target strolled south on Lincoln Avenue, he stepped down a curb to a narrow alley entrance. As Dillinger turned down the passageway, a half dozen agents closed in. The moment froze as Dillinger, his back to the pack, instinctively went for a cleverly-concealed .38—too late. Four shots were fired, three hitting their mark. Among a swarm of home-bound moviegoers and nearly a score of law enforcement officers, Dillinger went down. Chaos ensued.

According to the *Chicago Tribune*, Dillinger dropped at the feet of Mrs. Pearl Doss, a woman that recognized the fallen man as "Johnnie," a neighbor boy from her Indiana youth. Doss claimed that in that moment of recognition she was close enough to catch his classic last words: "They've got me at last." A nearby barkeep mistook the victim for his brother-in-law, sending his wife into hysterics. Tradition tells of passers-by running to dip their handkerchiefs in the still-flowing blood, anxious for gruesome souvenirs of the startling event.

Struggling for control, Purvis ordered that Dillinger be rushed to nearby Alexian Brothers Hospital. Dead on arrival, Dillinger's body was turned away at the doors. The strange party retired to the hospital lawn to await the deputy coroner.

That night the city awoke, electric. For weeks, Northsiders had been warned by police at the Town Hall and Sheffield district headquarters that the outlaw had been seen in Lakeview, North Center, and Uptown by various witnesses. A March 7th edition of the local *Booster* newspaper proclaimed:

> LOOK UNDER YOUR BED. SEARCH YOUR CELLAR. SHAKE OUT THE MOTHBALLS FROM LAST SUMMER'S CLOTHES. DILLINGER IS HIDING SOMEWHERE HERE. AND HE MAY BE HIDING IN YOUR BACK YARD.

One lifetime North Side resident, Frances Kathrein, recalls that sweltering July night in 1934, when she and her brothers and sisters lay sleeping on the front-room floor of their second-story flat, hoping for a breath of wind through the screen door. What wafted through that door was not a summer breeze, however, but a sudden sound of commotion on the street outside. Frances' future husband, Norbert, then 13 years old, tore down Cuyler Avenue with a group of newsboys full of papers and cries of "Extra!," delivering in loud voices the news: "Dillinger's Shot!"

In a report shocking for its day, the *Chicago Tribune* reported on the mob scene at the Cook County morgue, where the line of curiosity-seekers snaked through the building, apparently oblivious to rows of exposed corpses, and stretched down the block outside. The coroner, a man by the name of Walsh, after viewing the crowd "with apparent satisfaction," posed for photographs with the body. At his instruction, Dillinger's corpse was placed in a basement room behind a glass panel so that the crowds might be allowed to file past for a look at the expired Enemy. The scene was as absurd as might be imagined, and the *Tribune* presented it in all its brutishness, focusing particular attention on the women in the crowd, who

> pushed forward with massive shoulders and hips. Some of them sighed or groaned with a pretense of horror as they looked at the body, tilted at a 45 degree angle to give a better view. One or two with faces slightly less depraved than the others clucked their tongues and said as they went away: I wouldn't have wanted to see him except that I think it's a moral lesson, don't you? . . . One fat blonde woman, after leaving the basement, applied fresh lipstick and, preparing to join the waiting line to have another look, said, "I'm disappointed. Looks just like any other dead man."

The Biograph Theater manager declined a chance to speak to the press about the theater's role in the set-up, fearing possible ill-effects on his business. On the other hand, when one reporter, hoping to squeeze some information from Morris Oppenheimer, the proprietor of the bar next door, arrived at the tavern, he found that Oppenheimer had "already paint[ed] a sign, in blood-red letters, proclaiming: DILLINGER HAD HIS LAST DRINK HERE."

In light of the mania following Dillinger's death, it seems almost unbelievable that no unusual phenomena were reported at the shooting site in the immediate months and years that followed. In fact, it was not until the 1970s that passers-by on north Lincoln Avenue began to spot a bluish figure running down the alley, stumbling, falling, and disappearing. Accompanying such sightings were the typical reports of cold spots, feelings of uneasiness, and the sudden unwillingness to use the alley as a handy shortcut to Halsted Street.

In recent years, while paranormal tales of that alleyway have lapsed, its history and mystery remain. Visitors to the Biograph Theater can examine a diagram on the window of the old box office describing the complex set-up of Dillinger by Melvin Purvis' FBI. Led by the story, they can sit in the seat where Dillinger sat more than 60 years ago and afterwards emerge to walk his last path to the passage still known by older Chicagoans as "Dillinger's Alley."

There, just beyond the pool of neon light shed by the theater's brilliant marquee, the imaginative and the perceptive might well wonder about the supernatural survival of that most reluctant of victims.

Dillinger's will to live may continue to inspire us to doubt his death, a doubt that echoes that of Mary Kinder, a friend of Dillinger's. Kinder had certainly read the news about the shoot-out in the alley and had talked with a legion of reporters the next morning about her reaction to the fugitive's demise. Despite the undeniable fact of Dillinger's demise, the girl couldn't help asking, as some still do, "Is it true? Is he dead?"

◆

A second floor classroom in the former Our Lady of Angels school after the devastating fire there in 1958. (*Courtesy of D. Cowan*)

Our Lady of the Angels

The new parish school of Our Lady of the Angels is not "new" anymore. In fact, it has been nearly 40 years since its erection on the West Side spot where its earlier namesake once stood. There, on December 1, 1958, 92 children and three nuns perished in a blaze that claimed not only innocent life. Also destroyed were the psychological and physical well-being of an entire neighborhood; widespread trust in the city and its resources; and the faith of many people in the local clergy, the Archdiocese of Chicago, and the Church itself. To say that the fire touched many more than those 95 who died is to understate the profound impact of the event; to say that the city still feels its impact is to state the obvious. Yet, at this writing, not even a plaque exists at the site in commemoration of all that the fire destroyed. Some feel that the event is still too close for such a gesture. Others point to a striking memorial at Queen of Heaven Cemetery in suburban Hillside, marking the graves of 25 of the fire victims. A few still say, as they did at the new building's completion, that the new parish school is their memorial.

When David Cowan and John Kuenster combined their extensive research efforts to pen their 1996 volume, *To Sleep with the Angels*, they aimed to "set straight the record" on one of the most devastating fires in American history and, arguably, the most tragic event in Chicago's memory. To accomplish their grim task, they conducted countless interviews with survivors, friends and family of those who perished, firefighters and police, members of the Archdiocese of Chicago, and the reporters who documented the impact and aftermath of the event. The resulting documentary has surely begun to accomplish what the authors intended: "to provide a sense of closure to an historical void that . . . remained open for nearly four decades."

Like so many schools of its time, the parish school of Our Lady of the Angels was ill-prepared to challenge its fate. In the late 1950s, the building remained without sprinkler systems and smoke detectors, the second-floor staircases were without fire doors. The fire alarm rang only inside the school, with neither an outside alarm nor a fire station signal to assist it. In all, the school possessed just a single fire escape. Even the window ledges, 37½ inches off the floor, were too high for most of the primary and middle-grade children to climb over. Fourteen hundred students packed the main building alone, typical of the overcrowding common to elementary schools of the day. Notwithstanding what were by current standards grossly inadequate safety conditions at the school, the building had passed its last inspection just two months before the fire erupted. Governed as it was by a 1905 ordinance that contained neither provisions requiring construction with noncombustibles nor installation of fire-safety devices such as sprinklers and fire escapes, Our Lady of the Angels was unbelievably, legally safe.

In the aftermath, investigators isolated the spot where the blaze had begun sometime after two o'clock on that overcast December afternoon in a refuse drum at the bottom of the desolate northeast basement stairwell. After annihilating the container's debris, the fire had continued to smolder until the heat blew out a stairwell window and fed the area with a wave of oxygen. With nothing in its path but wooden and asphalt-tiled stairs, varnished woodwork, and two layers of rubberized-plastic paint on the walls, the fire shot up the stairwell and forged a swift path to a second floor corridor flanked by classroom doors. Every surface the fire touched dissolved into black smoke and burst the glass in transoms over classroom doors. By 2:45 p.m., as Engine 85 pulled up to the building, the upper floor of the north wing was mostly ablaze.

Nearly one-third of the roof was burned off before firefighters could halt the fire's advance. They were working against a nearly half-hour time loss. The fire had burned many minutes before an alarm was sent, help was sent to the wrong address, and a locked courtyard gate had to be broken through. Still, the firefighters' initial efforts resulted in the rescue of 160 children, some of whose falls they broke with their own bodies as children jumped from classroom windows.

One of Carl Sandburg's *Chicago Poems*, "Anna Imroth," tells of a young girl's death in a factory fire, after failing to survive a jump to safety. In that poem, commentators on Anna's misfortune charged her death to "the hand of God and the lack of fire escapes." In response to the fire at Our Lady of the Angels, the public was far from willing to so neatly split the blame.

For the fire at Our Lady of the Angels left far more than a building in ruins. Among the debris, Chicagoans and the world recognized the ashes of their trust, in the city, in the Church, in their neighbors. Everywhere the wronged sought a scapegoat for the fire. Families and friends cursed the city; the media targeted the Archdiocese; police and fire officials hunted for an arsonist. In fact, God was barely mentioned, except to be invoked in the millions of prayers and curses following the disaster. Still, though many were blamed, only one villain was truly rehabilitated—the existing fire safety requirements.

On January 21, 1959, the Chicago City Council adopted amendments to the city building code requiring automatic sprinkler systems in all frame schools over two stories tall with wooden floors and joints. By December 1964, every school in Chicago was brought up to speed with respect to the new fire safety codes, and within a year of the Our Lady of the Angels fire, more than 16,000 school buildings across the country had made major fire safety improvements.

During his ten years of research for *To Sleep with the Angels*, David Cowan made countless visits to the new school and to the fire memorial at Queen of Heaven Cemetery. Cowan describes the fire site in no uncertain terms. Of the new school, he firmly states, "That's sacred ground." This feeling was heightened after a 1995 commemorative mass, when Cowan and a friend visited the second-floor classrooms where the fire had played out. Describing the discomfort of "being in the same air space" as those who had witnessed the fire firsthand, Cowan, himself a firefighter and a Catholic, relates with discretion a number of unusual accounts he received in the course of his conversations with those close to the fire.

A young woman who attended Our Lady of the Angels in the early 1980s told of several occasions when she heard the sound of people screaming and felt a sort of presence while she was alone in the school hallway. Later, she drew sketches of faces she had seen in a dream—faces which she linked to the inexplicable sounds. Elsewhere, family members of the victims told of premonitions of death during the days before the tragedy. One mother had entered her son's room on the night before the fire to encounter a vision of him lying in a coffin. Others related experiences which occurred after the fire. One woman, resting at home after the ordeal of identifying her son at the morgue, woke to see him sitting on the couch, holding her hand and consoling her. In another case, a sister appeared to her grief-stricken brother, assuring him, "Don't worry. I'm going to watch over you." In one particularly compelling case, a survivor of the fire related how, after escaping the building, he and a friend went looking for his sister amid the frantic crowd gathered outside the school. Relieved at seeing her walking towards home down a nearby alley, he returned to the drama of the fire scene. However, when he returned home later that afternoon, he learned that his sister had died in the fire.

Although Cowan clearly trusts in the earnest nature of these accounts, there are other tales of the fire which invite his criticism; namely, reports that the fire memorial at Queen of Heaven Cemetery has at times exhibited the smell of smoke, a phenomenon to which he, during his countless visits to the site, was never privy. Whatever truth there may have been in any of these stories, it is certain that a great number of ghosts were laid to rest with the publication of *To Sleep With the Angels*.

David Cowan agrees. Reflecting on his years growing up in the parish neighborhood, his life as a journalist, and more than a decade of research on the fire, he remarks, "I always sensed a feeling of restlessness" surrounding the memory of the fire victims. Now, since the telling of their stories, "this blanket of serenity is over their graves."

◆

written on the wind

THE LAST RIDE OF THE GRIMES SISTERS

*P*hantom cars have driven in and out of the annals of parapsychology since the invention of the automobile. They are, however, rarely connected with any verifiable historical event. Chicago's psychic vehicles have typically adhered to this rule. Witness the ghostly sedans whizzing along the Midlothian Turnpike outside Bachelors Grove or the phantom drivers speeding past White Cemetery and St. Mary's. A glaring exception to this generality seems to have been occurring since the late 1950s in the southwest suburban town of Willow Springs, where in 1956, a month-long search for two missing girls ended and one of the most distinctive of the southwest suburbs' ample collection of haunting phenomena began.

It was December 28th of that year when Patricia and Barbara Grimes, aged 13 and 15 respectively, left their home at 3624 S. Damen Avenue, headed for the Brighton Theater at 4223 S. Archer, only a mile away. Having planned to spend a simple evening watching a new Elvis Presley movie, the girls would instead go missing for 27 agonizing days, until their nude, frozen bodies were found on a bank of Devil's Creek in southwest Cook County. The coroner's office announced that the girls, their bodies otherwise unharmed, had died from exposure and secondary shock.

A staggering 300,000 persons were questioned with respect to the murders of the Grimes sisters. Of these, 2,000 were seriously interrogated. The chief suspect in the case, Max Fleig, aged 17 at the time, was protected by law from subjection to a polygraph test. Chicago Police Captain Ralph Petacque persuaded the teenager to submit to an unofficial test. In the course of that interview, Fleig confessed. With no way to use the test as evidence against him, police were forced to let Fleig go free.

Angered and frustrated at a new Illinois law which prevented the administration of polygraphs to juveniles, the girls' mother, Loretta Grimes, lauded the efforts of police but damned the system's protection of a confessed murderer. In a gesture both symbolic and practical, the girls' mother insisted on taking a lie detector test herself to erase any doubt that might have surrounded her own statements.

A year after the tragedy, Grimes maintained that her daughters had, without question, gotten willingly into the car with their killer. It had been a bitterly cold night when the two sisters had ventured out and they were taking shelter in doorways every few moments to escape the weather. Two boys had seen them just before midnight near 35th and Seeley, apparently headed for the family's home just three blocks away. The girls would surely have accepted a lift from someone known to them, their mother insisted. She was as certain that they would never have gotten into a car with a stranger, regardless of their discomfort.

Sometime after the deed, the police investigated a second confession, that of Silas Jane, a skid row transient who was believed to have been involved in a string of murders in the Chicago area around the time of the Grimes' deaths. However, Jane's story unraveled and he retracted his confession.

Despite all the frustration, however, independent research continues in this grim search for justice. Recently, Oak Park resident Renee Glos began to drag another suspect into brighter light. Daughter of the late Harry Glos, chief investigator of the Cook County Coroner's Office at the time of the Grimes murders, Renee is determined to convince the public of the guilt of one Bennie Bedwell, a Tennesseean believed by her father and then-Sheriff Joseph Lohman to have been at least an accomplice to the gruesome deeds of that cruel winter. In fact, it was Bedwell that as part of his actual confession took police by the hand and pointed out the spot where the Grimes' corpses had been laid. He later claimed that he had been shown the site and pressed to confess by Sheriff Lohman. Whatever the truth may have been, by February, Bennie was out on bond. After a few additional entanglements with Florida law, he disappeared for all purposes from the face of the earth.

While research like Glos's certainly adds to the pool of knowledge on the Grimes slayings, other insights are attained through less traditional methods. In the case of Jerry Karczewski, a Chicago-area medium and psychic detective, a week before picking up a book discussing the Grimes case, he "had a vision of two black-haired girls, really sweet kids, 10-13 year range of age," who "came again, not staying long the second time." After discovering and reading the account of their deaths, the medium "knew who they were." A third "visit" by the sisters showed the girls "standing in front of the Brighton show," a glimpse of a young man driving a vintage model car, and a flash of wooded area.

Notwithstanding the wealth of clues of every variety, 40 years later, police and history are without an answer in the Grimes killings. The impact of the tragedy, along with the frustration of irresolution, continues to haunt Chicagoans who remember with sadness a time before such shocks. Meanwhile, in south suburban Willow Springs, where the girls' bodies were found nearly a month after their disappearance, local residents claim a more literal haunting.

This region itself has remained enigmatic for more than a century and a half, part of the watery and densely-forested stomping grounds of Resurrection Mary, the Sag Church ghosts, the phantom horses and carriage of Archer Avenue, and other oddities. Specifically, the eerie environmental impact of the Grimes slayings seemed to begin immediately after the discovery of the bodies, when a house near the site was abandoned by its owner, who left everything behind, including the car in the driveway. Though guesses have been made about the possible guilt of the escapee, no reason for the evasion has been established. The house was recently razed after having become a haven for drinking and other less innocent pastimes, at least as suggested by the satanic graffiti left by its transients. Even after the house's demolition, curiosity seekers sought out the site, tucked off the road, inexplicably drawn to the remains of its foundation and the broken furniture scattered among the trees.

But the atmosphere is only the setting.

Part of German Church Road, where the Grimes' bodies were found, is alleged to replay the last act of the 1956 murders. Since the discovery of the bodies in January 1957, Cook County police have received reports from those claiming to have heard cars pull up at the site and to have distinguished the sound of something being dumped in the road without any car or person in sight. In addition to recurrent cases of such "audio" phenomena, one woman reported having seen the bodies of two teenaged girls being dumped from a car. When police investigated the report, they found no trace of such an incident.

It is obviously impossible to judge just how many, if any, of these reports were made in earnest, and how many were simply conscious and callous fabrications. Putting aside the lone case involving visual phenomena, however, it is difficult to imagine many witnesses going to the police with reports of such bizarre experiences. If those events were truly related in good faith, it would seem that the audio phenomena must have been quite pronounced or that the events were related to police by those who witnessed them on multiple occasions.

Believers in the legitimacy of these reports have wondered if witnesses' experiences are audio hallucinations, based on previous knowledge of the site's notoriety and created in the witnesses' own minds. Others suggest that the intense anxiety of the killer at the moment of the dumping of the girls' bodies may have left an impression on the very physical environment, an impression that so-called sensitive individuals might perceive on their visits to the site.

Whether imagination or fabrication, subjective or objective reality, the tales surrounding German Church Road demonstrate an undeniable fact: the brutality and irresolution of the Grimes murders nearly undid the trusting mentality of 1950s Chicago. Forty years later, the impact of the deed on the city's former optimism is oppressively obvious, if not audible.

◆

The Death of Ioan Culianu

The dead say nothing
And the dead know much
And the dead hold under their tongues
A locked-up story.

—ITALO CALVINO
"Invisible Cities"

On May 21, 1991, a popular University of Chicago Divinity School professor was found dead in the men's room adjacent to his campus office, shot through the back of his head with a single bullet from a .25 caliber Beretta. About a year after the murder, a Prospect Heights resident began talking in his sleep about the murder of a man unknown to him. When the incidents continued, the man, David Jedlicka, asked his wife to write down his unconscious dictation and to question him while he was asleep, so that they might decipher what seemed like gibberish. When the couple realized the identity of the mystery dream victim as the recently-murdered Professor Ioan Culianu, they contacted Chicago author Ted Anton who, intrigued by the puzzling murder, had been investigating the story on his own. Anton's subsequent interviews with the couple uncovered an interesting fact: David Jedlicka and Culianu shared the same birthday.

Born in Iasi, Romania, Culianu blossomed even amid the squalor that remained after the Communist seizure of his family's estate. Raised on tales of the Culianus' earlier glory, Ioan grew up confused—the offspring of intellectual nobility, abandoned by his father, entrenched in poverty, and a prisoner of the Soviet-trained secret police, the Securitate. Culianu, a natural intellectual, soared through the University of Bucharest where he studied Jorge Luis Borges, Renaissance philosophy and magic, Sanskrit, Indian mysticism, astrology, and ancient religions. Key to his development, intellectually, socially, and culturally, was the work of the exiled

Romanian scholar, Mircea Eliade.

After Culianu had defected to Milan at age 22 and studied at the Sorbonne in Paris, Eliade, who had recognized in Culianu an obvious protege, assisted the eager Ioan in his quest for a tenure-track position at his own institution, the University of Chicago. An instant hit with the Chicago students, Culianu enticed young scholars with his darkly diverse lectures and occult dabblings, charmed admirers with his tarot readings and infected followers with his unappeasable thirst for knowledge. It was not until after his move to Chicago that Culianu discovered his mentor's alter ego. Eliade had ties to the right wing Romanian Iron Guard.

After the 1989 overthrow of Nicolae Ceausescu, Culianu followed Eliade's activist lead, becoming enmeshed in political debate and publishing his somewhat overstated opinions in radical journals and newsletters. For some months before his death, Culianu received death threats, worried that he was being followed, and at one point had his home computer stolen. The last of the death threats warned Culianu to call a number in Medellin, Columbia at one o'clock on the afternoon of May 21, 1991. Ioan evidently complied, reached a wrong number, then walked to the bathroom and died.

With no witnesses, no suspects, and no weapon, local and federal law enforcement officers were left to examine their only available clues—the intricate intellect and exploits of a most mysterious victim. In his recently-published *Eros, Magic and the Murder of Professor Culianu*, Ted Anton's own search for the killer's motive, apparently aided by Culianu himself via Jedlicka's sleeptime ramblings, leads him to a conclusion shared by many mourners, that the prolific and popular Culianu "signed his own death warrant with his increasingly vitriolic writings."

That fearless voice, expressed in life with a sometimes poison pen, lost its literary outlet on that fateful day in 1991, but only temporarily. Determined to be heard, Culianu seems to have foiled even the most foolproof attempts of his enemies to silence him. Whether his triumph will aid in bringing those enemies to justice remains to be seen.

♦

A Cynic's Survival

CLARENCE DARROW'S HYDE PARK HEAVEN

*Mr. Darrow sat listening to the eulogy of his dead friend and
tears filled his eyes. Then someone whispered . . . that a few
words were expected of him. . . . "We were old friends and
we fought many battles of the mind," said Mr. Darrow.
"And we were to have debated once more next week—on 'Is
There Immortality?' It was his contention . . . that there is
immortality." "But he is dead and he knows now, in the
negation and darkness of death, that he was wrong. . . . "*

—BEN HECHT
"Schopenhauer's Son," from *1001 Afternoons in Chicago*

---

*A*s illustrated by the few examples offered in this chapter,
Chicagoland haunting legends have often been associated with
the dark deeds that have plagued the city's reputation, from the
earliest massacre of the Fort Dearborn settlers to the impassioned
murder of John Lalime; from the bloody gangland exploits of the
earlier 20th century through the grim doings of murderers-at-large
like the Grimes' slayer. Curious, then, is the lack of haunting legends
associated with, for example, the murders perpetrated by hometown
serial killers like Richard Speck and John Wayne Gacy. Both are
gone to the grave now, owing to death in prison and capital
punishment, respectively. However, for many self-styled specialists
in the nature of hauntings, the failure of these tragic events to
produce ghostly manifestations simply aids in supporting the
hypothesis: hauntings primarily occur when wrongful deaths go
unavenged. Therefore, the capture of criminals like Speck and Gacy
would satisfy their victims' phantom quest for justice, allowing them
to retire peacefully.

When Clarence Darrow defended Nathan Leopold, Jr. and
Richard A. Loeb after their premeditated 1924 murder of Bobby
Franks, the great criminal lawyer's ultimate goal was to keep his

clients from the gallows. This task would not be an easy one to accomplish, but Darrow was not easily deterred.

Successful in procuring imprisonment for the criminals, it is not surprising that young Bobby Franks remained quiet in his grave, despite his tragically early death. Apparently, Franks did not require his murderers' execution to feel that justice had been served. When Leopold and Loeb were released from prison, however, some might have wondered if a riled Bobby Franks would show himself to protest the pardon. No such appearance ensued, perhaps owing to the remarkable reformation of Nathan Leopold who, upon his release from prison, moved to Puerto Rico, began a mission in San Juan, and eventually donated his eyes to science.

Famed attorney and cynic Clarence Darrow vowed to show himself after death—and does: sometimes on the back steps of the Museum of Science and Industry, viewed here from his memorial foot bridge. (*Photo by Ursula Bielski*)

The only paranormal activity tied in any way to the Leopold and Loeb "Trial of the Century," concerns the reportedly postmortem survival of the defendants' infamously cynical, flatly agnostic attorney, Clarence Darrow. Ever since his ashes were scattered across the Osaka Garden and Wooded Island of the Jackson Park Lagoon, near his Hyde Park home, wanderers behind the Museum of Science and Industry have claimed to catch glimpses of a figure of a man, dressed in suit, topcoat, and fedora, standing on the back steps of the museum gazing across the water. Some witnesses, familiar with the famous lawyer, have positively identified the apparition as Darrow. Others, initially unaware of the identity, have also made the connection after seeing photographs of Darrow following a sighting.

Fittingly, the ruthless opponent of capital punishment seems to have remained thoroughly opposed to death of any kind. Even now, long after the end of his own life in March 1938, many witnesses claim that Darrow himself refuses to allow his own spirit to be sentenced to death.

◆

VI

THE DEVIL HIMSELF

Chicagoans Encounter the Evil One

The Devil went down to Bridgeport: Kaiser Hall, where Satan once shimmied. (*Photo courtesy of Dale Kaczmarek*)

Steppin' With Satan

WHEN THE DEVIL CAME TO BRIDGEPORT

The prince of darkness is a gentleman.

—WILLIAM SHAKESPEARE

ONE OF THE MOST POPULAR AND UNIVERSAL FOLK LEGENDS HAS LOCALIZED ITSELF AND LIVED FOR A GOOD PART OF THIS CENTURY IN CHICAGO'S BRIDGEPORT NEIGHBORHOOD—HOME OF THE Daley family for generations and still an unmoving landmark of old Chicago politics, social relations, architecture, and economics.

Here, on street corners and front stoops, in barber shops and beauty parlors, and in the ubiquitous corner taverns, talk abounds, spanning many topics, many opinions, many generations. Listeners will be engaged by the most amazing of memories, including those recalling one unforgettable neighborhood night: the night the Devil came to dance.

Local tradition remembers it on a Saturday night in an old ballroom just west of Loomis Street on Archer Avenue. A young unescorted woman became enchanted by a mysterious and dashing stranger whose acquaintance she had made on the dance floor. As they whirled to the music with the other local couples, the girl happened to glance at the exceptionally deft feet of her partner.

Responding to her subsequent scream, the neighborhood men, assuming the stranger had made inappropriate advances, immediately pursued her escort who had quickly fled from the scene. When he was cornered near a second-floor window, the stranger alarmed the crowd by refusing to fight, instead leaping from the ledge to the pavement below. When the onlookers rushed to the window to observe his fate, they were amazed to discover that the man had landed squarely on his feet.

As he bolted across Archer, the furious crowd rushed from the building and after the fugitive. Once outside, however, the onlookers discovered the real reason for the young woman's scream. Imbedded in the concrete, in the spot where the stranger had landed, was a single but unmistakable hoofprint.

The legend of "The Devil in the Dancehall," according to folklore expert Jan Harold Brunvand, is a popular one in the Mexican and Latin-American traditions. As with all folk legends, the versions are many, but the story line is the same. A person at a dance, usually a young girl, dances with a charming stranger who turns out to have horse's hooves or chicken claws, the Hispanic versions of the rather generic American perception of diabolic "hooves." When the stranger's identity is thus discovered, he disappears in a puff of smoke, leaving only the smell of sulfur and an unconscious young woman as mementos.

When he wrote *The Vanishing Hitchhiker*, his classic first volume on urban folk legends, Brunvand had found no evidence that this legend had made its way into Anglo-American culture. For over half a century, however, the testaments of Bridgeport residents have proven otherwise.

◆

Dealing With the Devil at Hull House

*A*s a champion of women's independence and the founder of one of progressivism's most controversial institutions, much was asked of Jane Addams, most of which she was able to provide: shelter to the homeless, food to the hungry, encouragement to the hopeless, protection from abusive injustice. But there came a brief period in the life of her pioneering settlement house, Hull House, when the needs of its visitors became insatiable—when women began arriving there by the handful demanding to see "The Devil Baby."

From the beginning, Addams was incensed by a rumor circulating throughout the turn-of-the-century city that Hull House was sheltering a horned and hoofed newborn with the blood of Satan in its veins. After a first group of women pushed through the front door demanding a look at the child, the parade of the curious appeared unstoppable. Each day for six weeks, women of every class and culture streamed into the settlement house hoping to return home with a tale of the alleged incarnation. Each day, Addams turned them away with growing annoyance at what she saw as a pathetic oppression of immigrant women by their Old World superstitions, and "the 'contagion of emotion' added to that 'aesthetic sociability' which impels any one of us to drag the entire household to the window when a procession comes into the street or a rainbow appears in the sky."

Bewildered by the story's hold on the public imagination, yet unable to persuade the curious of the tale's falsehood, Addams resorted to private interviews with each of the older visitors. In the course of these sessions, she discovered a common quality of desperation among them. Listening with interest to their versions of the stories and the circumstances of their own lives, Addams became aware that the tale was serving a serious need—that of exhausted, ignored, and forgotten women to be heard. By hastening to Hull

House in search of this monstrous infant, they were rushing for a chance to win the respect of their husbands, children, and neighbors, to seize the spotlight for a moment before slipping back into a painful obscurity:

> Because the Devil Baby embodied an undeserved wrong to a poor mother, whose tender child had been claimed by the forces of evil, his merely reputed presence had power to attract to Hull House hundreds of women who had been humbled and disgraced . . . .

It is intriguing that for each culture represented by these women, there seemed to be a separate interpretation of the Devil Baby, but a moral common to them all—the father of the baby had been punished with the evil offspring for his ingratitude for the expected baby or mistreatment of his pregnant wife and her cultural traditions.

Dispossessed: Progressivist Jane Addams had her hands full when the Devil Baby came to Hull House. (*Photo by D. Cowan*)

Italian women described a young Catholic girl who had foolishly married an atheist. After she hung a portrait of the Blessed Virgin on their apartment wall, her husband ripped it down, proclaiming that he'd rather have the Devil in the house than such a picture. The Devil Baby was his punishment for that preference.

A Jewish version described the sheepish mother of a handful of daughters and a heartless husband in search of a son. When his wife became pregnant again, the husband clearly announced his preference that she give birth to the Devil before another girl. That bitter proclamation sealed the child's fate.

Just as the causes of the catastrophe varied, so did descriptions of the resulting imp. Though most described a simple horned baby, the more animated narrators added a tail or hooves. Many told of how the child had been born blaspheming and cursing its parents with unimaginable language. In other accounts, the child was fond of smoking cigars and laughing incessantly at its poor parents. Finally, after struggling to control the damned thing, the father hopelessly took it to the heroine of Hull House, Jane Addams herself. Allegedly, Hull House workers had the baby taken to a local church for baptism, but it struggled out of the priest's grasp and began to dance along the back pews. Unable to pacify the evil infant, Addams kept it locked under supervision in an upstairs room at Hull House, where, according to most later versions of the story, it eventually died.

Intriguingly, one obscure version of the Devil Baby story ties it to the urban legend known as the "Devil in the Dancehall," one incidence of which was alleged to have occurred in the Bridgeport neighborhood, a short distance from Hull House (See p. 153, "Stepping with Satan.") Some curiosity apparently arose as to whether the dashing and diabolical stranger who appeared in the crowd at that Bridgeport dancehall may have impregnated one of the young women at the dance, perhaps a Hull House resident out for an evening of merriment, a welcome reprieve from the sadness of everyday life. Believers in this connection point out the likelihood of a such a lonely and searching young woman to be charmed out of her sensibilities by the reportedly enchanting stranger of lore.

Though most accounts of the Devil Baby story begin and end at Hull House, others have speculated that the baby was taken out of the house and sent by the humanitarian Addams to a more isolated home, perhaps even the Waukegan retreat house which she founded on the North Shore.

Today, among believers in the existence of a so-called Devil Baby of Hull House, there continues a debate between those who believe that the baby was just that—an earthly manifestation of diabolical origin—and those convinced that the child was, sadly but simply, a deformed infant brought to Hull House by a destitute mother. Believers in the second likelihood also assume that the child either died at Hull House or was sent from public scrutiny to a quieter shelter outside the city.

Whether or not a baby, deformed or demonic, was ever brought to Hull House, belief in the fact has remained fierce. The widespread popularity of the Hollywood film, *Rosemary's Baby,* inspired by the Hull House story, has proven that the appeal of the tale is hardly provincial, though local accounts persist of an evil little mug that glares out of the upstairs window, as do reports of foggy upper windows and feelings of unease.

Adding to the building's mystery have been a few self-styled ghosthunters, whose photos of shadowy figures on the inside staircase are sometimes used to back up rumors of a woman's suicide having taken place in an upstairs room.

During her lifetime, Addams did what she could to prevent this "haunting" of Hull House. Soon after the phenomenon, she seized the opportunity to proselytize on the wretched state of women's lives, sharing her visitors' stories with the readership of the *Atlantic Monthly* in October 1916 and emphasizing her belief

> that the old women who came to visit the Devil Baby believed that the story would secure them a hearing at home . . . and as they prepared themselves with every detail of it, their old faces shone with a timid satisfaction.

These days, as busloads of ghosthunters eyeball Hull House hoping for a glimpse of a gruesome little face, a misty window, or a filmy form on the staircase, Jane Addams must turn often in her grave, disgusted by the enduring appeal of a foul and fantastic fairy tale. Yet, even the realistic progressivist was not altogether grounded in "modern" convictions. During her own administration of Hull House, Addams engaged in at least one superstition of her own— placing pails of water on the attic stairs to keep the ghosts away.

♦

The Uninvited: St. Michael's parishioners remember
a most unwelcome guest. (*Photo by Ursula Bielski*)

'The Scariest Ghost or Whatever It Was'

MEMORIES OF ST. MICHAEL'S

Once, early in the morning, Beelzebub arose.
With care his sweet person adorning,
He put on his Sunday clothes.

—PERCY BYSSHE SHELLEY
"The Devil's Walk"

*I*n the early 1970s, Old Town resident Arlene Zoch was interviewed by the *Chicago Tribune* regarding her experiences as a past resident of two of that neighborhood's many haunted private homes. Although her own experiences in those houses had at times been quite unnerving, Arlene maintained that '(t)he scariest ghost or whatever it was that I've heard about is the one that walked into St. Michael's Church . . . .'

For at least the past 25 years, rumors have passed from neighborhood to neighborhood about a horrifying incident that occurred at St. Michael's Catholic Church on Cleveland Avenue in the Old Town section of Chicago's North Side. According to Ms. Zoch's 1973 account, the tale was told of the late Fr. "Curly" Miller who had done a number of exorcisms during Arlene's girlhood in St. Michael's parish. One day, as the priest was leaving the church he noticed an elderly woman following him. As he moved to open the heavy door to allow her passage, he saw that the woman was without feet, bearing instead a pair of hooves, classic evidence of the creature's diabolical origin.

In later years, another episode reported to have taken place at St. Michael's began to gain popularity. In this story, which circulated in that parish throughout the late 1980s, a hooded, hoofed figure was seen in the communion line at Sunday mass, professedly by several members of the congregation. This atrocious violation of communion protocol may be hard to grasp by non-Catholics. It made a dramatic impact, however, on the parishioners of St. Michael's. Even now, the story is possibly one of the least discussed of Chicago's supernatural legends. Echoing the opinion of Arlene Zoch, the thought of it, especially to Catholics, is simply too unsettling.

Where did these stories originate? Fr. Miller's early experience seems as legitimate a report as they come, owing to his previous experiences as an exorcist. Whether looking at his case from a spiritual or psychological point of view, his vision at the rear of St. Michael's may certainly have been some "demon" coming back to haunt him.

Possibly, Fr. Miller's earlier experience led to some phenomenon akin to dubious theories of mass hallucination. Alternately, the congregation present may have collectively interpreted an apparition in accordance with their specific belief system. Most rationally, someone at that mass saw "something," an oddly-dressed congregant, a disfigured or disabled communicant, or the like, and subsequently convinced others present that they had all witnessed something evil. The final theory holds that some fraud was perpetrated on the community to perhaps mock the resident exorcist and his previous testimony, to shock the congregation, or simply to spite the larger Church.

Today, St. Michael's is the church of choice for the upscale population that has almost thoroughly infiltrated the surrounding neighborhood. The adjoining high school has been turned into condominiums and hardly a trace of the old Catholicism remains to remind the young parishioners of the days when the role of the exorcist was an important one, and when it was the exorcist's lot to face some bizarre and frightening realities.

What Fr. Miller saw that day at St. Michael's remains a mystery. Whether later stories of related visions are truth-based is also unresolved. That the rumors stubbornly remain, despite the parish's changing climate is, however, a fact. That they will continue to circulate for many years to come is a distinct probability.

♦

Rumors of Evil

SATAN AND THE FOREST PRESERVE
DISTRICT OF COOK COUNTY

*I*n the early 1970s, Fr. John J. Nicola, an expert on the paranormal and its relation to Catholicism and spirituality, spoke to a *Chicago Tribune* reporter about the huge increase in reports of supernatural phenomena. Fr. Nicola felt that the surge was due largely to a massive trend by youth towards satanically-inspired culture. Interestingly enough, Nicola was far from disturbed by this, claiming that there is naturally a greater frequency of so-called diabolical activity in places or times of great good, for example, during Christ's lifetime or during the Middle Ages, when the cathedral builders were so fervently inspired to express devotion to their god.

Nicola may have observed the disturbing paranormal incidents occurring in 1970s Chicago with cool confidence, trusting the city's great concentration of religiosity as exhibited in its background of Native American spirituality or the faith of its tightly-knit Roman Catholic parishes. Residents of the Chicago area, however, were often far from calm about newspaper reports of the activities of local satanic cults, the involvement of teenagers in such activities, and rumors of inexplicable phenomena that seemed rooted in the diabolical.

Cook County residents seemed to follow the lead of McHenry County when they cited satanic or other occultist practices in explaining local paranormal activity. In that northerly county, the Stickney Mansion's poltergeist-like activity that began in the 1970s was often attributed by locals to its occupancy by "devil-worshipers" in the 1960s. (See "The Inevitable Haunted Houses," p. 186.)

In Cook County, Bachelors Grove Cemetery (discussed previously) was the extreme example of what many locals thought to be an interplay between deliberate satanic practice and the frighteningly uncontrollable phenomena it invited. One writer suggested that the hooded apparitions reported within cemetery confines were a product of diabolical summonings by inexperienced practitioners, since such figures have only been seen since the rumors of satanic activity began to circulate. In addition, many have reported a chanting chorus of voices that follows on the heels of visitors to the site, another phenomena that seems to date only as far back as do the reports of demonic worship. Chanting has been documented by visitors to at least two other sites in the Chicago area, both of which have become established in local lore as ritualistic grounds for rumored satanists.

Simultaneously with Bachelors Grove, but on the Northwest Side of the city, the LaBagh Woods Forest Preserve was beginning to earn a sinister reputation among teenagers as the meeting grounds of formidable, yet unnamed, satanic cults. Accompanying these rumors have been documented discoveries of bodies found in the woods, sometimes hanged from trees. The ensuing murder cases have gone unsolved. Over the past 20 years, however, wanderers in these woods off Foster Avenue have reported an elusive chanting sound seeming to emanate from the surrounding trees. Such reports seem to have ebbed in recent years, returning the preserve to its pre-stigmatized status as a safe and serene recreational park.

Further west, another preserve is fighting to regain its peaceful status. During the 1970s, at Camp Fort Dearborn, groups of Boy Scouts and other campers were disturbed to find makeshift stone altars, trees filled with nooses, and bizarre symbols scratched into trees and rocks in the woods around their campsites. At one evening gathering, dozens of Boy Scouts heard what sounded like a large group of chanting voices. The increasingly amplified whisper seemed to surround the group and suddenly diminish.

Because these preserves are the stomping grounds of so many Chicago-area teenagers, it should not be surprising that a number of local youths have very definite ideas about the source of their infestation by paranormal presences, demonic or otherwise. One far Northwest-side 14-year-old, Chris Williams, speaks with great sobriety of the activities known to have occurred at the various preserves in and around the city. With an authority obviously based on careful consideration of the subject matter, Williams expounds on his own theories regarding the mysteries of the Forest Preserve District. On the matter of the hooded figures reported at Bachelors Grove and other sites, Williams surmises that, if occult groups have indeed practiced magic at these sites, perhaps the energy created by a focused concentration of believers somehow imprinted on the landscape some of the images present in their rituals, much as a camera imprints real time images on film. For example, if hooded garments were worn during these rituals, perhaps visitors to these sites occasionally view "imprints" of these hooded figures.

Another of Williams' theories leans less towards the scientific and more towards the spiritual. Discussing the ancient belief in dryads, or tree spirits, Williams reasons that, if in fact such entities exist, the density of trees in the District's preserves would allow for the existence and manifestation of more than a few of these blossoming spirits.

Whether the paranormal phenomena experienced by visitors to these preserves during the 1970s and after can be connected in some way to occultist practice is, of course, unknown. What is certain however, is that at least for a time, the two were undeniably meshed in local perception. As for the question of the existence of dryads, in the Forest Preserve District or elsewhere, only the trees, infinitely silent and secretive, hold the answer. And, at least so far, the trees won't tell.

◆

VII

THE INEVITABLE
HAUNTED HOUSES

*A house is never still in darkness to those who listen intently.
. . . Ghosts were created when the first man awoke in the night.*

—SIR JAMES MATTHEW BARRIE
"The Little Minister"

A "haunted jukebox" at 505 N. Sheridan Road on the North Shore is only one of that house's many wonders. (*Photo by Ursula Bielski*)

*I*N 1991, THE NEW YORK STATE SUPREME COURT WAS FORCED TO ADMIT ITS BELIEF IN GHOSTS. RULING IN THE LANDMARK CASE OF *STAMBOVSKY VS. ACKLEY*, THE COURT CONCLUDED THAT THE purchaser of a Nyack, New York house was entitled to cancel a $650,000 contract because the seller, well aware that the house was reputed to be haunted, withheld that information from the buyer. In addition to the voiding of the contract, the buyer's $32,500 down payment was returned to him.

The Supreme Court's decision, which reversed that of a lower court, pointed out that the presence of ghosts reduced property value, making the seller guilty of non-disclosure. The court also ruled that the ghosts were in violation of another part of the contract: that which stated that the property was to be delivered to the buyer vacant.

Real estate agents in many other states are still lucky. Most are not legally required to inform potential buyers about alleged hauntings. An increasing number of agents, though, choose to fully reveal such matters to their clients. According to many such agents, "haunted" houses end up categorized as "stigmatized properties," a distinction which dumps them right in with murder sites and the like. As such, these houses are pushed and usually sold at prices about 20 percent below their potential. Nonetheless, the problems avoided by full disclosure of hauntings make the profit losses seem well worthwhile. As parapsychologists and ghostbusters well know, when residents find a ghost in the house, "negative responses range from mild goosebumps to total terror."

Quite to the contrary, some buyers actually request haunted houses when home shopping. Aside from ghosthunters who wistfully dream of their own personal Amityville Horrors, those embarking on commercial ventures may feel that a ghost or two is just the thing to jump-start a restaurant, bar, or other business. Additionally, many clients, especially celebrities and wealthy eccentrics, consider ghosts to be a distinctive status symbol.

Although Chicago appears devoid of haunted houses owned by wealthy eccentrics, the city has certainly had its share of houses haunted by them. Some of those houses still stand, ghosts and all.

◆

Ghosts of Houses Past

With Chicago ranking as one of the top architectural centers of the world, it is hardly surprising that the ghosts of disgruntled architects should remain some of the most aggravated spirits in the Chicago area. From Prairie Avenue to McHenry County, the building of homes has created some of the region's most intensely emotional situations—situations which some researchers argue are the stuff of which ghosts are made.

In old Chicago, as the newly rich struggled to establish their place in society, the vision of an imposing and enduring family home drove more than a few wealthy businessmen. Sometimes, though, the establishment of such a mansion was foiled by the early death of the visionary. Their plans were often abandoned due to mournful or uninterested family members, a lack of funds, or other postmortem circumstances. The responses of these willful personalities have not always been passive.

At the southeast corner of Aberdeen and Taylor streets stood the Fanning House, what was supposed to have been the pride and joy of Peter Fanning, a thriving Chicago stone cutter who began the building of this dream house in the 1870s. Notwithstanding his fantastic plans for the mansion, all that Fanning lived to complete were a massive wraparound stone wall, connected at the entrance by iron gates, and a monstrous stone foundation complete with an iron vault in which Peter intended to store his fortune. When the rather mad Fanning died, his daughters topped the costly foundations with an unassuming and cheaply-built house.

According to legends that circulated throughout the late 19th and early 20th centuries, Peter Fanning's troubled spirit took its revenge on the commercial structure that was later built on the corner of the Fanning lot. Each business that occupied the building met with financial disaster. In turn, the disgruntled and displaced businesses attributed their failures to the nasty attitude of the deceased stone cutter.

Just a few blocks away was the more infamously haunted Schuttler Mansion. Peter Schuttler, a carriage manufacturer, chose the corner of Adams and Aberdeen streets for the building of his home, but died of blood poisoning before its completion. Despite its unfinished state, his widow and their children occupied the home until Mrs. Schuttler's death. Afterwards, the house was vacated and remained abandoned for many years, acquiring dust and disrepute. Contemporaries of the Schuttlers claimed that the house had become haunted and identified the specter as that of Peter Schuttler. According to speculation, here was another frustrated visionary, laid to rest (or unrest) before his architectural plans could be realized.

Significantly, however, these stories diminished as the years rolled by. New ghosts came to haunt the realm of the old Schuttler spirit. In fact, by 1911 when the mansion was demolished, local legend held that the house was occupied by an eccentric old man who "years ago" had been kept prisoner in the long-deserted mansion.

In addition to these well-established haunted houses, others flourished as well, thanks in great part to word-of-mouth testimony and an occasional mention in the city's news pages. William Leonard, writing for the *Chicago Tribune Sunday Magazine* in the 1950s, wondered in one of his pieces, "Whatever Happened to Chicago's Haunted Houses?" For example, the one at Washington Boulevard and Green Street, where, after midnights, a phantom couple sat smoking clay pipes in an upstairs window. Or the home built by Elizabeth McCarthy at 3530 Cottage Grove in the 1870s. After McCarthy's death, her daughters locked up the room where their mother had spent most of her last years on earth. The daughters McCarthy made numerous attempts to rent the house on the condition that the room be kept locked, but not surprisingly, no takers could be found, and the house fell into ruin. Apparently, Elizabeth herself didn't mind the lapse; she was seen on several occasions by a number of South Siders, a silent sentinel at her usual window. Meanwhile, over on south Anthony Avenue, another house was establishing its notoriety, thanks to its foreboding appearance and a father who, after his daughter married against his will, shut himself in and died. Stories abounded, as they did at North Side spots like the house on Erie Street with human bones in the backyard, whose neighbors frequently heard the phantom deliveries of cadavers to the National Medical College which the building had previously housed. The horse and carriage, the sound of heavy boxes being unloaded, the footsteps that came and went—all were heard but never seen. According to Leonard, however, even these beautifully haunted houses had become thoroughly unhaunted.

Around the time of these classic hauntings, an altogether unusual case was developing 50 miles south of Chicago, in Watseka, Illinois. Behind the doors of the Vennum House on July 11, 1877, a 13-year-old girl named Lurancy Vennum began her climb to fame as "The Watseka Wonder." That summer day was the first of many occasions on which Vennum reportedly slipped into catatonic states that ushered her to the heavens to converse with spirits. During these trance-like periods, which occurred three to 12 times a day on some occasions and lasted up to eight hours at a stretch, Lurancy would astound onlookers by speaking in dozens of voices. Often, she claimed to be delivering messages from discarnate beings.

Doctors huddled and sent the girl to the state insane asylum at Peoria, where she remained throughout the autumn and part of the winter. Then, in January 1878, Asa Roff visited the Vennum family and begged for their attention. According to Roff, his own daughter Mary had suffered the same attacks as Lurancy. The difference was, Roff believed that his daughter had actually communicated with the dead. Notwithstanding her father's efforts on her behalf, Mary Roff died several years earlier after she also had been committed to an asylum. Determined to save Lurancy Vennum from a similar death, Roff persuaded the Vennums to allow Dr. E. Winchester Stevens, a spiritualist physician, to examine young Lurancy. To the amazement of all present during the examination, Lurancy seemed to become possessed by none other than the dead Mary Roff. When Mary refused to leave Lurancy's body, the Vennums allowed the Roffs to take Lurancy home with them, hoping that Mary might take leave of the daughter once she returned to her own house. For three months, Mary's personality acted through Lurancy's body, aware of family members and neighbors, talking intimately about past family events, and giving every indication that the dead Mary had returned home.

Finally, in May 1878, Lurancy's voice asserted itself over Mary's, announcing her desire to return to the Vennum home and her family. Reclaiming the puppet body from its invader, Lurancy was cured of the apparent possession, yet maintained a thankfulness to Mary Roff for saving her from the unknown entities which had originally plagued her. In gratitude for this bizarre act of kindness, Lurancy occasionally returned to the Roff home and allowed Mary to re-enter her body. During these brief possessions, the Roffs conversed with their dead daughter as naturally as ever. This unique arrangement continued until 1896 when Lurancy joined her husband in a move to Rollins County, Kansas. The occupants of Vennum House, now a private residence, have not reported any similar events.

Far north of Chicago's South Side is the city of Waukegan, an industrial Lake Michigan port town. Reaching Waukegan via the winding roads of the North Shore demonstrates the harsh juxtaposition of affluent towns like Lake Forest and Lake Bluff with the obvious economic decline of North Chicago and Waukegan. Entering Waukegan with its ramshackle bungalows interspersed with boarded-up shops and gas stations, the great blue stretch of Lake Michigan shocks with its beauty as does the stream of stunning mansions that line the drive up Sheridan Road from Chicago. Amidst this richness and residue, it is difficult to imagine that in the mid-19th century, Waukegan was one of the busiest harbors on the Great Lakes. It grew with remarkable speed after the Potawatomi ceded land comprising modern Lake County to the United States government. As merchants reliant on the lake were turning the town into a bustling commercial center, another aqueous feature was drawing hundreds of visitors annually: the alluring natural mineral springs that flowed through Waukegan's ravines.

Various of these springs were commercialized as bottlers shipped the ostensibly healing waters to eager consumers around the United States. One group of five springs was located near the center of Waukegan and another, the Glen Flora Springs, eventually lent its name to what is today the Glen Flora Country Club just west of Sheridan Road. Before the building of the club, this land was the site of the Milner House, where the spirit of Mary Willard appeared to the ailing Belle Milner, urging her to go west to save her failing health. (See "Dead and Buried," pp. 48-49.)

Just south of the Milner House, at the corner of Washington and Sheridan, stood the Dr. Norman J. Roberts House, the 1891 home of a world-famous oral surgeon. Roberts, a prominent

Waukegan citizen until his death in 1939 was known for his sure-handed performances of difficult jaw operations. The doctor had also established himself as a fine student of archaeology and anthropology. Local lore places an Indian burial ground behind his house and maintains that he used an Indian axe head as a doorstop.

Beyond such minor eccentricities were his curious dealings with patients. Roberts allegedly kept famed author Pearl S. Buck waiting in his dental chair 45 minutes, jaws propped open, while he chatted with a neighbor in the backyard. Another favorite story tells of the woman who sat in that same chair from 10 a.m. until 5 p.m. while the doctor attended to various tasks around the office, stopping now and then to do a bit of work on his bewildered patient. One more in-house activity should be noted: in the front parlor of the towering mansion, the doctor's wife, Helen, gave violin lessons to Jack Benny.

For those who remember the Roberts House, the memory of it is as clear as a snapshot. The life in that house, it seems, was trapped in every corner. Unaware passers-by were drawn to the energy the structure seemed to have collected:

> The old house snags the mind like a picket fence snags the
> blowing leaves of winter, and holds them until, through
> desperate struggle, they wriggle free and scatter on.

There is apparently no reason why this house, occupied for years by a respected and endearing family, should have invited the phantoms that were said to claim it after the good doctor's death. Rather, like so many of history's haunted houses, the bad reputation seems to have flowered in conjunction with the deterioration of its physical state. Journalist Joe Manning observed how the house appeared both occupied and abandoned before demolition: "In daylight the old house looks as if it were made of rust and would crumble at the slightest jarring—like a house of cards . . ." And yet, perhaps because of some plays of light, "the only conclusion is that the house is inhabited . . ." And so it was, at least according to caretaker Leonard Vukadin and a whole lot of locals, until the very last.

During his 30 years in the house, Vukadin confined himself

to a modest portion of the first floor and surrounded himself with blaring radios and televisions to block out inexplicable sounds, like that of the piano playing by itself. During those dozens of years, "presences," glimpsed often by visitors as well, came and went through the locked doors and eventually scared Vukadin into the isolation of his first floor quarters. After several years in the house, he would not set foot in the attic, and further, wouldn't go to any of the upper floors after three o'clock in the afternoon. After all, Vukadin did consider the ghosts to be dangerous, having read once that spirits have been known to push people down stairways.

Vukadin's most disturbing experience came one day when he and his son were tacking up plastic sheeting over a window and looked over to see a nurse staring at them. The dark-haired young woman vanished after approximately 30 seconds. After the incident, Vukadin refused to go to the third floor again and could barely be convinced to enter even the second story. He would later assume that the woman he saw was the spirit of one of Dr. Roberts' nurses.

The Sheridan Road Investment Trust bought the house from Mrs. Roberts' estate in 1973. Thereafter, there was talk of moving it from its site in order to preserve it. The house was appraised, however, as practically worthless, due greatly to a fire that damaged much of the third floor in the 1960s. The Trust offered to sell the house for one dollar to anyone willing to move it at a cost of about ten thousand dollars. No one did. In 1978, the house was razed.

♦

Poltergeists

Several so-called haunted houses in the Chicago area were not actually place-centered, but seem to have been person-centered or poltergeist cases. One of these cases played out at Oak Park's Hephzibah Children's Home, at 946 North Boulevard. According to speculations by those involved, the activity was focused in a disturbed child residing there who was allegedly capable of provoking impressive RSPK. (See p. 37.)

Another relentless poltergeist supposedly followed a family from residence to residence during August 1957. For more than a week, the family of James Mikulecky was harassed by objects whizzing through the air of their Wilmington, Illinois home until Mrs. Mae Vlasek gave the frazzled family refuge in her home. All assumed that they had left behind a haunted house. When the unsettling events continued at the Vlasek house, it confirmed researchers' hunches that this was no haunting, but the work of a bona fide poltergeist.

In 1988 and 1989 another such case occurred in Orland Hills at the Gallo Residence, 8800 169th Street. The spectacle drew *Life* magazine to the scene to report on the dozens of incidents of inexplicable and often dangerous physical effects taking place there, all seemingly focused on 16-year-old Deana Gallo. The family was terrorized by, among other phenomena, menacing flames of fire repeatedly shooting from various wall sockets of their suburban home. Paul Hamilton, then an employee at a nearby Orland Park camera retailer, remembers the extraordinary time, recalling the rolls and rolls of infrared film brought in each day by the Orland Park Fire Department, which investigated the baffling situation without success. Some accounts explain that the Gallo's poltergeist was another unhappy example of what happens when modern developers encroach upon sacred land; the house in which the family was living was built on the site of an old Indian burial ground.

The Gallo case reminded some investigators of the locally-known Macomb Poltergeist, in which an emotionally fraught teenaged girl was blamed for the setting of farmhouse fires via psychokinesis, what parapsychology has more recently named "anomalous perturbation." After her parents' divorce proceedings, when the custody of the girl was awarded to her father, Janet Willey was sent to live on her uncle's farm. She was thereafter believed to have used her paranormal abilities to wreak utter havoc on the property until she was allowed to leave the farm to live with her mother.

Some researchers have come to believe that some distinctive quality of a property itself may encourage the development of paranormal activity. One such theory of poltergeist disturbances suggests that some areas of land may contain a special type of energy. This energy presumably remains untapped until a certain type of person, like the volatile Janet Willey, comes in contact with it, thereby channeling the energy and causing poltergeist effects. Some venture that so-called hallowed ground might contain this type of energy and that this is why researchers find ostensibly paranormal activity frequently associated with burial grounds and cemeteries, churches, and the like. Although we often speak of poltergeist agents as necessary conduits for this energy, in theory such a force does not require an agent or channel to manifest itself. Thus, we might explain that events such as recognitive hauntings (see p. 37) occur only when past impressions can tap into an energy source inherent in the property itself, such as a videotape can only be viewed if its VCR is plugged into a live socket. Basically, haunting RSPK or true ghosts can only manifest themselves on property that contains such an energy source, as in the case of so-called "cold spots," when a purported spirit is thought to draw all of the heat from the area it is occupying.

Of course, another view of poltergeists maintains that Deana Gallo would have caused the disturbances in question regardless of where she was residing. According to this theory, the human body is the source and not merely the conductor of the energy required for poltergeist disturbances.

Another likely poltergeist occurrence deserves a more detailed description. The scene of the brief but affecting disturbance was a 21st-floor condominium at 4250 N. Marine Drive. There, on Good Friday 1995, this quiet and comfortable apartment hosted an unnerving sequence of inexplicable events. Five days before, Robert, the owner and occupant of this residence and a nutritionist at a local hospital, had taken a Sunday trip to Elmwood Cemetery over Chicago's northwestern border. Videotaping the cemetery landscape, and in particular, the gravesite of a recently deceased friend, he intended to send the tape to the wife of that friend, then living in Eastern Europe, to assure her of the tranquility and beauty of her husband's final resting place. After a quarter-hour of taping with his new video camera, he packed up his equipment and headed for home.

That evening at about six o'clock, he was back home on Marine Drive watching television. As he sat, he thought he glimpsed some movement of the leaves on a palm plant in one corner of the living room. Looking for an open window, he found all of them closed and no draft from any other source. Easily dismissing the event, he was reminded of it the next evening when the same thing happened again at around six o'clock. He was content to ignore the replay, but became a bit perplexed when the same event occurred a third time on Tuesday evening. Eventually, he told his housekeeper about the strange happenings, but she ignored them suggesting it was his imagination.

Finally on Good Friday, sometime before ten o'clock in the evening, he heard a distinct knocking from the hallway, apparently from his bedroom. Although he went to investigate, the knocking had ceased by the time he reached the room. After returning to the living room, the knocking began again, and again he went to find the source. Failing to discover anything, he went back down the hall towards the living room and stood in the foyer to listen for the noise. The hallway was lined by closets, with slatted, hinged doors that folded open by pulling on round handles. As he stood and listened, he was alarmed to see one of these doors begin to move ever so slightly and then begin to fold open. Frozen to the spot, he watched as the door opened completely. Puzzled and a little shaken, he pushed the door shut; a few moments later, the same process began again. Once more, he pushed the door closed. Wondering at the cause of the phenomenon, he rushed to retrieve his new video camera, hoping to film the event should it repeat itself.

It did.

Robert succeeded in capturing more than ten minutes of

inexplicable events on videotape, including the opening of the hall closet, knocking sounds coming again from the bedroom, and the bedroom door opening and closing. Perhaps most astounding is the final event which Robert recorded: the opening of a bedroom closet door and the steadily-increasing movement of clothing inside that closet, a movement which Robert abruptly brought to an end by moving the door closed with his foot.

Now thoroughly upset by the evening's events, Robert hastened to call a suburban friend, expressing his fear of spending the night in the apartment. As she tried to reassure him, Robert felt something grab the upper portion of his right arm. When he dropped the phone in alarm, his friend was finally convinced that something was wrong.

Three months before he had purchased the condominium over a year earlier, the previous owner had died in the apartment. Knowing this, Robert's friend suggested that the spirit of this woman may have remained. As both she and Robert were religious, his friend directed him to find a bottle of holy water that Robert brought home from the Jordan River on a trip to the Holy Land. While he did this, she told him of a traditional prayer which, she explained, was used when a person died in the home to assure that the person's spirit would not linger there. As Robert toured the apartment with his friend on the other end of the portable phone he sprinkled holy water and repeated the prayer she dictated. Nothing unusual happened during the tour; in fact, nothing ever happened again.

The next day, Robert reported the night's events to his housekeeper and showed her the videotape he had taken. She promptly quit. Some time after, he ventured to show the tape to a friend in the building, who thereafter refused to enter Robert's apartment. Saddened by the loss of these acquaintances, Robert was nonetheless still bewildered by his experience and anxious to find some explanation. After mentioning the event to a nun at the hospital where he worked, he agreed to let her view the tape. She encouraged Robert to have a priest come to bless the apartment. Although nothing unusual had occurred since that one night, he agreed.

Robert, attempting to make sense of that evening offers some possibilities, all of which depend on the presence of an entity. This suggests haunting RSPK (see p. 37) or perhaps even a visit from an "evil spirit" or other non-human presence. At first, he wondered if the activity began because he was watching a religious television program. Perhaps, he proposed, there was some religious—or irreligious—presence that was inspired or disturbed by Robert's observance of the holy day. Another possibility was that one or another of his deceased parents was making their presence known to him as a result of his prayers and increased thoughts of them during Holy Week. Or as his friend speculated, it was the spirit of the previous owner who needed assistance in moving on to the next life.

Though all of these possibilities are compelling in their own ways, most parapsychologists would probably categorize the disturbance at Robert's apartment as poltergeist activity, basing this conclusion on two facts, the brief nature of the events and the absence of apparitional sightings. For although it is unusual to find a non-adolescent poltergeist agent, it is not altogether unheard of. In fact, certain cases suggest that even significant adult stress may at times produce RSPK.

In Robert's case, the emotional stress of Holy Week and his extended bereavement of his parents and friend may have compounded to trigger an episode of RSPK. An appeal to the agent's religious belief system (i.e., by his blessing of the apartment at his friend's suggestion) may have changed his "energy" and halted the RSPK. Additionally, haunting RSPK in which a discarnate entity is thought to produce the physical disturbances typically lasts for long periods of time, often years, and is almost always accompanied by the sighting of apparitions.

A similar case, this one longer and livelier, occurred in the Waukegan Milakovich Home in 1922. On every Monday night of that year, "something" tormented Mrs. Milakovich by raiding the pantry, spreading flour on the floor, and throwing coal lumps everywhere. Exasperated, the woman finally called the local priest. Fr. Joseph Lauerman, moved by her frustration, agreed to keep watch at the Milakovich home with two neighborhood men, Duke Nolan and Russell Edwards. No one saw a ghost, but Nolan did lose his revolver. Another local, Michael Dozema, now alarmed that a ghost should be walking around armed, began his own vigil. At around two o'clock in the morning as Dozema attempted to light his pipe, his match blew out, as did each of several successive matches.

He later claimed to have seen a shadow on the wall and testified that a hand had grabbed his shoulder, causing him to throw his pipe to the floor. The pistol was never found; the ghost was never heard from again.

Like Robert's experience, this seems to have been another poltergeist case, owing to the apparent lack of apparitional sightings, dismissing the "shadow" as just that, the relatively short-lived nature of the events, and the probable mourning of Mrs. Milakovich following her husband John's death. Accounts of this case do not state whether Fr. Lauerman made a blessing of the home before he and his colleagues began their vigil. Perhaps such action would have eliminated the phenomena immediately, as was the case with Robert. Another interesting aspect of the Milakovich case was the restriction of the activity to one day a week—Mondays. Researchers might theorize that this was the one day each week which Mrs. Milakovich "set aside" for unconscious release of her emotional turmoil. Of course, to those who are privy, or subject, to such experiences, it is difficult to imagine that one is bringing on the events unconsciously. Further, it is currently impossible to conclude that poltergeists are indeed created by individuals and are not just what they have been termed: noisy ghosts.

Robert is still apprehensive about the events that he witnessed and filmed on that disturbing night. Despite its apparent departure, he still worries that whatever upset his household might return unexpectedly. It is tempting for researchers to say that if Robert believes the disturbances have ended, then they will not begin again. At this point in the development of poltergeist theory, however, it is difficult to make such a definite assessment.

What is certain, however, is that there exist innumerable accounts of this sort of event occurring not only in Chicago, but all over the world, in every kind of setting, to people of varying beliefs. Although they may be brief and unexceptional, such events almost always have an extraordinary and lasting effect on those who witness them. Their origins, therefore, are ultimately less engaging than their impact.

◆

Ghosts of Houses Present

While most of the houses already discussed have long since been kissed by the wrecking ball, the John Glessner House retains all of the vitality envisioned for it by its architect, Henry Hobson Richardson. Located at 1800 S. Prairie Avenue, the house is popularly believed to have been Richardson's last commission. In July of 1885, however, more than a year after the plans were drawn up for Glessner House, Frank Mac Veagh, who would later become Secretary of the Treasury of the United States, requested that Richardson design a home at 1220 N. Lake Shore Drive. The architect agreed, and went on to witness the completion of his design for a lakefront Romanesque brownstone after that of Glessner House, his next-to-last commission. According to Glessner's accounts, Richardson toured the lots at south Prairie Avenue and 18th Street and drew up the sketches for the house the very next day.

Glessner, loving the house as much as the architect did, wrote a book for his children about his time there. Through its doors, the elite of Chicago came and went, but it was only a few short years before the neighborhood, which both Marshall Field and George Pullman also called home, changed. Industry grew up around Glessner's tailor-made estate, so that upon his death in 1936 the house had already begun to assume the glaringly displaced appearance which it retains today.

Glessner was not Henry Richardson's last creative gesture, but to him and the majority of architects, it was the pinnacle of his genius. It should not be surprising then that this is where his spirit is rumored to hang out. For years, inhabitants have identified their unseen boarder as the house's designer and not its owner. While Richardson haunts the Glessner House, phantom horses reportedly gallop through the streets of the Prairie Avenue Historic District.

Perhaps the most striking of the city's haunted houses is that which sits atop a hill at 103rd Street and Longwood Drive in the far South Side's Beverly neighborhood. The Givens Mansion, or "The Irish Castle," was built in 1886 for developer Robert Givens, who reportedly requested a home resembling the 13th and 14th century estates of his native Ireland. Until the present, stories have persisted that Givens had the castle built for his bride-to-be. When she died before the house could be occupied, the building's title began its long, strange passage to its current occupancy by the Beverly Unitarian Church. The more likely version maintains that Rebecca was unhappy with the showy mansion. The Commission on Chicago Landmarks designates it as Chicago's only castle since the Potter Palmer castle on Lake Shore Drive was demolished in the 1950s. Indeed, its startling gray limestone prominence suggests an influence quite removed from that which contributed to the surrounding neighborhood.

Over the generations, a manufacturer, a doctor, and the Chicago Female College have called the castle home. Local legend traces its haunting to that last tenant, specifically, to the death of Clara, a young girl struck ill during a flu epidemic while in residence at the school in the 1930s. Testifying to the presence of the girl's spirit is the Reverend Leonetta Bugleisi, pastor of the Unitarian Church, who saw two small arms embrace her husband's waist just minutes after her installation as the church's pastor in February of 1994. Though on the receiving end of such affection, her husband claimed to have felt nothing. More than two decades before the Bugleisis arrived at the Givens mansion, psychic Carol Broman claimed to sense two personalities inhabiting the castle. One of them, she insisted, was a young girl.

In addition to Bugleisi's experience, neighbors have claimed to have seen the glow of candles in the castle's windows when the building was empty, and a number of specters have been glimpsed during wedding receptions held on the premises. Moreover, during these and other parties, vases and utensils have gone missing, and half-full wine glasses have mysteriously emptied themselves between visitors' sips. Paranormally notable was one New Year's Eve party when a woman in red stepped down the south staircase and through the door to the sleeping porch, which silently opened in front of her. Outside, a female figure was seen walking away in the snow; she left no footprints behind. Other apparitions include that of a woman in a white nightgown wandering the grounds and the interior of the building, a young girl with an Irish brogue who wistfully reminisces about the castle's history, and a woman seen in the old gardens, said to be the spirit of Eleanor Veil, who occupied the castle and tended its landscape during the Depression.

Apart from visual apparitions and other playful manifestations, the castle is host to various audio apparitions as well, most frequently noise once described by Bugleisi as "jingling," the sounds of a dinner party's tinkling of glasses and silverware, and unintelligible voices coming from uninhabited floors.

While the building housing the Beverly Unitarian Church remains perhaps the most displaced-looking structure in Chicago, the surrounding suburbs host a few eye-catching and eerie abodes of their own.

Resembling a stark English country house, the ostentatious Stickney Mansion in Bull Valley has been called "as out of place as a medieval castle in a junkyard." When planning its construction in the 19th century, George and Sylvia Stickney chose a site off a still-deserted country highway, at 1904 Cherry Valley Road. To this day, the strangely lovely house looks for all the world as if it's scared everyone away.

The Stickneys, however, made no effort to bring life to this dull spot. In fact, they did quite the contrary. As avid spiritualists during the movement's heyday, they insisted on a distinctive feature for the house's design and gave an engaging explanation for their orders. Since the couple planned on holding frequent seances in their future home, they specified that the structure must not have a single square corner. Spirits, they reasoned, get stuck in perpendicular corners. Therefore, to facilitate the building's spiritual activity, it would be built with only rounded edges. It has also been suggested that George Stickney may have thought that evil lurked in corners, a belief typical of the period. In fact, experts on farm architecture confirm that barns with rounded edges were occasionally designed for particularly superstitious farmers.

Whatever the reasons for the precaution in planning, legend states that—whoops!—one corner of one room ended up with the dreaded 90-degree measurement. And it was here that George Stickney was allegedly found one day, dead from no traceable cause.

The two-story oddity, featuring arched windows, wood porticos, and a second-floor ballroom covering the length of the building, often served as a guest house for Civil War soldiers, who were treated to the sounds of McHenry County's first piano there. Later, the opulent ballroom was converted to a seance salon, where Sylvia Stickney gained fame as a gifted medium. Her abilities may have been enhanced by a fervent desire to keep in contact with the Stickneys' children, seven of their 11 perished in infancy.

Though riddled with the memory of death, the house seemed peaceful enough until the 1970s, when Rodrick Smith moved in. He moved out several years later claiming that strange noises and the unwarranted barking of his dogs made the place uninhabitable. A local antique dealer claimed he saw a real estate listing containing a picture of the house in which a woman in a wedding gown and a butler opening a curtain could be clearly seen at separate windows. The photographer later testified, though, that no one had been home at the time he snapped the photo. The tenants who replaced Smith claimed to have experienced nothing unusual, but moved out after several years when plans to restore the house fell through.

Believers in the house's paranormality point to the occupancy of the house in the 1960s by a group of alleged devil-worshipers. These tenants were in fact a group of hippies who painted the rooms in dark colors, built open fires in the middle of several rooms, and upon their departure, left drug paraphernalia and bizarre graffiti as mementos of their stay. Whether satanists or not, they apparently effected some very negative change in the property, at least according to Rodrick Smith, that went far beyond physical damage.

There seem to be two rather aggressive schools of thought about the haunting of the Stickney's former home. One is held by local officials, including Mayor Jean Dooley and the Stickney House Restoration Committee. Both agree that the house has been grievously abused by vandals as a result of the unfounded haunting legends. While these parties have partially restored the house as the local police headquarters, they continue to face expensive repair bills. In fact, at one time the bulldozing of the house was a serious consideration.

The other perspective is that of locals like Bill Nelson, a neighbor who lives across the street from the Stickney House itself. Several years ago, Nelson succinctly communicated to the *Chicago Tribune* the widely-held local opinion about the menacing structure.

Reflecting on the house for perhaps the millionth time, he stated simply but ominously: "It gives you the feeling that it's alive."

Heading back toward Lake Michigan, travelers will hit the North Shore, full of 19th-century mansions and winding, sloping, tree-lined roads which run north along the coast from Evanston, just north of Chicago, to Waukegan. With crashing waves on the eastern border and ancient and dangerous ravines, the houses of the North Shore simply beg for ghosts. Indeed, many of these looming structures, nearly caricatures of themselves, have more than their share of spirits to offer curious drivers up Sheridan Road. Others, most likely devoid of legitimate specters, seem nonetheless to have been singled out and proclaimed as haunted, usually by local youths with dynamic imaginations. Adolescents or teenagers intent on finding a haunted house or other site will usually prey on the reputations of dilapidated structures, unkempt cemeteries, or similarly neglected locations. Occasionally, however, an old story, an eccentric resident, or even a house number, can curse the reputation of even the loveliest of places. Consider the unlucky victim who lived at 666 N. Maple in Lake Bluff.

Sometime during the Truman administration, a Waukegan schoolteacher, returning to this Lake Bluff address, discovered that her room had been ransacked. Alarmed by the apparent break-in, she was significantly more disturbed to find the mutilated body of a sailor in another room of the house.

The dead man, a recruit at nearby Great Lakes Naval Training Center, had apparently committed suicide after feeling remorse for his attempted burglary. A penciled note found by police contained the following words:

> To whom it may concern:
> Please notify commanding officer at U.S. naval training station that William Irwin, seaman recruit, is dead—B-23551-32—and also my parents who I have caused a lot of worry and regret. No use bringing any more anguish and disgrace to my family at all. This is my last writing at 11:30 a.m. Look—my parents are Mr. and Mrs. Monroe Irwin, RFD 4, Jamestown, N.Y.
>
> [signed] William Howard Irwin.

To this day, the house is known among local adolescents as a haunted one. Although there are no accounts of specific phenomena, the tragic memory of one sailor's story—shut up behind a door marked "666"—seems to have provided enough evidence to taint its reputation, at least in young and vivid imaginations.

Infinitely more legitimate is the haunting of 505 N. Sheridan Road, where the Dunham family—Bill and Teddy, and their children, Ritchie and Leslie—has been experiencing all manner of unusual phenomena since the family's arrival 14 years ago. Not only does the house shelter a classic female phantom, complete with long, flowing hair, it has also been known to swallow up mylar balloons, tools, and even live birds. It is also home to a spooked jukebox which turned itself on, Halloween 1996, the anniversary of the death of Teddy Dunham's grandfather. The family has repeatedly spotted fleeting figures in their peripheral vision, heard after-dinner conversations of unseen guests, and has generally accepted the fact that they are living with other non-human entities besides their pets, a dog named Dusenberg, Lexus the cat, and their hermit crab, Viper.

One particular room, a certain spot in the room, in fact, attracts the psychically sensitive—an upstairs bedroom which Teddy feels may have been a nursery. One psychic friend who asked if he could walk around the house, walked into the same upstairs room and said, "Something has happened in this spot, I just know it." Teddy herself does not experience any unusual feelings in that room. She recalls, however, that "babysitters said that the kids before . . . always had that room. And they always went up, put the kids in bed, and ran back downstairs." Laughing off such reactions, the Dunhams are pretty insistent on the positive influence of their invisible housemates, citing several occasions where the house or children may have been seriously endangered were it not for some bizarre circumstances that saved the day. Case in point: the day the entire toaster burned up, leaving its surroundings almost completely undamaged. Teddy explains that, in light of such experiences, "our attitude has always been, if we have a ghost, she's been very good to us."

Another Dunham House, this one the Dunham-Hunt House in St. Charles, has hosted some interesting phenomena since the Dunham family brought home various artifacts related to General

Washington. Mysterious noises and sensations abounded in the parlors and bedrooms of this landmark overlooking the Fox River. Most notable were the footsteps that are still seen walking across one of the carpeted rooms, the evil presence felt to crouch in a downstairs hallway, and an antique desk that housed at least one pesky spirit. One past administrator was so harassed by the Dunham-Hunt haunts that he called on a team of exorcists from a local progressive church. This so-called "A-Team" reportedly uncovered a "nest" of ghosts in the house's basement which the team immediately proceeded to banish with nearly perfect success. After a harrowing series of days during which the house apparently sounded like it was being ripped apart from the inside out, all that remained of the nest were the baffling imprints of footfalls, padding silently across that same carpet.

Back on the North Shore, among the lavishly-forested lairs of the Lake Forest rich, stands the peerlessly decorated Schweppe Mansion. Despite its 20 bedrooms and 18 bathrooms, not a living soul inhabited this elaborate structure for nearly 50 years after its owner, Charles Schweppe, killed himself with a bullet to the head in 1941. Charles moved into the Tudor and Gothic masterpiece on Mayflower Place upon his marriage to Laura Shedd whose father, John G. Shedd, had built the house for Laura as a wedding gift. When Laura died in 1937, Charles lived a lonely life of apparent emotional torment, roaming the house's staggering 33,000 square feet. His suicide note explained little of his ghastly experiences in the echoing house, though he tried to express the relentless turmoil he'd endured. In two lines, he tallied his awesome misery: "I've been awake all night. It is terrible."

Thereafter, as the house stood empty for 47 years, rumors spread that Charles remained in torment, haunting the mansion's master bedroom. Of particular interest to *psi*-searchers is a window overlooking the driveway. According to ongoing testimony, this lone pane has never needed cleaning, even when the house has been otherwise covered in grime. Over the years, these eerie tales only added to the house's grim atmosphere, keeping many vandals and potential buyers at bay. Then, Donna Denten Desplenter bought the house and immediately started its renovation. When she began her overhaul, Desplenter discovered a curious reality: the mansion has what its caretaker has called a "doorway to hell." Apparently, this entryway in the basement leads only to narrow, black corridors, turning into other snaking passageways, dead ends, and desolate rooms. Such a wonderland, especially nestled in a reputedly haunted house, necessarily drew the braver party-goers of the area's teenagers. The purchase of the home by Desplenter has once again put the Schweppe Mansion on the path to livability, driving out the potential vandals and relieving the neighbors. Still, while local interest in the haunting of this haven has certainly dissipated, it is uncertain whether Charles' spirit has done the same.

Far from the North Shore, both physically and spiritually, is Moline House, a private Berwyn home, located at 3101 Wesley Avenue. According to its owners, the house is inhabited by a mischievous apparition who seems to cause the relocation of objects, sometimes moving them instantly from one spot on to another distant site or simply hiding them from the house's residents. There have been no speculations about the spirit's origins. In fact, the family seems nearly oblivious to this uninvited and sometimes pesky lodger.

Necessarily more attentive are the residents of Old Lobstein House in south suburban Forest Park. A fine example of a Victorian Painted Lady, the house has reputedly been haunted for half of a century. Residents have variously reported deafening banging sounds, the unmistakable echo of pacing footsteps across the attic floor, and the scampering of children in an upstairs hall, as well as the classic cold spots. Even neighbors are privy to the house's bizarre show. Many have glimpsed a shadowy silhouette at the attic window. November 6th seems to be a red-letter day for the unseen forces of Old Lobstein House. Annually on that date, the attic comes alive with inexplicable sounds. Tradition says that the property retains the spirits of two children. The first is that of Addie, the daughter of the house's architect, John Lobstein. The second belongs to Addie's half-brother, "Charlie," who reportedly committed suicide in—yes—the attic. Inevitably, lore assumes the house's peculiar behavior each November 6th to be its way of "commemorating" the rumored date of Charlie's tragic demise.

One final house deserves a special note and a visit, especially since tours of the oddity are available. Located near

Gurnee, in far northeastern Illinois, the Gold Pyramid House is something to behold. A one-hundredth scale reproduction of the Great Pyramid at Giza, the house holds a Chariot Room housing ancient artifacts and reproductions, among them a life-sized gold-covered sarcophagus lid depicting the death mask of the boy king Tutankhamen. Even the terminally unimpressed might pause for another eyeful—a full-size gold-dipped model of the king's chariot. The bizarre history of this American monstrosity began during the house's construction, when bulldozers struck an outcropping of gold ore, the only such strike to ever have been reported in the state of Illinois. Later, after the structure was in place, a spring gushed forth at the center of the pyramid, although no underground water had been found during surveys of the property. The water proceeded to form a moat around the building and, amazingly, was so pure that the property owner was given license to bottle and market the stuff as spring water. By 1986, more weirdness developed. Ravens began to attack those who attempted to enter the Chariot Room from the north, echoing an Egyptian legend that tells of black birds that protect the north entrance to Tut's tomb at Giza.

Obviously, some of Chicago's so-called haunted houses are more inhabitable than others. What is common to them all, however, is the fascination of residents, neighbors, and the larger culture itself with these phantoms that variously open closets, steal balloons, wash windows, host dinner parties, switch on jukeboxes, and sometimes, overpower the personalities of their human hosts.

Every Chicago ward and every outlying town has its haunted house, a structure that shelters the old way of life from the encroachment of the changing, surrounding culture. These pages have collected only a handful of such havens, but there are as many of these habitations as there are neighborhoods to welcome them. No matter how many are demolished, the world's haunted houses can never be lost. Constantly contributing their own additions to the original structures, future storytellers will faithfully rebuild them, generation after generation, in the shared space of local memory.

♦

VIII

BELIEVING IN MARY WORTH
Myth, Imagination, and Chicago's School Spirits

Every time a child says, "I don't believe in fairies,"
somewhere, a little fairy falls down dead.

—UNKNOWN SOURCE

More chilling than these stone statues of Chicago children at suburban Forest Home Cemetery are the tales traded by their flesh-and-blood counterparts. (*Photo by Matt Hucke*)

EMEMBERING CHANGES IN THE COMPOSITIONS OF THEIR CLASSROOMS OVER THE YEARS, VETERAN ELEMENTARY SCHOOL TEACHERS ON CHICAGO'S NORTH SIDE INEVITABLY RECALL some periods more than others. Without a doubt, one of the most vivid influxes of children occurred in the 1950s and 1960s, when hundreds of families migrated to Chicago from the southeastern United States. The children of those families, some in school for the very first time, brought to their urban classmates an eye-opening awareness of an enthralling distant culture—tales of days spent free and open, of life side by side with wild animals, of landscapes of hills and forests. For the northern-born kids, however, the best baggage brought by their new classmates was welcome cargo indeed—a wholly new, and wholly horrifying, collection of "ghast" stories.

Some wise educators encouraged the exchange of regional cultures and valued the storytelling abilities of these kids "straight out of the hills." Kids like Clitus Blackburn, clad in a man's fedora and coat, were allowed to share with one captive classroom the spine-tingling southern stories which had stowed away on the trip north. Such stories fell on ready ears; Chicago children were well primed by their own ethnic backgrounds for belief in the supernatural realms of other regions.

Despite the joy in sharing their tales from beyond, these young migrants also experienced a predictable despair. Many educators, quick to recall the assimilation of southern children to their mid-century classes are struck by a singular impression: it wasn't an easy transition. One retired Chicago teacher reflecting on the newcomers' often acute sadness remembers that they "missed the South so much . . . the country . . . hunting, fishing, running through the woods." One such student, remembered only as "Charles," would sulk all morning until the break; then, outside at recess, climb up in the only nearby tree and refuse to come down "because he wanted to go home to West Virginia."

As the '60s ebbed, children like Clitus and Charles became somewhat acclimated to their urban environs. What remained in the elementary schools, however, was a sort of communal receptiveness to the unknown, an ache for mystery that arose from a nostalgia for the remembered, or imagined, wilderness, from urban ethnic life seasoned by Old World customs, and from religious interminglings. As the Clituses and Charleses were becoming familiar with the mysteries of urban life, a new kind of mystery began to seep into the larger culture, trickling into the schools through some young parents and newly certificated teachers, the alternative culture of the 1960s.

Suddenly, the unknown seemed closer than ever before. Kids, perhaps more than anyone else, sensed the new proximity of the unseen and responded appropriately. Take the case of one North Side school which in the early 1970s gained a reputation as "haunted" when an enchanting teacher captured the imagination of the student body.

One school day around 1972 or '73, two teachers at the old Horace Greeley Elementary School were standing in the hallway talking; at their side was a young charge, a girl who was being detained for some act of mischief. As the teachers carried on their discussion, a class filed down from the third floor and went into the library. Heading the class was the teacher rumored to be a "witch," a piece of gossip even the faculty had difficulty in dismissing. One of the observing teachers remembers: "She had the greenest eyes . . . . She knew all about the occult and satanic things and all that. The kids would go in the library and they'd sit there and they'd look like they were zombies." On this particular day, after the class had passed into the library, the two teachers and their silent little shadow remained in the hallway. All of a sudden the trio spotted something

like a cloud coming down the hall . . . just fog . . . coming.
Coming from the library. We thought at first it might have
been eraser dust. Well, it wasn't eraser dust.

One of the teachers started to back up and the other followed
suit, with "the little girl's eyes getting bigger and bigger . . . and it
[the cloud] was just rolling . . . ."

The dumbstruck group watched as this eerie cloud, which
extended about three feet to eight feet off the floor, rolled between
the teachers, continued to the stairs, ascended the staircase, and
actually made a turn to complete the climb. When the cloud reached
the third floor, one of the teachers, who, amazed, had followed it,
observed the cloud as "it went right into the classroom where the
class had just come out of." When she looked in, it was gone. Later,
she remembers telling the teacher but "she didn't believe us." She
wasn't the only one, "The principal thought we were both crazy."

Notwithstanding the initially "mature" dismissal of this
incident, the account was destined for survival. Inevitably, "the little
girl started saying she saw a ghost." After the story began to spread,
students began to believe that the ghost was none other than that of
Horace Greeley, the school's namesake. After the identity became an
accepted fact, students naturally began to take appropriately
cautionary measures. In particular, according to one faculty member,
"There was this portrait of Greeley hanging in the library, and they
were afraid to go in there because of the picture." Although many
teachers at the newly-haunted school must surely have grown
exasperated by such fears, other teachers gently encouraged rumors
of a local ghost, conspiring with fellow faculty in whistling through
the ventilation system or spreading news of ever-new phantom
encounters.

Charmed by their new though invisible mascot, students and
teachers dubbed the school's newspaper *The Greeley Spirit*. Its first
issue, released to the student body in May 1983, featured a piece
entitled, "Does Horace Greeley's Ghost Still Roam Our Halls? Some
Say Yes, Some Say No, Some Say Wait and See." Alongside the
copy, the article's author, Nam Hee Kim, drew a cartoon of "Horace
. . . The Greeley Spirit" floating on a presumably ectoplasmic cloud
above the school buildings. Briefly summing up the experiences

One student's rendering of the ghost of Horace Greeley Elementary School, as it appeared in the school newspaper, *The Greeley Spirit*.

already mentioned, this young writer verified some other instances when the life, or afterlife, of Greeley School seemed to imitate the artistic imaginings of students and teachers, echoing the testimony of one teacher who remembered that "things would fall off the shelf. Like books would plop right off. And things would disappear and then reappear in the same spot."

A real Greeley ghost? No one will ever know. The old Horace Greeley School was torn down in recent years after its replacement in 1978 by the new sparkling and carpeted version that now stands several blocks away. As our then-aspiring journalist wondered, "We don't know if the ghost followed us. Do you think so?"

♦

*Y*et while there were new tales to tell, the old were, and still are, king. But with the telling of tales comes the duty of issuing warnings, not always against ghosts, but against things perhaps much worse, such as mysterious childhood dangers like Mary Worth.

For at least two generations at slumber parties across the country, adolescents have challenged each other to lock themselves in a darkened bathroom and whisper into the mirror, "I believe in Mary Worth." In some versions, the routine requires the candidate to spin around and call on the name of "Bloody Mary." At that point, the legendary Worth is alleged to reach out from the mirror and scratch the face of her victim. As one Chicago teacher recalls of her own past students: "The kids . . . all believed that . . . . [They] were so superstitious." Superstitious, perhaps. But the ritual goes on, though few practitioners grown to adulthood have ever wondered how or where it began.

Not so in the case of one Larry Rawn, who believes he has traced the Worth legend to Lake County, a region stretching northward out of Chicago along Lake Michigan.

According to Rawn's compelling research, Mary Worth made a name for herself during the days of the Civil War, when she lived on the Old Wagon Road, now Dilly Road, just west of Gurnee. There, famed throughout the region as a witch of the most heinous variety, Worth was known as a catcher of runaway slaves whom she would keep chained in her barn to be used in her diabolical rituals.

Rawn first learned of Mary Worth in the 1960s from a Lake County resident in her 90s who, as a girl of four or five, had watched Mary burned at the stake by furious locals outraged at Worth's atrocities. According to tradition, after the unofficial execution, the body was buried in nearby St. Patrick's Cemetery, called by Rawn "the most vandalized cemetery in Lake County." Rawn strongly denounces this theory, though, reasoning that in the late 19th century a known witch would never have been allowed a Christian burial.

True. But for those who insist on sticking to the story, Rawn supports his assertion with a most beguiling piece of evidence.

Several decades ago, a friend of Rawn's purchased the Worth property, a big old sprawl of land holding a new home and barn and marked by an ancient tree out front. Fully aware of the lot's history, the farmer and his wife lived on the foundations of the very barn where Worth had kept her second-hand slaves and practiced her craft. The barn had been burnt to the ground following her demise. The couple was also aware of the grim fact that a girl had committed suicide in what was to be their new home. Unhindered by this gruesome legacy, and with intentions to cultivate the property, the farmer at once set out to clear the land to make way for the sowing of oats. Though the land was generally free of debris, one small boulder, remarkably square, stood stubbornly in his way. Frustrated in his efforts, he moved the rock to the front of the house, to be used as a stepping-stone.

From that day on, the property took on a life of its own. His wife repeatedly found herself locked in the barn, and in the house, plates popped out of spring-loaded hangers and crashed to the floor. As the bizarre antics worsened, a terrible question arose in the farmer's mind: had he inadvertently moved the marker over the real grave of Mary Worth? The fearsome phenomena seemed to answer with an almost-audible yes.

Anxious to restore the equilibrium of his investment, the farmer set about relocating the stone; unfortunately, he never found the exact spot from which he had moved it. After years of unexplained and often dangerous events, the house burned down in 1986, allegedly due to arson.

Afterwards, the Worth property was bought by a contractor who aimed to build on it, but the deal went bankrupt, as did two others that followed. Finally, a developer successfully completed a cluster of houses, but the home built on the property nearest to where the farmer's house had stood burnt at least once, some say twice.

Notwithstanding these incidents and their seeming linkage to the removal of the curious stone, St. Patrick's Cemetery continues to be visited by those seeking a sighting of the real Mary Worth. Here, the curious gather around the alleged Worth grave and the widespread ritual at the site of its inception, calling on the name of the witch and professing with scared but steely tongues their belief in her existence. Some claim to have been scratched to bleeding by an unseen thing, and some even show photographs of themselves or others bearing these marks of otherworldly abuse.

Adding to these bizarre tales is the legend that St. Patrick's Cemetery is itself cursed. According to this story, a priest refused to let a local resident be buried in the cemetery. In response, a member of the man's family told the priest that the burial ground would have no peace until the man's body was allowed inside.

During the mid-1970s, young Chicago fans of the supernatural sustained themselves by recycling old stories told by their parents and classmates and by embellishing or fabricating rumors of school hauntings. Thanks to new waves of Latin-American immigrants that arrived in Chicago beginning in the 1970s, however, and increasingly in the 1980s and '90s, Chicago kids eager for the unknown did not go hungry for long. Puerto Rican and Mexican newcomers would furnish surprisingly familiar food to local appetites. As a result, in today's schoolyard circles, pre-adolescent Hispanic girls hold court with their tales of the supernatural, telling third and fourth generation American playmates of mingled prayers and spells that worked, and some that failed, of run-ins with long-departed relatives, of the wonders of psychic reading and healing, and of little laughing men conjured with candles and ouija boards. Building on a remarkable faith founded on Mary Worth and all her attendant phantasms, wide-eyed classmates huddle together and gobble each offered morsel, however improbable. And once encouraged, every child, it seems, has a story to share.

◆

In spite of their democratic acceptance of all ghosts, for Chicago children in the 1990s, one folk legend has remained without peer since its recent emergence: the mind-numbing concept of Candyman.

The cinematic evolution of the old Mary Worth, Candyman wins hands down against the mirrored terror in sending chills down young Chicago spines. Smile and whisper, "Candyman" to a Chicago kid and one can almost see her blood run cold. For candyman is not a tale to be told lightly, and certainly not a name to

Sweet Home Chicago: Candyman's Cabrini-Green Kingdom.
(*Photo by D. Cowan*)

be laughed at. For Candyman, they will tell you, lived in Cabrini Green, the notorious Chicago housing project. And Candyman is real, as proven by his appearance in the Clive Barker film named for him.

Hollywood itself created the story of the unfortunate young African-American man who suffers a horrible death and lives in infamy as an urban legend, preying on those who don't believe in him.

The son of a slave living in 1890s Chicago, the boy who became Candyman was gifted with superior artistic talent. A prominent townsman recognized his ability and commissioned the young man to paint a portrait of his daughter. Of course, artist and subject fell in love and the young woman became pregnant. The irate father called on the men of the town to avenge his daughter's supposed victimization. Needing no coaxing, the mob seized the young man and carried him to a field, the future site of Cabrini Green, where they cut off his right hand with a saw. Then, spotting a nearby beehive, the men broke open the hive, covered the boy with honey and watched as the angry bees stung him to death. Through some otherworldly mechanism, the young victim became trapped between the real and imagined worlds, where he lives in the figure of a towering, cloaked stalker, with a bloody hook for a hand.

Like Mary Worth, the wronged Candyman won't bother those who fear him, provided of course that they refrain from provocation, provocation which consists predictably of facing a mirror in a darkened room and calling his name.

In the film, the legend of Candyman is investigated by a graduate student at the University of Chicago. The unsuspecting young scholar delves into a world where the violence of Cabrini creates a universe where reality and nightmare hopelessly overlap. Confident of her own scholarly superiority over superstition, our would-be sociologist flippantly tests the legend's verity, inevitably provoking her own destruction at the hands of the mythical monster.

The tragic content of the Candyman myth, magnified by exceptionally violent screen imagery, lodged deeply in the minds of Chicago schoolchildren who recognized all too well the familiar landscapes of their own city. Although it is impossible to foresee the specific fate of the Candyman legend in Chicago folklore, it is easy to guarantee a long and interesting life for its motifs.

◆

$\mathcal{S}$ince they spend their grammar school days rejoicing in the supernatural, it is hardly surprising that after entering high school these same youngsters continue to spend much of their time in pursuit of the unknown. And, in fact, elementary schools have not been the only Chicago schools to gain and maintain haunted reputations over the years. Across the city and suburbs, a variety of legends created and cultivated in young minds have become firmly rooted in various halls of learning. Lourdes High School on the city's Southwest Side and Benet Academy in west suburban Lisle have both been reported to harbor resident specters. How else to justify the inexplicable footsteps and music at Lourdes and the various unaccounted for occurrences at Benet, previously St. Joseph's Orphanage, where one or more orphaned phantoms are rumored to make the fourth floor a most enticing, though off-limits, area.

Still, although several haunted high schools have emerged in and around Chicago, far fewer ghosts tend to be walled up in school buildings after the elementary years. Suddenly, there are weekends and hanging out and all of the territory outside the structured life of family and school. Suddenly, the academic environment is no longer the only hauntable realm; the whole world becomes a blank page on which to scrawl fantastic tales. Running on a chaotic mix of childhood fantasies, oddly meshed with an opposing longing for maturity, high schoolers everywhere and at all times have sought a physical place apart, a place where the thrills of freedom and imagination could survive their own desires to grow up. For Cook County teenagers, the forest preserves have provided the most natural remedy to reality. The woods are where the best of Chicago legends thrive: in the miles of trees lining Archer Avenue; down the dirt path to Bachelors Grove Cemetery; scattered along the DesPlaines River in LaBagh Woods.

Although many of the stories focused on these preserves stretch far back through Chicago youth culture, the cultural changes of the 1960s and '70s certainly stoked their illicit campfires.

Working with imaginations encouraged by pop-cultural concepts of altered consciousness, liberation, and occultism, local teenagers began to circulate haunting legends and other tales with a new enthusiasm. Inadvertently mimicking the efforts of their parents and grandparents, young voices began to credit many accounts of eerie happenings to the work of the Devil. In the southwest suburbs, the tales of Satan worship at Bachelors Grove were gingerly accepted by kids and adults alike. Similarly, North Side high-schoolers in the '70s and '80s knew enough about the diabolical activities at LaBagh Woods to stay away. Naturally, they didn't; its picturesque groves became the place to party.

Cemeteries, too, have possessed a universal appeal for teenagers. Chicago-area burial grounds have been no exception. In addition to the obvious intrigue of darkness and death, many Chicago cemeteries offer the added bonus of resident phantoms, the search for whom has at times become a familiar part of high school life.

Consider the case of Resurrection Cemetery. On the Southwest Side, a long-standing tradition mandates that upon getting one's first driver's license, the new driver must drive that certain stretch of Archer Avenue in search of the infamous Mary. Recall also how the students at Proviso West High School have been known to leave school dances to line up along the fence of Mt. Carmel Cemetery hoping for a glimpse of the ghost of Julia Buccola. Finally, although the Peabody graves have now been moved from Mayslake, the thrilling legend surrounding that coal mogul's burial still draws teenagers to the estate for a variety of youthful initiations.

♦

After commencement, those graduates who go to college rarely shed their common superstitions; rather, local legends are stuffed into suitcases along with sweatshirts and popcorn poppers, to be offered to new acquaintances during the course of endless collegiate talk sessions. For Chicago-area co-eds, whether at a nearby private college or a state university swaying in the cornfields, urban legends continue to be the most powerful of icebreakers. Here, among beanbag chairs, bunkbeds, and beer cans, faded stories

reaching back to childhood are whitewashed by enthusiastic retelling to totally new audiences who undoubtedly take them home
over breaks to share with their own hometown comrades.

Yet, while tales from home are a mainstay of collegiate
folklore, they eventually pale as new kinds of legends are discovered
and created—on-campus ghost and horror stories, as well as those
"heard about" other area colleges and universities. And, of course,
stories about nearby woods, cemeteries, and other predictably
appealing sites.

Students at Eastern Illinois University in Charleston, for
example, will be glad to tell you about a ghost named Mary who
reputedly haunts Pemberton Hall, a female dormitory. Mary, who
has been reported to lock doors left open, turn off lights and stereos,
and perform other small caretaking acts, is allegedly the spirit of a
counselor who was beaten to death by a maniacal custodian in the
1920s. And while the legend bears a striking similarity to a common
urban legend, that of the "Roommate's Death," students at Eastern
will prove that the legend is true by pointing skeptics to a memorial
plaque hanging in the dormitory.

A similar story, this one more detailed, is often traced to
Northern Illinois University in DeKalb. Because of the specifics, the
tale is a chilling one.

One evening in the 1970s or '80s, a female student living on
campus at Northern found herself feeling ill and wanted to turn in
early, hoping that a good night's sleep would hasten her recovery.
Her roommate, sympathetic but studious, elected to do some
research at the library. Wishing her friend a good night and better
health, she left the dorm and started towards the library, a good walk
across campus. After several hours of study, she was invited by
another student to go to a local bar with a group of mutual friends.
She said yes, but arranged to meet the others at the library entrance
in 20 minutes, having left her ID back in her room. The others
agreed, but urged her to hurry. Picking up her books, the young
woman walked quickly back to her dorm. When she entered, her
room was dark and, not wishing to disturb her sick roommate, the
young woman fumbled in the closet for her ID. Closing the door
quietly behind her, she walked back to the library where her friends
were waiting. The group left campus for town and spent several

hours at a popular bar.

When the group arrived back at school, the driver returned to the library where some had left their cars. Those who lived on campus went their separate ways. Our young woman headed alone towards her dormitory.

As she came within view of the building, she was startled to see that the parking lot was lit up with flashing lights, and that all of the dorm's residents were standing outside. As she approached the crowd, the young woman saw that many of the residents were sobbing, while others stood pale and silent. When she was spotted by some friends, they looked at her blankly, then rushed to her side warning her away from the building. Alarmed, she ran past the police guard, through the entrance, and up the stairs to her floor. Outside her room, town and campus police were milling around. When they spotted the young woman coming towards the room, they moved to block her path. Screaming that the room was hers, she managed to break past them and in through the door. Immediately, she regretted her action.

There on the floor, in what seemed like a lake of blood, lay her roommate, brutally mutilated and barely recognizable. More blood covered the walls of the room and of the small entryway. Overcome with nausea, the horrified roommate rushed from the grisly scene to the bathroom, followed by the anxious cries of detectives. After vomiting, she staggered to the sink and splashed her face with water. Slumping against the closed door, she looked up at the large bathroom mirror. There, scrawled across the glass in blood, her roommate's slayer had left a message especially for her: "Aren't you glad you didn't turn on the lights?"

♦

Not all disquieting collegiate tales are horror stories from urban legend. Some accounts are firsthand reports of seemingly paranormal occurrences. At Maryknoll College, a Roman Catholic seminary in Glen Ellyn, students in the 1970s frequently reported run-ins with a phantom priest who would gently touch their cheeks and then dematerialize as suddenly as he had appeared. His presence most often occupied the photography lab, where his appearances were accompanied by roving cold spots.

At Barat College in Lake Forest, students and staff have encountered the strong scent of flowers in the chapel. In recent years a psychic traced the odor to an invisible bouquet of flowers carried by the spirit of a nun.

◆

Benedictine University, previously Illinois Benedictine College, in west suburban Lisle, another nearby Catholic university, has also hosted a variety of unexplained phenomena. Over the years, several students have reported the feeling of an unseen presence in a particular room of Jaegar Hall, an underclass-men's dormitory. But these creepy sensations are hardly the only paranormal events alleged to have taken place at this quiet college.

Throughout the years, various stories have centered around a wooded area on the outskirts of the campus, containing a murky slough and a tiny cemetery with the graves of the school's founding brothers and other members of their Procopian community. The usual rumors of slough-side satanic rituals abound here, where the murdered corpse of a DuPage County woman showed up in recent years. Her ghost is believed to haunt the area where the body was found, but she is hardly the most famous of the Procopian community's phantoms. That distinction belongs to an erstwhile monk named Zombie.

Before he was released from his vows, one of the Abbey's monks, dubbed with the unfortunate nickname because of plain old ugliness, lived according to the rules of his order and took special care in one of his duties: tending the little cemetery where community members were laid to eternal rest. So passionate was his care for these grounds that he would hide inside the cemetery fence at night and literally scare away any students who tried to hold drinking parties on the premises. Though Zombie was a devoted brother, his dedication was marred by a fatal flaw—he refused to take communal meals preferring to eat in the solitude of his own room. When this quirk began to come between he and his fellows, he wrote to Rome requesting to be excused from compulsory participation in shared mealtime. In response, Zombie was released entirely from his vows. The Abbey community, however, allowed the orphaned brother to remain with the community as a volunteer. Happily, he was also allowed to continue his caretaking of the cemetery. When Zombie's Maker called him, he happened to be in the cemetery at the time, and where he fell, he was buried. According to a strong tradition, Zombie continues to guard his beloved burial ground from a most convenient perspective. And whether one believes the tale of Zombie's continued devotion, what is true is what happened when long after his burial a bunch of football players aimed to spend an evening drinking on Zombie's turf. The party broke up almost before it began, the gridders leaving all the beer behind. Then, in 1990 or '91, several male students purportedly took a ouija board into the locked campus cemetery where all hell really did break loose that night.

Accounts say that one of the young men became "possessed," screaming and howling uncontrollably, incapable of being restrained by his companions. Reportedly, campus police were called to assist in dragging the young man back to his room in Kholbeck Hall where he continued to resist efforts to calm him. A priest was called from the Abbey to offer prayers and to counsel everyone involved. The apparent victim of possession eventually had to be taken to the hospital and medicated. The real story? According to more sober sources, several students did go out to the cemetery with a ouija board, not in search of Zombie, but in a half-hearted attempt to contact the spirit of the murdered DuPage woman. Unfortunately, one of the pranksters became overexcited and his hysteria convinced his companions that something had gone very wrong.

Notwithstanding the natural explanation of the event, the basic story was embellished over the next several days with some interesting flourishes. Most notable was the insistence that campus police had initially taken the screaming young man up to the fourth floor of Benedictine Hall and locked him in a room hoping he might tire himself out. When he quieted down and they unlocked the door, the young man was sitting quietly on a chair looking out a window covered with swarming flies. Needless to say, when the star of this drama returned to campus, he faced a variety of looks, some respectful, some suspicious, all intrigued, and left a wake of whispering behind him.

During the following several weeks, ouija boards enjoyed a spurt of popularity among campus residents. Some credited the devices with fearful powers. One group blamed their ouija board for a fire that broke out in their room at Neuzil Hall, claiming that they had left it on the sofa where the fire had started and that the board's remains were nowhere to be found.

♦

*T*he ouija-centered tales of Benedictine University are not the only such stories in Chicago-area campus folklore. Students at a number of other colleges continue to draw on experience and legend in cautioning against the far from innocent ouija board, touted by its modern manufacturer, Parker Brothers, as "the mystifying oracle." At River Forest's Dominican University, previously Rosary College, students offer their own stories. Many focus on the ouijia's apparent power to invest certain individuals with superhuman strength. Not surprisingly, some students and alumni have named adjacent Thatcher Woods as the home of the evil thought to manifest itself through the boards, claiming that satanic worship is a regular occurrence at this otherwise soothing preserve.

Eerie, yes. But here at Dominican University, the most chilling experience requires no conjuring, no packaged and patented mediums, no adjacent evil. Rather, the school houses one of the most startling samples of permanent paranormality free for the gazing. Walk through the darkly atmospheric dining hall of the gothic campus and raise your eyes to the lintels above the south entryways. There, flanking the lengths of stone are artfully sculpted heads set into the door frames. One crucial element is missing from these renderings. The faces have all been removed, seemingly chopped off and raked over with mortar and trowel.

Tradition tells of a time when these trimmings were intact. Rumors began to circulate, however, that the expressions on the stone faces were altering themselves with some frequency. As such reports grew, school officials most likely huddled and decided to have the questionable countenances axed from their settings to avoid further gossip or future transfigurations. Apparently, the plan worked. No disturbances are known to have followed on the heels of this remarkable administrative action, though the faceless sentinels remain as a testament to the unusual decision.

◆

*R*egardless of the abundance of the unexplained in the logbooks of resident life, the intimacy and idle time of dorm living are hardly a necessary condition for post-high school consumption of the preternatural. Case in point: Morton College, a commuter college in southwest suburban Cicero, harbors a haunt of its own, which expresses itself in disembodied footsteps and clouds of mist that drift through classrooms.

◆

*W*hether shared during pre-kindergarten milk and cookies or post-doctorate coffee breaks, stories of the supernatural continue to make growing up in Chicago a truly spirited experience. Utilizing stories smuggled in from their parents' and grandparents' birth countries, rumors about nearby cemeteries and preserves, universal but localized urban legends, and eerie tales of their own alma maters, area youth have never failed to remain faithful to the unknown, delighting in its well-established manifestations and cataloging new ones every day. Appealing to their own apprehensions about the reality of adult life, the world of myth and imagination provides a safe haven during young people's uncertain years. Shivering under stars at Bachelors Grove, creeping through the woods of the Peabody Estate, or calling boldly on Candyman, Chicago kids can save the real world for another day.

Not that the tales are necessarily dismissed as unbelievable. For those like 8-year-old Adam McMahon of west suburban Naperville, the anomalous can seem as acceptable as everyday life. Like many of his elders, Adam carries with him one special story of the supernatural, that of the strange events reported at North Central College. Learning of the alleged haunting of one of the campus buildings from his Uncle Terry, an employee at the college, this aspiring storyteller earnestly related the details:

Not all schools are happy, for example, haunted schools like North Central. About 50 years ago, a kid of the school died somehow in Pfeiffer hall. A man was a security guard [there], of course, brave. His name was Terry McMahon. But remember, ghosts can't hurt you. A piano went playing and also an electrician said that when one light went on, all the others go on, but they go on one at a time. Remember, ghosts are real.

♦

IX

A DIFFERENT WORLD
The Native American Connection

This anomalous photograph of Dave Black was snapped when he noted strange sensations during an investigation of Robinson Woods in February of 1998. *(Photo courtesy of Supernatural Occurrence Studies)*

*I*N RECENT DECADES, THE CONNECTION OF PARANORMAL EVENTS WITH NATIVE AMERICAN CULTURE HAS EMERGED AS AN INCREASINGLY STRONG IMPULSE IN POPULAR MEDIA. WITNESS the story line of the motion picture *Poltergeist*, in which real estate developers building on an Indian burial ground bring the ancestral wrath upon unsuspecting suburbanites. Recall the earlier fate of a similarly-situated house in *The Amityville Horror*. Remember the power inherent in Stephen King's *Pet Sematary*. In these fictional situations and others like them, when foolish skeptics have ignored Native American warnings about sacred ground, a knowing public, along with the audience, shakes its collective head as if to say, You're asking for it.

In examining Chicago's folklore, one might compile a whole separate casebook of similar, "real life" situations. Many local paranormal phenomena have been explained by their occurrence on or near former American Indian tribal sites, trails, or burial grounds. Cemeteries like Bachelors Grove and St. James-Sag are supposed to have had previous existences as Indian tribal and burial sites, respectively. The Gallo home in Orland Hills was likewise alleged to have been built on such a site, contributing presumably to the devastating poltergeist activity which occurred there in the 1980s. Most notably, Archer Avenue's beginnings as an Indian trail have led some researchers, especially ley hunters, to believe that the phenomena associated with Route 171 are fact, and that they draw on the geographic energy created or identified there by Native

American cultures.

Although this book has already touched upon the wonders of Archer Avenue and other locations, several other Chicagoland sites beg for examination by those intrigued by the possible relationship between Native American culture and *psi* effects, most notably, a colorful totem pole in Chicago's Lincoln Park and an old Indian burial ground situated in Robinson Woods on the city's far Northwest Side.

Driving east on Addison Street from Wrigley Field, explorers will quickly arrive at the threshold of the first of these curiosities—Lake Shore Drive, across which stands the impressive tower of intriguing totems. Donated to the city by food magnate J.L. Kraft, the sculpture has since its erection provided a meeting place for lakefront visitors and a prime spot for Gold Coast sunbathers. Bright sunshine notwithstanding, a shadow of mystery has long encircled the artwork. Some observers, comparing photos taken over the years, have alleged that one of the pole's figures, a spear-wielding man riding a whale, has moved. The faithful have cited a native belief in the totem's power to come to life; skeptics have shrugged off the apparent alterations, blaming optical illusion.

Like the totem pole in Lincoln Park, Robinson Woods Indian Burial Ground is also part of a recreational area, the Indian Boundary Division of the Forest Preserve District of Cook County. The physical atmosphere of the latter site, however, tucked a few steps off the street from the intersection of River Road and Lawrence Avenue, is significantly less cheerful. In fact, even investigators known for nerves of steel have found their hearts a-flutter when left alone at this tiny Potawatomi burial ground, where 40 years of *psi* phenomena have gone largely unexplained. To understand the nature, if not the cause, of the site's unusual occurrences, researchers have looked to the history of the area's eternal inhabitants, the family of Chief Che-che-pin-quay, or Alexander Robinson. Indisputably, Alexander Robinson left one of the deepest sets of handprints in Chicago's foundation, both recognizing the need for sincere diplomacy between the native populations and the white settlers and doing what he could to aid in those relations. Equally dedicated to the opposing cultures running through him, Robinson spent his life attempting to be true to both.

The mixed son of an Ottawa Indian mother and a Scottish trader, Robinson grew up among the Potawatomi near St. Joseph, Michigan. He was apparently traveling to Chicago in 1812 when he received news of the massacre at Fort Dearborn. After spending some time camped along the mouth of the Calumet River, Robinson joined Antoine Ouilmette, remembered by the town of Wilmette, in cultivating the gardens of the deserted fort, becoming a permanent Chicago resident in 1814.

Robinson was a devoted Chicagoan from the beginning, settling at Hardscrabble, now Bridgeport, where Racine Avenue meets the south branch of the Chicago River. In 1826, Robinson married Catherine Chevalier, becoming the son-in-law of a mixed blood Potawatomi chief known as Shobonier. According to traditional accounts, John Kinzie, Chicago's first antihero, performed the ceremony. Upon the death of Catherine's father, Robinson assumed his role as the new chief, Che-che-pin-quay, a name which means Winking (or Blinking) Eye. Working as a translator for Alexander Wolcott, an Indian agent, Robinson became enmeshed in the mixed culture of Chicago, establishing himself as a faithful friend of both Native Americans and whites.

In July 1829, the Potawatomi made a large cession of land in the Treaty of Prairie du Chien. A portion of this land was set aside for Robinson at Lawrence Avenue and River Road on the DesPlaines River in appreciation of the chief's peacekeeping efforts as an interpreter. In addition, Che-che-pin-quay was awarded a lifetime annuity of $200, which was increased several years later by the Chicago Treaty to $500 a year.

In 1830, Robinson opened a tavern at Lake and Canal streets; five years later, he bid good-bye to his tribe and headed west to Council Bluffs, Iowa. As the Potawatomi fled the encroachment of white settlement, their chief, firmly pledged to the development of Chicago, returned to live on his 1,200 acres on Chicago's far Northwest Side. He remained there until his death in 1872.

As it turned out, Robinson's adopted name was truly fitting. Every time he blinked, it seemed, the chief found that the whole world had changed, often by the work of his own hands. Born in a Potawatomi village in George Washington's inaugural year, he settled in a volatile environment and remained true to the city that grew up there. Between 1816 and 1833, he signed four treaties with the U.S. government, essentially giving away an empire. Remaining behind in the wake of his own tribe's exodus from Chicago's threatening urbanization, Robinson did all he could to help make the transition from fort to city one of relative peace. Ironically, his last year left him reflecting on the destruction of that city in the Great Fire of 1871.

Throughout the first half of the 1900s, the lively goings-on at the Robinson house, nestled in the woods off Lawrence Avenue, made for exciting conversation among Anglo-Chicagoans, whose ever-deteriorating opinion of the indigenous population stretched well into the century. Rumors of wild living were spread by Chicagoans suspicious of the Robinsons' famous hospitality. Notwithstanding their place's shady reputation, Robinson's family continued to enjoy their life in the woods until the spring of 1955, when the Robinson house, still occupied by Alexander's granddaughter, burned to the ground.

After more than a century as the centerpiece of tribal ceremony, impromptu celebration, and everyday life, the remains of the Robinson house mixed with the soil of what is today Robinson, or Che-che-pin-quay Woods. There, a dozen yards from Lawrence Avenue and its manicured bungalows, the Robinson family rests at a tiny burial site in a clearing of trees, flanked by two benches, and marked with a single boulder bearing a short inscription.

In 1973, the last of the Robinson ancestors died and sanitation officials worked to block his burial at the Robinson gravesite. Thereafter, peculiar events began to be reported by visitors to Robinson Woods, and rumors of paranormal phenomena spread quickly. These first-hand accounts ranged from the sighting of Indian faces and strange lights among the trees, to the unmistakable sound of tom-toms, to a sudden and pungent scent of lilacs at the Robinson gravesite, even in winter. Among various investigations conducted at the site over the years, one of the most compelling was conducted by students from Northeastern Illinois University, which at the time offered a course of study in parapsychology. That investigation yielded some interesting evidence in favor of witnesses' allegations, including audio tape recordings of the beating of drums. In addition, recent investigations by Dave Black and Jason

Nhyte of Supernatural Occurrence Studies have produced some especially compelling photographic images of the site, a site which is known for producing visual evidence. In further testimony, Uri Geller's *Unexplained* magazine recently printed several photographs of Robinson Woods taken by Clarendon Hills resident James Hunter, which seem to include human-like forms nestled among the trees.

Psychics claim to experience vivid visions at Che-che-pin-quay Woods. Lucy Solis, a southwest suburban student of Native American descent reports having at least two "vision dreams" of the site. One happened while visiting the physical location and a second occurred during sleep. During the first, Solis beheld a medicine man about 5'8" tall wearing a round brimstone hat with a grey feather on the side and a worn jacket over dark trousers. He spoke silent and foreign words to her. She wrote them down and took them to the professor of her Native American Studies course at Moraine Valley Community College

> my words weren't gibberish but had meaning. The words were similar to "Washnita Taka Hielo." The medicine man pointed to me and his chest repeating these words to me. My instructor said he was speaking Lakota.

Working from her instructor's translation, Solis interpreted the words as having a personal meaning for her—"Go on thy sacred path"—which made perfect sense to a student who at the time was engrossed in tracing her Native American ancestry. A later dream brought a supporting, similar message: "Kashniwa Taka Hey—Washnita": "Go sacred younger one. Go sacred on thy path." Why there should be a Lakota presence at this Potawotami memorial ground is an unanswerable question, one that—at least for Solis—in no way undermines the vitality of the message.

In very recent years, other theories have arisen concerning the "haunting" of Robinson Woods. Such theories have generally been tied to the Schuessler-Peterson murders of nearly 40 years ago, when the bodies of 14-year-old Robert Peterson, and John and Robert Schuessler, 13 and 14 respectively, were found near the Che-che-pin-quay Woods in October 1955. The Schuessler-Peterson case marked the beginning of an era which would watch the easygoing trust and security of Chicagoans dissolve into despair. Only a year after the murders, teenagers Patricia and Barbara Grimes would leave their South-side Chicago home one December night only to be found several weeks later, their bodies dumped near a drainage ditch in suburban Willow Springs. Two years more, and the tragic fire at Our Lady of the Angels School would extinguish nearly 100 young lives and all but the most stubborn stores of community trust. It is not surprising that some visitors to the Robinson graves should credit the Woods' unrest to the long-unsolved murders of the victims once found among its flora.

In 1994, however, Kenneth Hansen, a stablehand and admitted pedophile, was found guilty of the Schuessler-Peterson murders. In 1998, Hansen's attorney announced his intentions to seek a new trial, based on a startling claim made by Hanover Park resident, Margie Mack, who insisted that it was her late father Jack Reiling, and not Kenneth Hansen, that committed the triple homicide. To demonstrate the earnestness of her claim, Mack gave the prosecutors copies of a diary she allegedly kept while investigating the belief in her father's guilt, a belief which Reiling's own wife was said to have shared.

Mack said that her mother remained convinced of her husband's guilt even after Hansen's sentencing four years after Reiling's death, and that she had borne an intolerable burden of guilt for what she insisted was a wrongful conviction. It was at the time of that conviction that Margie Mack began questioning her family members in her own investigation of her father's connection to the infamous case.

Almost immediately after her public claim, however, a prosecutor held that Mack's mother, Joyce Saxon, had made up the story of her ex-husband's guilt so that her daughter would not idolize Reiling, for whom Saxon harbored ill feelings. Soon after, a Cook County Circuit judge denied Hansen a new trial.

Whether future questioning of the Schuessler-Peterson verdict will lead to the quieting of Robinson Woods ghostlore is yet to be seen. Meanwhile, investigators and passers-by will continue to marvel at the allegedly ethereal atmosphere of this urban but enchanted forest.

♦

X

A MILITARY PRESENCE

Fort Sheridan's "Dead House." (*Photo by Ursula Bielski*)

Great Lakes Revelations

WHEN IN THE EARLY 1980s JIM STONECIPHER BEGAN WORKING ON THE RESTORATION OF AN OLD PIONEER CEMETERY AT GREAT LAKES NAVAL Training Center, he had no idea of the questions that would be unearthed as the project progressed. As the group of volunteers sought permission to extend their explorations, fearful of future building over Native American and military burial sites, a curious theory began to take shape. Some of their discoveries taken together may actually bring about a revision of current Chicago history.

As Stonecipher began to explore the first settlement at Fort Dearborn and its relationship to the fort's outpost at Waukegan, known then as "Little Fort," he became aware of obvious discrepancies between written accounts of the second Fort Dearborn's geography, which describes deep ravines suggestive of the North Shore, and the actual topography of the Chicago site, an expanse of prairie on a lake-bound river. Stonecipher asks, would the government build a second fort on a site like the one at Chicago, especially after the location was proven by the first fort's destruction to be ineffective for such use?

A tour of Great Lakes with Stonecipher clarifies his remarkable hypothesis. Above the barracks and classroom buildings, officers' residences and administration buildings, the bluffs of Waukegan tower over the tree-choked ravines, inspiring Stonecipher's oft-repeated question: Wouldn't this have been a much better place for a fort? Picturing the flatlands flanking the Chicago River and the predictable fate of the troops at the first Fort Dearborn, one must agree. Yes, this would have been a better place for a fort; and now that you mention it, why would the government build a second fort on the site where the first had failed?

If these initial arguments stop short of persuasion, Stonecipher presents a perplexing piece of evidence, a "General's Map" dating to the time of the second Fort Dearborn. That map, charting the stretch of shoreline from Chicago to Wisconsin, clearly marks the site where an observer would place Waukegan. When Stonecipher pulls a hand away, however, and dramatically reveals the name written across the site, his enthusiasm becomes understandable. Affixed to that unmistakably North Shore site is the clear label: "Fort Dearborn."

The topographical argument placing the second Fort Dearborn at Waukegan certainly presents some appeal to reason, which the General's Map might reinforce. Stonecipher has other arguments to offer as well, though some of these would be called downright unreasonable by his critics. The North Shore resident and ex-Navy man believes that a stretch of property on the base could provide the most compelling evidence of all for his hypothesis. A house on the property is believed by some, including Stonecipher, to harbor the ghost of a West Point graduate who died in a farmhouse-turned-hospital at the second Fort Dearborn. For Stonecipher, the ghost's presence at Great Lakes would prove that the second Fort Dearborn was here in Waukegan and not in Chicago as current history maintains.

Quarters 63 sits on a lot between Ross Theater and Quarters 64, bordering the parade grounds at Great Lakes. Over the years, a resident of Q63 would often stand at the window ironing, between one and two o'clock in the afternoon. During these hours, she would sometimes be surprised by a man walking back and forth in the front yard as if on sentry duty. Friends of hers from Japan reportedly saw the same man combing his hair in an interior room. Both parties described a man in a gray uniform, although the officer who lived in the house was in the Air Force. When the family of Q63 was preparing to move, they needed the previously-executed power of attorney to authorize the transfer of property. Searching the house, they were unable to find the document. Finally, after expressing their anger over the missing paper, the family found it mysteriously stuck behind a picture hanging in the house.

In addition to the relatively recent happenings at Q63, Stonecipher believes that the haunting of the structure may have already been apparent to residents some time ago. John Philip Sousa, who lived at Great Lakes in 1918, supposedly spoke of his house there as haunted. Stonecipher has reason to believe that Sousa's haunted house may have been none other than Q63.

To one side of Q63, in a house numbered Quarters 64, the marvelous has likewise become mundane. Dogs shy from the basement stairs, lights and windows appear to do as they please, a toilet seat refuses to stay up or down. On one occasion, a table was found moved from one room to another. Most startling of all, a resident awoke one night to find herself staring into the bearded face of a six-foot tall, 170 pound man in uniform. Before she could fret, he disappeared.

Stonecipher believes that the activity occurring on these properties may be attributed to one or more officers buried in the area stretching from Ross Theater, across Q63, to the end of Q64. As for the officer in uniform seen by occupants of both residential units, Stonecipher wonders if this might be a second lieutenant by the name of McDuffy, a West Point graduate who died at the second Fort Dearborn two weeks after graduation. Pointing out the ravine directly behind the frame structure dubbed Q63, Stonecipher tells of descriptions of the hospital at Fort Dearborn which "was in the basement of a farmhouse, across a ravine." Stonecipher doesn't stop there, however. If the fort hypothesis fits, then, according to his research, the property under the three buildings is the military cemetery which current research places outside the farmhouse hospital at the Chicago fort.

The sometimes unusual goings-on at Ross Theater may also suggest that Stonecipher is onto something. The building is supposed to host the "typical disturbances" associated with poltergeist cases, including noises, movement of objects, problems with technical equipment, and so on.

Moving away from this supernatural stretch of land, ghosthunters will want to make a beeline for Building 18, which was once the base hospital. More than 100 persons died inside this imposing structure and at least one just outside—when a nurse reportedly committed suicide by jumping from an upper window. Over the years, the building's occupants have reported seeing and even speaking with a major who turns out to be less than tangible and with a nurse believed to be the suicide victim. Behind the hospital building, strollers on the bluff overlooking the ravine may distinguish "footers" in neat rows, as well as sunken portions of grassy earth which workers like Stonecipher believe to be evidence of another burial ground.

Another suicide has been tied to Quarters A, that of a maid in a corner house. The cause of death was questionable; some claim she was killed. Believers in her murder have told tales of a Woman in White who is seen on the top floor of the house. During his teen-age years in the house, the son of an admiral told his parents that he had seen "Satan" in his bedroom. Stonecipher wonders if the boy in fact saw the disheveled and destitute spirit of an early settler.

For researchers, the USO Building sets yet another plate of phenomena on the smorgasbord of *psi* that is Great Lakes. No families were ever quartered in this building. Nonetheless, one night a public works person distinctly heard the sound of a little boy's giggling accompanied by recurrent knocking. Thinking that one of the sailors was playing a joke on him, the worker went to his car to get a hatchet, hoping to turn the tables and scare the culprit. When he returned, he found the room empty and the bathroom door swinging wildly. No one had come out of the locked building, nor was anyone hiding inside. Over the years, several similar incidents were reported to have occurred on the premises. Accompanying such reports were claims that furniture and other objects had sometimes moved by themselves.

Even if further research validates Jim Stonecipher's theories about the history of Great Lakes, this impressive institution will never run short of mysteries. Remembering, and often replaying, the experiences and memories of the thousands of men and women who have lived, worked, and died here, Great Lakes will long remain a popular port for wayfarers into the unknown.

♦

The Phantoms of Fort Sheridan

*I*llinois can claim only the scantiest handful of American tall tales, but what the region lacks in quantity, it makes up in quality, especially in the forested coastal areas surrounding north suburban Fort Sheridan. For it is this wild and rocky region that is supposed by American folklore to have been part of Paul Bunyan's logging territory, the Great Lakes themselves having been gouged out by a fall taken by Bunyan's Great Blue Ox, Babe. Even without the whoppers, however, the history of Fort Sheridan remains fully American, richly anecdotal, and often eerie.

Fort Sheridan was built along the Indian trail connecting Green Bay, Wisconsin, a French trading post and mission established around 1670, and the Native American hunting grounds and villages in and around Chicago. Tribes of mostly Illinois and Potawatomi would travel northward along the road from what is now Diversey Avenue in Chicago, hugging the lakeshore and heading up what is now Clark Street. With the 19th century came a series of treaties between the white settlers and the Native Americans. The last was negotiated in Chicago on September 26, 1833, in which the Potawatomi ceded to the U.S. all of their remaining Illinois land.

Not long after, the trail was employed increasingly by traders and settlers traveling between Green Bay and Chicago. Because of the trail's use as a passage for military-escorted pioneers traveling from Ft. Dearborn, it was also known as the Military Road. Eventually, the road became the central highway connecting Chicago and Green Bay and was officially named Green Bay Road.

By the late 1860s, Chicago had become a regrouping point for Eastern pioneers headed westward. The Division of the Missouri, quartered in Chicago and led by Lieutenant General Philip Sheridan, played a large part in these pioneers' protection. Sheridan's special burden was to make sure they obeyed the law in the frontier regions (i.e., most of the land west of Chicago). From the Division's headquarters at Washington and LaSalle streets, Sheridan met the challenge and established himself and the Division as indispensable to the peace and safety of Chicago and vicinity. In the days of looting that followed the Chicago Fire of 1871, Mayor Roswell Mason responded to the chaos by declaring martial law and putting the city in Sheridan's hands.

Although Mason's decision caused an outrage in the governor's office, Sheridan carried out his commission, gaining esteem in the eyes of the city's administration and in the hearts of its citizens. A dozen years after the Great Fire, Sheridan was reassigned to the War Department, leaving in tears a Chicago that would remember when 'all eyes were turned to him' in those chaotic days 'when men's hearts failed them, and ruin and desolation stared us in the face. . . .'

With such a strong reputation, it was natural that Sheridan came to mind several years later when Chicago businessmen, concerned about the violent potential of labor unrest, met to discuss plans for a military installation near Chicago. With fresh memories of the Haymarket Riot of 1886 overshadowing the city, the moguls recalled the power of the military to restore order on that devastating day. Accordingly, they decided that a ready source of military force would be crucial if business were to proceed without serious future threat from workers.

On November 8, 1887, Companies F and K of the Sixth Infantry Regiment pulled into Highwood from Utah. 80 soldiers were commanded by Major William J. Lyster, who set up camp near the wild shoreline set aside for the fort. With five men to each tent, the companies started out poorly, with no vegetables, undrinkable water, and the looming realization that the elite of Chicago were relying on the soldiers' readiness to take on urban unrest.

Major Lyster nonetheless persevered in his duties, and by the time he ended his command in late summer of 1890, the erection of permanent buildings had begun. Nearly ten years later, Congress appropriated several hundred thousand dollars for permanent structures to house six companies of infantry and four troops of cavalry, as well as a wharf, water tower, cemetery, and rifle range. The construction proved tedious, if ultimately successful. Water had to be pumped from the lake and driven to the building sites by horse-drawn tankers. Construction materials had to be transported through ever-present mud. Adding to all the frustration within the fort, were still more problems outside of it.

With the establishment of the fort came the development of the village of Highwood. Originally planned in 1868, Highwood's settlers came from Chicago after losing their homes in the Chicago Fire, hoping to establish farms on the North Shore. Less than a year after Lyster's arrival, Highwood had become inextricably tied to the military post and was renamed the village of Fort Sheridan. Although the town and the fort suffered few conflicts of interest, one was enough to test their relationship—the question of liquor.

Worried that the town would become a "den of iniquity," and pointing fingers at the dram shops (i.e., taverns) that catered to soldiers and construction workers, residents banned the sale of liquor, though "blind pigs" remained in business peddling alcohol in defiance of the law. Finally, liquor licenses were established, at a $1,000 a pop and issued to anyone who was willing to pay the price and to promise not to sell to "lunatics, idiots, insane persons, minors, and habitual drunkards." Not surprisingly, illegal liquor sales continued, as did the arguments. Finally, in 1908, taverns were closed and stayed shuttered until state laws took over liquor sales.

Amid such squabbling, the physical fort was quietly and admirably taking form. Designed by the pioneering Chicago firm of Holabird and Roche, the fort would eventually attain status as a National Historic Landmark. After a movement that began in 1979, an Historic American Buildings Survey found 94 of the fort's buildings, beginning with its massive 150-foot water tower, worthy of designation as a National Historic District. These buildings deserve reverence, but not merely or even mainly for their artistic or military significance. As silent witnesses to the struggles of countless individuals, these structures are venerable ultimately for the stories they shelter.

Among the hundreds of thousands of anecdotes grown dusty in these landmarks, the most moth-eaten are the humdrum tales of day-to-day army life. But, even the strangest realities inevitably became typical; the most bizarre of personalities just another among hundreds of buzz-cut heads. For example, a mess sergeant assigned to the Anti-Aircraft Military Training Center (AATC) who ate razor blades, nails, tacks, buttons, and even drinking glasses before enlisting in 1941. After he swallowed a wristwatch, doctors predicted an imminent demise. Instead, the sergeant went on to a great career with Ringling Brothers Barnum and Bailey Circus.

Although most of Fort Sheridan's more colorful characters have since passed away, a few still linger. Curiously, the most famous do not seem to be military. Instead, the fort's two most active spirits are working class unenlisted going about their respective business. Best known is a so-called "Woman in Orange," seen during random sunrises at Building 31, the Community Club Building. Building 31 previously housed the officers' mess hall and the El Morocco Lounge, an officers' club which once hosted George S. Patton. The Woman in Orange, so dubbed for the stunning orange dress she wears, seems perpetually concerned with the perfection of her catering skills. She, by the way, is rumored to resemble Mamie Eisenhower.

Meanwhile, at Building 1, the old fort hospital, a custodian eternally tends to his duties, stoking the furnace and tapping the pipes. Across the road out back, the hospital morgue, nicknamed the "Dead House," still stands, although its ivy-covered walls and skylights have disappeared. The tiny, solid structure, bearing blind windows and crosses in relief, housed a neat interior with sink, sewer, and a room for autopsies. It is interesting that the Dead House was designed by Holabird and Roche, while the fort hospital itself was built from standard plans.

Other strays at the nearly deserted fort include a 19th-century chaplain named Charles Adams; a drill sergeant who scares the dickens out of witnesses by hollering orders to his long-dead enlisted; the galloping shade of a horse on Patten Road; and the festive strains of accordion music from the site of a former German POW camp.

Today, a drive through the roads of Fort Sheridan, set grandly on the edge of awesome Lake Michigan, is a bittersweet trip. The abandonment of such an opulent array of architectural gems remains a puzzling reality even in the face of all the facts, figures, and logic that explain the fort's closing. Explorers should not be deterred from seeking out its secrets. For while this richly historical setting has been emptied of most human life, a warm welcome awaits from at least some personalities who remain eternally present and accounted for.

♦

XI

EAT, DRINK, AND BE SCARY
Imbibing With the Otherworldly

A lot of Chicago lives in the neighborhood taverns . . .
a bit of the old country grafted into a strong new plant . . .

—BILL GRANGER

That (shuttered) Steak Joynt: Nasty Ghosts for Sale.
(*Photo by D. Cowan*)

SOME OF THE CITY'S MOST MALEVOLENT GHOSTS LOVED THAT STEAK JOYNT, A CHICAGO INSTITUTION THAT UNTIL VERY RECENTLY STOOD AT 1610 N. WELLS STREET IN THE OLD Town neighborhood. Before the restaurant closed, patrons had for decades reported hearing disembodied footsteps and other noises, especially on the central staircase. The building reserved its more sinister manifestations, though, for the restaurant's staff; particularly the waitress working on the second floor who was reportedly dragged along the carpet to the brink of the stairs, to be left with a heel broken off her shoe and deep fingerprints around her wrist; and a bartender who came face to face with a pair of glowing yellow eyes while working on the books one evening.

Over the years, owner Billy Siegel allowed several seances and numerous investigations of the property. The most recent of the latter was conducted by members of the locally-based Ghost Research Society who recorded temperature and electromagnetic field anomalies, visual apparitions, and other evidence of possible *psi* activity. According to popular accounts, the turn of the century witnessed two as of yet unsolved murders in the old Piper's Alley, a previously open, winding alleyway next to the restaurant. Siegel has wondered if the murders may have initiated the bizarre activity in his now shuttered establishment.

With the boarding up of That Steak Joynt, local enthusiasts of the paranormal lost a particularly favorite haunt. Not to worry. Chicago and the surrounding suburbs have plenty of other paranormal pantries to raid, wide open and chock full of fascinating phenomena.

♦

*O*ne of the most widely-known of these, both for its fare and its phantom, is located slightly west of the city in suburban Clarendon Hills. A popular restaurant and bar in its own right, the Country House Restaurant does not need to rely on its ghost for its business success. Diners and drinkers come from other towns to spend an hour or two at this darkly-lit beer and burger hideaway just off Clarendon Hills Road. In fact, with atmosphere aplenty, it might be necessary to invent some in-house haunts, if only for an excuse to have another round and move closer to the comforting fire. Alas, no need to bother: the Country House has a true blue beasty or two of its own.

Since 1974, when David and Patrick Regnery bought the former bar and grill at 241 55th Street, strange occurrences have been reported by the owners, their staff, and customers. Confused and a little concerned about slamming doors and haywire thermostats, inexplicable voices, and shutters that opened by themselves, the Regnery brothers considered the possibility of a haunting and consulted researchers to determine the cause of the disturbances. Psychics explained that the restaurant's ghost was that of a young blonde woman who was killed in a car accident outside the old bar and grill in 1957 following a fight with one of the bartenders. According to psychics, she was killed when her car hit a tree or telephone pole a half mile from the building.

When David Regnery heard the psychics' story, he talked to the previous owner, Richard Montonelli, who agreed, except he said the year was 1958. According to Montonelli, the woman had come into the bar on a Sunday afternoon, wanting to leave her child for the staff to watch. When the owners refused, the woman left, distraught. Soon the news reached the bar that the woman had run off the road and was dead. Her child, however, was unharmed.

There have been few lapses in unusual happenings at the Country House since its opening. Further, the phenomena have never discriminated. The owners, the customers, the waitstaff, and the cleaning crews all have their own stories to tell: the jukebox that went on by itself; footsteps heard walking up and down the stairs; customers waiting for tables hearing their names announced only to discover that no staff member had paged them. But perhaps the most disconcerting phenomena are of the presences of a woman and child. The latter has been heard crying for hours on end by cleaning crew members and has been seen by at least one customer, beckoning from an upstairs window. The former has been reported as appearing in and vanishing from the women's restroom.

In addition to the psychics who first interpreted the haunting of this house, at least one group of independent researchers conducted a field investigation of the property. In 1990, James Houran, an undergraduate psychology student at Illinois Benedictine College, secured permission to investigate the Country House, intending to use it as a case study in a thesis discussing methods in parapsychological research. Employing a team of five researchers and apparatus including camcorders, tape recorders, a parabolic microphone, and still cameras loaded with both infrared and black and white film, Houran staged an overnight investigation using a series of sweeps of the property and the compilation of subjective and collective experiences that occurred that evening. His investigation also involved interviews of witnesses and a follow-up without technical equipment. Much of the phenomena experienced during the structured investigation did, in fact, echo the occurrences reported by the restaurant's staff and customers, including reports of doors opening and closing and the sounds of disembodied voices and footsteps.

In recent years, other psychics have added their own impressions to initial readings of the property, responding to some staff members who had begun to feel that the presence in the building had turned menacing. Touring the structure after receiving such reports, some psychics determined that a malevolent male entity had joined the restaurant's spiritual realm and was causing the feelings of discomfort reported by some of the employees.

♦

Lincoln Park's popular Red Lion Pub at
2446 N. Lincoln Avenue. (*Photo by Ursula Bielski*)

*I*n Chicago proper, a pair of pubs have for decades provided customers with more than bottled spirits. On the Near North Side, The Red Lion caters to a clientele of part upscale workaholics, a handful of students from nearby DePaul University, a sprinkle of homesick Britons, and the occasional glint-eyed ghosthunter. If customers aren't dining on the scrumptious English eats, watching TV, or waiting for a movie at the Biograph Theater directly across the street, they can catch an earful of the unusual from owner John Cordwell, his son Colin, or one of the handful of waitstaff and bartenders familiar with the pub's unseen clientele.

This comfy but curious tavern distinguishes itself as perhaps the best-known of Chicago's haunted public places. Rightfully so, for The Red Lion is utterly poised for paranormal infiltration. Staring almost right into the box office of the Biograph Theater, The Red Lion stands a gunshot away from the alley said to be haunted by the late, "great" gangster John Dillinger and a mile or so from the site of the St. Valentine's Day Massacre. Neighbor to a handful of mobsters, including Al Capone, who dwelled in the apartments of 1930s Lincoln Park, the building housing The Red Lion snuggled right into its seedy surroundings, gaining notoriety as a bookmaker's joint in the 1940s and playing a part in what manager Colin Cordwell calls the neighborhood's 'bad karma.'

The pub's inexplicable occurrences began well before the Cordwells arrived. According to Colin Cordwell, Dan Danforth, owner of the building's previous establishment, Dirty Dan's, was well aware of the haunting and often invited neighboring businesspeople to come over and meet the ghosts. Another previous tenant who had occupied an upstairs apartment ran into trouble while trying to renovate. After spending time working on the interior, he would lock the doors behind him, only to return later to find his work ruined, boards and nails pulled up, and tools thrown about.

One of the most enduring haunting legends of this property is of a beautiful young woman who either died or was killed in one of the upstairs apartments. Psychics, wildly attracted to The Red Lion, seem to support the tale. Many have claimed receiving psychic impressions of a young flapper-type girl undergoing terrible suffering. However, Lou Demas, a next-door neighbor whose family owned the Red Lion's building for many years, disputes such romantic ramblings, countering them with his own memories of a young mentally retarded girl named Sharon, who used to sit on the porch outside the building with her elderly parents, who also died in the building.

Plump and plain, Sharon would unlikely be generating the glamorous impressions gleaned by sensitives. That's not to say she couldn't be responsible for locking women in the upstairs restroom, sometimes for 15 or 20 minutes before freeing the well-powdered prisoners. Some researchers also believe that another phenomenon, the sudden strong smell of perfume, might be attributed to a simpleminded girl like Sharon who wouldn't be aware of the subtlety involved in donning perfume.

Whoever this female presence may be, she is only one of a number of spirits believed to live on at the Lion. Others, like an unshaven young cowboy, a bearded and black-hatted masculine figure, and a blonde man with Slavic features, manifest themselves by walking across the bar, calling out people's names, and throwing things around the upstairs rooms.

Among the Lion's sundry lingering guests, the most intriguing spirit of all for John Cordwell is the one he believes to be that of his own father. A successful architect and native Englishman, John met his wife Justine in Africa 40 years ago while inspecting the progress of a university he had designed. A Chicago anthropologist, Justine brought John to her home city, where he began an architectural firm. With 80 architects on board, John retired from his own firm in the mid-1980s, and went into real estate development. As a retirement project of sorts, John decided to open the English-style pub that would become The Red Lion. In 1984, he bought the then-102-year-old property at 2446 N. Lincoln Avenue and began renovation. As a finishing touch, John hung a gorgeous stained-glass window on the stairway as a memorial to his father, an artist, whose grave in England was without a headstone. John also placed a brass plaque under the window dedicating it to his dad. In an interview with one researcher, Cordwell stated his belief that "everything seems to emanate from that point. I think he was very pleased by it."

If John's father is pleased by his son's tribute, he shows his approval in some funny ways. Upstairs customers standing next to the stairway and John himself have reported sudden and inexplicable dizzy spells and taps on the shoulder. Receiving such reports with a certain expectancy, John interprets these subtle scenes as gentle reminders of his father's notable faith in the spirit world, recalling the elder Cordwell's promise to "come back and contact" his son after death.

◆

*F*urther north, the Edgewater neighborhood harbors a resident bogey of its own, within the walls of St. Andrew's Inn, at 5938 N. Broadway. This far North Side pub gained supernatural status during its stint as the Edinburgh Castle Pub, when the previous owner Jane McDougal and her son, Blair, endured exploding and flying glasses and reports of drinks being drained by unseen tipplers. The culprit is supposedly Frank Giff, the rollicking proprietor of the tavern which once occupied the site. According to those who knew him, Giff was a serious drinker who indulged in nightly vodka binges. Often, Frank would close his bar and keep drinking until he fell asleep in one of the booths lining the barroom walls. One morning in 1964 Frank was discovered thus with his head on the table. But this time, he wasn't passed out; he was dead.

Another version of Frank's death insists that Giff died by falling off a barstool, receiving a fatal head wound. Whatever the specifics of Frank Giff's death, two facts remain: that he died here in the bar he loved and that he was unquestionably intoxicated at the time.

When they sold the property the family left old Frank behind at this distinctively Scottish stomping ground. Despite the several changes in ownership, customers of the successive establishments have been introduced to Frank's boisterous energy. Whether polishing off the pints of patrons, caressing the knees of young women, or generally making a loud but affectionate nuisance of itself, Frank's spirit will always be a regular there.

◆

*F*or ghostwatchers who like a little shimmy with their shooters, a handful of nightclubs are said to provide spirits, both kinds, and a variety of music, for dancing or just dramatizing the hunt. In the River North area, Excalibur and the Dome Room, both previously discussed (see "Dem Bones," pp.107-108.), are glam and glitzy options, filled with tourists, suburbanites, and the dedicatedly dance-minded, for sipping cocktails and scouring the building's cavernous rooms for ethereal infestation. Later, night owls might head to the Rush and Division area, in search of specters at the reputedly haunted Hangge-Uppe at 14 W. Elm.

Farther north, Cabaret Metro, 3730 N. Clark, continues to invite the more nonconformist of city and suburban youth to live shows in a darkly splendid old Lakeview Theater. But while the club has always attracted the more morbid members of the city's alternative music scene, most of these patrons have remained unaware of the supposed haunting of the building's upper floor.

Finally, patrons in the know won't be surprised to discover a paranormal presence at Thurston's, 1248 W. George Street. Once a slaughterhouse, the bar was reportedly haunted by the spirits of butchered animals until owner Mark Romano brought in a priest to bless the building. Customers can decide for themselves whether this oft-successful method was effective. Before the second or third round is the recommendation of at least one seasoned ghosthunter.

◆

Conclusion

ROM THE MOMENT MARGARET ANDERSON FIRST SPIED LAKE MICHIGAN FROM HER CHICAGO-BOUND TRAIN, THE WRITER KNEW THAT SHE HAD ENTERED UPON "ENCHANTED ground." That conviction, sensed by countless other writers and poets, artists and musicians, planners and reformers, continues to express Chicagoans' heartfelt awareness of their city's striking natural setting, rich cultural life, and relentless historical development, even in the face of devastations like the Fort Dearborn Massacre, the Great Fire of 1871, and a number of twentieth-century tragedies. As both folklorists and phantom-hunters have observed, Chicago's mindfulness of its own life is evidenced in one way by the city's rich ghostlore.

As shown in this collection, that ghostlore does not discriminate. It includes men, women, and children of all natures and doomed to any of a million fates: both the headstrong and the helpless; the nearly sainted and the prototypically cynical; the conquerors and the conquered. A look at the city's history demonstrates that Chicago was created by a continuous melding of these natures and fates. For a city formed by such interminglings and nurtured between the mystery of the prairie and the dreamy expanse of Lake Michigan, the enchantment of Chicago was nothing less than inevitable. Moreover, because all of Chicago had helped to create it, that enchantment was the city's free gift to anyone willing to acknowledge it.

Even now, or perhaps especially now, when much of the city has been reshaped and highly polished into a generic and franchised urbanity, the enchantment remains. Despite all attempts to drive them out, Chicago's ghosts, too, have stayed on, sheltered by the old cultures and nourished by the new.

The city, then, is as haunted as ever, by both recollections and wishes, by experience and imagination, but also by an often painful consciousness of its own passions—past, present, and future.

Ultimately, Chicago is, as Floyd Dell reflected, "a city haunted everywhere by the memories of love . . . its pain and glory."

♦

NOTES

*I*n one sense, this work was intended as a popular collection of accounts and not as a scholarly study. Accordingly, I have avoided the use of footnotes within the text. Nonetheless, I know there are readers who will wish to further explore the accounts contained in this volume. It is with those readers in mind that I have compiled the following list of notes and selective bibliography, the latter of which details the works on which this writing relied most.

Introduction

Page 4
Fr. Julian vonDurbeck alerted the author to LaVey's discussion of the "Law of the Trapezoid" and its application to Chicago architecture.

Streeterville, the posh neighborhood which the Hancock calls home, is traditionally considered by Chicago buffs to be a cursed tract of land. Cap Streeter, a somewhat loony entrepreneur, sailed up to the city one day, dropped anchor, and set up camp on the lakeshore of early Chicago. From there, he sent word around that all citizens could dump garbage on "his" land for free, saving their payment of the normal fees demanded by the city. The result was a rather impressive sprawl of refuse that created an entirely new, if noxious, shoreline. Streeter declared himself mayor of "Streeterville," an office he filled only until the city threw him out of office and made Streeterville an official part of Chicago, leading the irate eccentric to curse his erstwhile empire.

Chapter I

The phenomenon of the vanishing hitchhiker is addressed in various volumes, including those I've consulted: Jan Harold Brunvand's *The Vanishing Hitchhiker: American Urban Legends and their Meanings*, Spencer and Well's *Ghostwatching*, and Michael Goss' *The Evidence for Vanishing Hitch-hikers*. Brunvand reveals the phenomenon as quite well-established; in fact, he reminds his readers of the *New Testament* episode in which Philip baptizes an Ethiopian who picks him up in a chariot and then disappears. Later, folklore would tell of young women who would jump on the backs of men's horses, only to disappear upon arrival at their destinations. According to Brunvand, the phenomenon was known in the states by the turn of the century, with horses or carriages as the vehicles involved, replaced by the automobile by the time of the Great Depression.

Intriguingly, Brunvand discovered a number of Chicago-area versions of the vanishing hitchhiker story. One of these was alleged to have occurred in December of 1941, when a Chicago cab driver picked up a nun in the downtown area. According to his account, the two drove to the destination given, while listening to the radio and discussing Pearl Harbor. When the cab arrived at the address the nun had specified (a convent) the cab driver found that she had disappeared from the back seat. Alarmed, he inquired after his fare. Inside the convent, he spotted a photograph of the nun on a wall behind the Mother Superior's desk and pointed her out as the woman he'd escorted. The Mother Superior quietly informed him that the nun had been dead for ten years. A number of people reported similar occurrences around the time of the Century of Progress Exposition of 1933. In those accounts—which, incidentally, pre-date reports of "Resurrection Mary," people traveling by car to the fair are hailed by a woman by the roadside, carrying a bag. When the party picks her up and engages her in conversation, the woman tells them that the fair is going to slide into Lake Michigan in the coming months. Of course, when they reach the woman's destination, she is found to have vanished. At the address, usually a house, they meet a man who recognizes the woman of their description as his long dead wife.

Of course, the mysterious stranger known as "Resurrection Mary" is indisputably Chicago's most famous vanishing hitchhiker. A variety of sources were consulted in reconstructing her story, including the following volumes: Beth Scott and Michael Norman's *Haunted Heartland*, Rosemary Guiley's *The Encyclopedia of Ghosts and Spirits* and Joan Bingham and Dolores Riccio's *More Haunted Houses*. Additionally, the following should be noted:

Page 10
Sean Tudor's article, "Hells Belles" appears in the December 1997 edition of *Fortean Times*, pp. 36-40.

Page 14
Jerry Palus's account was included in an October 25, 1992 *Chicago Tribune* article, "Deathly dancer: Resurrection Mary still wanders amid the myths on frightful nights," a thoroughly researched and fascinatingly

detailed piece, which proved indispensable to this author's work.

Pages 15-16
Vern Rutkowski's discovery was discussed in an article which appeared in the S*outhtown Economist* on January 22, 1984: "SW ghost legend revived: Woman wonders: was Resurrection Mary her friend?"

Page 16
John Satala was quoted in a *Southtown Economist* article published on October 30, 1983: "Behind the ghost of Resurrection Mary."

Pages 21-22
The account detailed here was reported to Chicago folklorist Richard Crowe, and is included in Brad Steiger's volume, *Psychic Chicago.*

Page 22
Quotations are from the October 25, 1992 *Chicago Tribune* article, "Deathly dancer" (see detail for p. 8).

Page 26
Gail Ziemba gave her opinion of the phenomenon during a conversation with the author in December of 1996; Prusinski's account was related to the author by the management of Chet's Melody Lounge, also in December of 1996.

Pages 26-27
Quotation is from Kenan Heise's novel, *Resurrection Mary: A Ghost Story.*

Details of the story of La Llorona were taken from the volume *Haunted Heartland.*

Noted cemetery historian Helen Sclair discusses the remarkable physical beauty of St. Casimir Cemetery in her essay, "Ethnic Cemeteries: Underground Rites," which is included in Melvin Holli and Peter d'A. Jones' volume, *Ethnic Chicago.*

Chapter II

All information on Rosehill Cemetery and related history was provided by David Wendell, the cemetery's erstwhile historian and archivist, during the course of various interviews conducted in 1996 and 1997. Historical information on Graceland Cemetery was taken from *A Walk Through Graceland Cemetery and Greater Chicagoland Cemeteries* and from the *Chicago Tribune* article, "Burial treasures: Joan Pomaranc's grave and glorious tales make cemeteries come alive," published on November 6, 1991.

A detailed history of Bachelors Grove Cemetery was presented in the South Suburban Genealogical Society's Fall 1995 issue of *Where the Trails Cross*, which provided much of the factual information for this section. Additionally, the following should be noted:

Page 57
Norman Basile is quoted in *More Haunted Houses*.

Page 58
The quotation regarding the 1973 vandalism incident appeared in the *Chicago Tribune* on September 14, 1973. Brandon's assertion appears in his *Weird America*.

Page 59
Quotation is from an anonymous personal account related to the author in July of 1996.

Page 62
Dale Kaczmarek, of the locally-based Ghost Research Society, has suggested that the Bachelors Grove quarry pond was used as a dumping site for gangland victims. This belief is documented in several sources, including *The Encyclopedia of Ghosts and Spirits*, which also recounts the results of the psychic's visit in the 1980s.

Page 63
The description of the Bachelors Grove tombstone phenomenon as simulacra was found in the Bachelors Grove Cemetery article which appears in *The Encyclopedia of Ghosts and Spirits*. This article also furnished a good summary of the phenomena alleged to have occurred at the site.

Page 64
The account regarding phantom vehicles on the Midlothian Turnpike is from a written testimony given to the author by Laura Cleveland in October 1997.

Pages 65-67
Brunvand discusses the legends of "The Hook" and "The Boyfriend's Death" in his volume, *The Vanishing Hitchhiker: American Urban Legends and their Meanings*.

Page 67
Quotation is from an anonymous personal account related to the author in the Fall of 1996.

Page 70
The quotation regarding St. Mary's Cemetery appeared in the *Chicago Sun-Times* article, "13 ghosts you can meet," published on October 31, 1980.

Chapter III

Personal accounts attesting to the paranormality of Archer Avenue are a dime a dozen on the Southwest side of Chicago; this chapter relies almost exclusively on such sources. Years ago, local author Kenan Heise encountered this rich folklore and documented it in part in his *Chicago Tribune* article, "Meet the folks on Archer Avenue—the dead ones"; the quotation on p. 74 appears in his novel, *Resurrection Mary: A Ghost Story*. The author is deeply indebted to Norma Johnson of the Lemont Historical Society for providing a detailed account of the "lost" legend of Cal-Sag Cemetery, including the quotes from the *Lemont Observer* and the *Chicago Tribune*, as recounted on pp. 75-78. The discussion on ley lines incorporates information from Paul Devereaux's *The New Ley Hunters' Guide* and from Colin Wilson's *Poltergeist: A Study in Destructive Haunting*. The latter source additionally provided the quote on p. 81 regarding Tellurianism.

Chapter IV

Although the legends associated with Holy Family Church are fairly well known around Chicago, they are addressed with special care by folklorist Richard Crowe, as interviewed by Brad Steiger in his volume, *Psychic Chicago*. Several St. Ignatius alumni provided their own versions of the haunting of their alma mater by Arnold Damen, including the graduate who so generously shared the experience recounted on p. 88.

Information regarding Queen of Heaven Cemetery's Marian phenomena was adopted in part from personal accounts; additional detail was discovered by Matt Hucke at the Apparitions Web site, specifically: *web.frontier.net/Apparitions/Hillside.homepage.html*.

The author is greatly indebted to the DuPage County Forest Preserve District, the Mayslake Landmark Conservancy, and especially Joseph Pinter for providing both written and oral information regarding the Peabody Estate and its legacy.

Chapter V

Various sources were consulted in compiling the historical background of Fort Dearborn, especially Donald Miller's *City of the Century: The Epic of Chicago and the Making of America* and *Ethnic Chicago*. Additionally, the following should be noted:

Page 101, 102, 103, and 105
Quotations are from Nelson Algren's *Chicago: City on the Make*.

Page 103
Both quotations are from *City of the Century*.

Page 105
Eckert's *Gateway to Empire* is discussed in the volume, *Hands on Chicago* by Kenan Heise and Mark Frazel.

The author is indebted to David Wendell for his research regarding the death of John Lalime and the removal of his remains to the CHS, as well as for information in this section regarding the temporary housing of the *Eastland* victims. The article "Ghost Stories: Bumps in the night haunt clubs," that appeared in the October 31, 1996 edition of the *Chicago Sun-Times* provided additional information on The Dome Room and Excalibur.

Historical background of the Cloes Brickyard legend was provided by Elmer Vliet's volume, *Lake Bluff: The First Hundred Years*.

Details of the *Eastland* disaster, including the quotes on pp. 113-114, were provided by *The Chicago Daily News* of July 24, 1915; additional background was furnished by David Nelson of the *Eastland* Museum and by the volume, *Chicago Sketches* by June Skinner Sawyers.

The quote on p. 120 in the "Making His Mark" section is from "April's hand of death," which appeared in *Firehouse* magazine, April 1983, pp.53-54.

The St. Valentine's Day Massacre was reconstructed with the aid of several sources, including the volume, *Capone* and the June 12, 1988 *Chicago Tribune* article, "Here reel gangsters were for real."

Tales regarding the Tivoli Theater were related to the author in several anonymous personal accounts. The National Pastime Theater was featured in the *Chicago Tribune* article, "Spirits of the speakeasy," as published on January 6, 1997; quotations on p. 128 are taken from that story. In reconstructing the story of John Dillinger, the author relied substantially on the *Chicago Tribune* of July 23, 1934; Tribune quotations on pp. 129, 130, and 132 through 135 were taken from that edition. An account of Dillinger's *ante mortem* misadventures in plastic surgery was provided by David Wendell. Also note:

Page 130
East Chicago's then-police chief, Martin Zarkovich bore a vendetta against Dillinger from this day on; the FBI would have Zarkovich instruct Anna Sage to wear red when she accompanied the fugitive on that later, fateful trip to the movies. It was Zarkovich, too, who would fire one of the three fatal shots that night. In 1998, a San Francisco auction house received a $25,000 bid for Zarkovich's .38 caliber Smith and Wessen revolver.

David Cowan and John Kuenster thoroughly documented the events and aftermath of the fire at Our Lady of the Angels in their volume, *To Sleep with the Angels: The Story of a Fire*. Details of the tragedy, and the quotations on p. 137, were taken from their account. Additional information and insights were provided during the author's interview with David Cowan held in December of 1996; the quotations on pp. 139-140 were extracted from that interview. The quotation from Sandburg's "Anna Imroth" (p. 138) is from that poem as it appears in his *Chicago Poems*.

The events surrounding the deaths of the Grimes Sisters were reconstructed with the aid of several sources, including the 1997 *Chicago Reader* article, "Death and the maidens," as published on March 21, 1997. Rene Glos's research, mentioned on p. 142, was discussed in Lucia Mauro's article, "Author wrestles with unsolved murders," which appeared in the *Pioneer Press*, February 11, 1998, p. B4. Jerry Karczewski's experiences, recounted on pp. 142-143, were related to the author in the spring of 1998.

The death of Ioan Culianu is ardently investigated by Ted Anton in his 1996 volume, *Eros, Magic and the Murder of Professor Culianu*; biographical details regarding Culianu were taken from that volume and from Umberto Eco's article, "Murder in Chicago" which appeared in the

New York Times Review of Books on April 10, 1997.   The quotation on p. 146 was taken from a review of Anton's work which appeared in the January 5, 1997 edition of the *Chicago Tribune*.

Chapter VI

Jane Addams' writings, as quoted on pp. 155, 156, and 158, on the Devil Baby at Hull House appeared in the October 1916 issue of the *Atlantic Monthly*; additional background was provided in part by the volume, *Twenty Years at Hull House*. A connection between the devil at the Bridgeport dancehall and the Devil Baby at Hull House stories was made by Dylan Clearfield in *Chicagoland Ghosts*.

Regarding St. Michael's Church on p. 161, Arlene Zoch was quoted in the *Chicago Tribune* of February 4, 1973.

Father John Nicola's observations on p. 163 appeared in the *Chicago Tribune* article referenced directly above.

Chapter VII

The quotation on pp. 169-170 was taken from the *Chicago Tribune* article, "Out of this world. Search for true haunted house can be spirited indeed," as published on October 30, 1994.

Information on Chicago's "old time" haunted houses was found in the 1957 *Chicago Tribune* article, "What's happened to haunted houses?"

Details of the "Irish Castle" were taken from the June 9, 1995 *Chicago Tribune* article, "You won't find Casper, but city's only castle a haunting experience." Additional information on the Beverly Unitarian Church was provided to the author by members of the church's congregation and staff.

Historical background and quotations regarding the Stickney Mansion appeared in the *Chicago Tribune* on September 5, 1989 and October 31, 1973.

The suicide note found at 666 N. Maple in Lake Bluff appeared in an unidentified newspaper article provided by Janet Nelson of Lake Bluff's Vliet Center.

Quotations regarding 505 N. Sheridan Road were taken from a personal interview of the author with the Dunham family in the Fall of 1996.

Chapter VIII

Accounts appearing in this section were collected over several decades and from innumerable sources. However, the author is particularly grateful to those teachers, students, and alumni who took the time to relate their own experiences and recollections especially for inclusion in this volume.

Chapter IX

Biographical background on Alexander Robinson (Che-che-pin-quay) was graciously provided by Virginia Barber of the Mitchell Indian Museum at Kendall College; additional detail was furnished by the volume, *Chicago Sketches*. A brief summary of the phenomena discovered at Robinson Woods by Northeastern University researchers was related to the author in a 1995 conversation with Joseph Troiani. Information on the Mack-Reiling "confession" that appears on p. 220 was provided by articles in the May 28, 1998 editions of the *Chicago Sun-Times* and the *Chicago Tribune*, written respectively by Terry Wilson and Lorraine Forte.

Chapter X

The author is greatly indebted to Jim Stonecipher for his thorough introduction to both the history and ghostlore of Great Lakes Naval Training Center.

General information on Fort Sheridan was graciously provided by Leah Axelrod and Paul Melichar. Additional historical background and quotations are from the volume, *A View From the Tower*, by Martha E. Sorenson and Douglas A. Martz.

Chapter XI

Information on the Country House restaurant was taken from the article, "Ghostburgers: A spook oversees the cooking," which appeared in the *Chicago Tribune* on June 12, 1988. The formal investigation of the restaurant is detailed in Jim Houran's *A Night at the Country House*

Restaurant.

Colin Cordwell's description of the Lincoln Park neighborhood's 'bad karma' appears in Arthur Meyers' *Ghostly American Places.* John Cordwell's statement, as recounted on p. 228, appeared in an article on the Red Lion Pub in the volume, *The Ghostly Gazetteer.*

Additional information on Chicago's haunted clubs was provided by "Barfly's haunted bar tour," which appeared in *Barfly's* August/September 1996 edition.

♦

SELECTIVE BIBLIOGRAPHY

Addams, Jane. *Twenty Years at Hull House*. New York: New American Library, 1981.

Algren, Nelson. *Chicago: City on the Make*. Chicago: University of Chicago Press, 1987.

Anton, Ted. *Eros, Magic and the Murder of Professor Culianu*. Evanston, IL: Northwestern University Press, 1996.

Auerbach, Loyd. *ESP, Hauntings and Poltergeists: A Parapsychologist's Handbook*. New York: Warner Books, Inc., 1994.

Bettenhausen, Brad L. "Batchelors Grove Cemetery," *Where the Trails Cross*. Volume 26:1 (Fall 1995).

Bingham, Joan and Dolores Riccio. *Haunted Houses USA*. New York: Pocket Books, 1989.

_____. *More Haunted Houses*. New York: PocketBooks, 1991.

Brandon, Jim. *Weird America: A Guide to Places of Mystery in the United States*. New York: Dutton, 1978.

Brunvand, Jan Harold. *The Vanishing Hitchhiker: American Urban Legends and their Meanings*. New York: W.W. Norton & Company, 1981.

Bryan, Mary Lynn McCree and Allen F. Davis, eds. *One Hundred Years at Hull House*. Bloomington, IN: Indiana University Press, 1990.

Calvino, Italo. *Invisible Cities*. New York: Harcourt Brace Jovanovich, 1978.

Clearfield, Dylan. *Chicagoland Ghosts*. Michigan: Thunder Bay Press, 1997.

Conzen, Michael P. and Kay J. Carr, eds. *The Illinois & Michigan Canal National Heritage Corridor: A Guide to its History and Source.* DeKalb, IL: Northern Illinois University Press, 1988.

Cowan, David and John Kuenster. *To Sleep with the Angels: The Story of a Fire.* Chicago: Ivan R. Dee, 1996.

Devereaux, Paul. *The New Ley Hunter's Guide.* Somerset, England: Gothic Image Publications, 1994.

Emert, Phyllis. *The 25 Scariest Places in the World.* Los Angeles: Lowell House, 1995.

Enright, Richard T. *Capone's Chicago.* Lakeville, MN: Northstar Maschek Books, 1987.

Finucane, R.C. *Ghosts: Appearances of the Dead and Cultural Transformation.* Amherst: Prometheus Books, 1996.

Forest Preserve District of Cook County. *The Chicago Portage and Environs.* Illinois Department of Commerce and Community Affairs Bureau of Tourism, 1996.

_____. *Tinley Creek Division Picnic Areas and Trail Map.* Forest Preserve District of Cook County, (n.d.).

Goss, Michael. *The Evidence for Phantom Hitch-hikers.* (n.l.): Aquarian Press, 1987.

Greeley, Andrew. *Death & Beyond.* Chicago: Thomas Moore Press, 1976.

Guiley, Rosemary Ellen. *The Encyclopedia of Ghosts and Spirits.* New York: Facts on File, 1992.

Hauck, Dennis William. *Haunted Places: The National Directory.* New York: Penguin, 1996.

Hecht, Ben. *1001 Afternoons in Chicago.* Chicago: The University of Chicago Press, 1992.

Heise, Kenan and Mark Frazel. *Hands On Chicago*. Chicago: Bonus Books, 1987.

Heise, Kenan. *Resurrection Mary: A Ghost Story*. Evanston, IL: Chicago Historical Bookworks, 1990.

Hendrick, George and Willene, eds. *Carl Sandburg: Selected Poems*. San Diego: Harcourt Brace & Company, 1996.

Holli, Melvin G., and Peter d'A. Jones. *Ethnic Chicago: A Multicultural Portrait*. Grand Rapids: William B. Eerdmans Publishing Company, 1995.

Holmes, Torlief S. *The History of Waukegan*. Waukegan, IL: Waukegan Historical Society, 1994.

Houran, James. *A Night at the Country House Restaurant: A Scientific Inquiry into a Documented Haunting*. (Unpublished MS) 1991.

James, William. *The Will to Believe*. (n.l.): Dover, 1956.

Johnson, William H. *Chicago*. New York: Newson and Company, 1941.

Lanctot, Barbara. *A Walk Through Graceland Cemetery*. Chicago: Chicago Architecture Foundation, 1988.

Miller, Donald S. *City of the Century: The Epic of Chicago and the Making of America*. New York: Simon & Schuster, 1996.

Myers, Arthur. *Ghostly American Places*. Avenel, NJ: Wings Books, 1995.

_____. *The Ghostly Gazetteer*. Avenel, NJ: Random House, 1995.

Rhine, JAB. *New World of the Mind*. New York: William Morrow & Company, 1973.

Roberts, Nancy. *Haunted Houses*. Chester, CT: The Globe Pequot Press, 1988.

Sandburg, Carl. *Chicago Poems*. New York: Henry Holt and Company, 1916.

Sawyers, June Skinner. *Chicago Sketches*. Chicago: Loyola Press, 1995.

Sclair, Helen, ed. *Greater Chicagoland Cemeteries: Guide #3, 1994 Conference of the Association for Gravestone Studies*. Worcester, Massachusetts: Association for Gravestone Studies, 1994.

Scott, Beth and Michael Norman. *Haunted Heartland*. New York: Dorset Press, 1985.

Sorenson, Martha E. and Douglas A. Martz. A *View from the Tower: A History of Fort Sheridan, Illinois*. Highwood, IL: Colonel Wilbert W. Sorenson, Jr., United States Army, 1985.

Spencer, John, and Tony Wells. *Ghostwatching: The Ghosthunters' Handbook*. London: Virgin Books, 1994.

Steiger, Brad. *Psychic City: Chicago, Doorway to Another Dimension*. Garden City, NY: Doubleday & Company, 1976.

U.S. Department of the Interior. *Historical Map & Guide to the Illinois & Michigan Canal National Heritage Corridor*. (n.l): Canal Corridor Association, 1993.

Vliet, Elmer. *Lake Bluff: The First Hundred Years*. Lake Bluff: Elmer Vliet Historical Center, 1985.

Wendell, David. *The Civil War at Rosehill*. (n.l.): Rosehill Cemetery & Mausoleum, (n.d.).

Wilson, Colin. *Poltergeist: A Study in Destructive Haunting*. Llewellyn: St. Paul, 1993.

INDEX

A

E

F

ℋ

I

N

T

y

Z

On Your Own

SELF-TOURS FOR THE SELF-ASSURED

*H*opefully, it has been made evident that nearly every part of the Chicago region harbors a dim but distinguished host of haunts. For the would-be ghosthunter, then, plotting an afternoon or evening of investigation should not be a difficult task. Nonetheless, the wise will bear in mind a few common-sensical precautions:

Forest Preserves are just that: natural wooded areas that come complete with all the dangers of the natural environment—plus a sizeable population of undesirables that frequents them. Enjoy and explore, but go in a group and during the day, unless you're prepared to defend yourself against both seamy strangers and the notorious Forest Preserve District Police, neither of whom will welcome you warmly.

Private Houses are private homes. Drive by for a quick look at reportedly haunted properties, but never, ever ring a bell or approach a resident on their property. If they wanted an investigator, they would have called one.

Museums are for learning—but usually not about ghosts. If your ghosthunting brings you to a museum, step carefully. Pay the normal entrance fee and join the offered tour. Take photos as allowed. Show interest in the surroundings and exhibits. When your tour is finished, wait for a time when you can speak privately with your guide or with a guard, who will likely appreciate your discretion in asking about the site's alleged paranormality.

Churches do not exist for the sake of ghosthunting. Visit these sanctuaries for a service or drop in before or after for a bit of silent observation. If you wish to take photographs, ask permission of an usher or caretaker first. Likewise, rectories are private homes. Do not ring doorbells with the intention of grilling the priests or receptionist on the nuances of their local haunting.

Schools. Elementary and high schools are off-limits, due to safety laws. Colleges and universities, however, are often unsecured. Stroll the halls of the public buildings, being careful not to disturb classes or employees. Steer clear of residence halls; these too are private homes. If you are at all in doubt about whether you may access an area, play it safe: ask a security guard or administrator.

Bars & Restaurants are places of business. Patronize them. After enjoying your drinks or dinner, ask your bartender or waitperson if they've heard about the haunting of the site. Find out if you can speak to the manager or owner as well.

Cemeteries are sacred, and the managements of many are understandably chagrined by the queries of ghosthunters. In particular, the Catholic Cemeteries of Chicago are adamantly anti-ghost. If you're looking for a haunted site, don't mention the haunting. Use a proper name and ask to be directed to the lot number of the deceased. Drive carefully and walk softly. Take photographs discreetly. Never try to linger past closing time.

GROUP TOURS FOR THE LILY-LIVERED

A number of organized tours are available to those interested in the Chicago area's haunted history. Though some are held only seasonally—that is, in the weeks surrounding Halloween—some are conducted year round. As October approaches, watch local weekend sections of the newspapers for additional tours by other local investigators like Howard Heim and Norman Basile. Call for availability and reservations.

Excursions into the Unknown are conducted by Ghost Research Society president, Dale Kaczmarek, and originate in southwest suburban Oak Lawn. For information, write Mr. Kaczmarek at P.O. Box 205, Oak Lawn, IL 60454-0205; or call (708)425-5163. Or visit the GRS Web site at *www.ghostresearch.org*.

Supernatural Research Tours with Supernatural Occurrence Studies are specifically designed for small groups (2-10 people) and involve participants first-hand in research and evidence collection at a variety of classic and SOS-exclusive haunted sites around Chicagoland. Visit the the SOS Web site at *www.sos-chicago.com*.

HAUNTED?

*T*o request on investigation of an active private site—your home, office or business—or to report Chicago-area paranormal phenomena, contact:

Supernatural Occurrence Studies, a Chicago-based research team, offers haunting confirmation, consultation, and explanation through the use of standard photography and recording equipment, heightened awareness to strange energy, new-school theories and methods, historical research, and a healthy sense of skepticism.
Contact SOSChicago@msn.com
www.sos-chicago.com

The Ghost Hunters Society, based in the Chicago's northern suburbs, utilizes a state-of-the art computer system in tracking paranormal activity.
Contact Mike Komen, Poltermike@worldnet.att.net

The Ghost Research Society, based in the southwest suburbs, utilizes various methods—including psychics' assessments—in conducting investigations as part of its membership activities.
Contact Dale Kaczmarek, (708) 425-5163
DKaczmarek@ghostresearch.org
www.ghostresearch.org

If you would like to discuss a current haunting or other paranormal occurrence, or if you have a personal account of a past experience that you would like to have considered for a future edition of *Chicago Haunts*, please write the author in care of Lake Claremont Press.

Also by Ursula Bielski

More Chicago Haunts: Scenes From Myth and Memory
Graveyards of Chicago (with Matt Hucke)

Coming soon from Ursula Bielski

Creepy Chicago (children's edition)
Chicago Haunts (audiobook)
Chicago Haunts (Spanish edition)
A Gardener's Guide to Chicago

ABOUT THE AUTHOR

*U*rsula Bielski is a local historian, ghosthunter, and parapsychology enthusiast, who has been involved in numerous investigations of haunted sites in and around Chicago. She regularly speaks on the connections between the city's history and its ghostlore. Bielski holds a M.A. in history with an emphasis in cultural and intellectual U.S. history.

◆ ◆ ◆

Editor, **Bruce Clorfene**, has been an advertising account executive, attorney, writer and producer of radio humor, managing editor of a suburban weekly newspaper, and manager of a mystery bookstore. He is currently a screenwriter, freelance writer, writer and producer of newsletters, and freelance editor. He lives in Evanston, Illinois.

Cover artist, **Timothy Kocher**, is a graphic designer who lives and works in Chicago.

Publisher, **Sharon Woodhouse**, edited, typeset, designed the interior, and created the index for *Chicago Haunts*.

Lake Claremont Press staff members, **Susan McNulty**, **Brandon Zamora**, and **John Keagy**, assisted with various aspects of proofreading, typesetting, and indexing the manuscript. Additional help was provided by **Sandie Woodhouse**, **Sheryl Woodhouse-Keese**, and **Brian Keese**.

Lake Claremont Press is...

Ghosts and Graveyards

More Chicago Haunts: Scenes from Myth and Memory
Ursula Bielski
Chicago. A town with a past. A people haunted by its history in more ways than one. A "windy city" with tales to tell . . . Bielski is back with more history, more legends, and more hauntings, including the personal scary stories of Chicago Haunts readers. A new favorite!
1-893121-04-6, October 2000, softcover, 312 pages, 50 photos, $15

Graveyards of Chicago:
The People, History, Art, and Lore of Cook County Cemeteries
Matt Hucke and Ursula Bielski
Ever wonder where Al Capone is buried? How about Clarence Darrow? Muddy Waters? Harry Caray? And what really lies beneath home plate at Wrigley Field? *Graveyards of Chicago* answers these and other cryptic questions as it charts the lore and lure of Chicago's ubiquitous burial grounds. Grab a shovel and tag along as Ursula Bielski and Matt Hucke unearth the legends and legacies that mark Chicago's silent citizens.
0-9642426-4-8, November 1999, softcover, 228 pages, 168 photos, $15

Haunted Michigan: Recent Encounters with Active Spirits
Rev. Gerald S. Hunter
Within these pages you will not find ancient ghost stories or legendary accounts of spooky events of long ago. Instead, Reverend Hunter shares his investigations into modern ghost stories—active hauntings that continue to this day—and uncovers a chilling array of local spirits in his tour of the two peninsulas.
1-893121-10-0, October 2000, softcover, 207 pages, 20 photos, $12.95

More Haunted Michigan:
New Encounters with Ghosts of the Great Lakes State
Rev. Gerald S. Hunter
Rev. Hunter invited readers of *Haunted Michigan* to open their minds to the presence of the paranormal all around them. They opened their minds . . . and unlocked a grand repository of their own personal supernatural experiences. Hunter investigated these modern, active hauntings and recounts the most chilling and most unusual here for you, in further confirmation that the Great Lakes State may be one of the most haunted places in the country. *More Haunted Michigan* brings you antique ghosts

from Jackson, theatrical ghosts from Dowagiac, a growling ghost from Mackinac Island, and even a feline ghost from Otsego. There are ghosts who hang out in mirrors, a territorial creature that curses a Christmas tree farm, an angelic janitor, a talking cemetery, and a family terrorized for decades because their house sits on a portal to the spirit world. Join Hunter as he tours the state, documenting the unexplainable and exploring the presence of the paranormal in our lives.

1-893121-29-1, February 2003, softcover, 231 pages, 22 photos, $15

Regional History

Chicago's Midway Airport: The First Seventy-Five Years
Christopher Lynch

Midway was Chicago's first official airport, and for decades it was the busiest airport in the nation, and then the world. The story of Midway can be viewed as a reflection of America, encompassing heroes and villains, generosity and greed, boom and bust, progress and decline, and in the final chapter, rebirth. Lynch captures the spirit of adventure of the dawn of flight, combining narrative, essays, and oral histories to tell the engrossing tale of Midway Airport and the evolution of aviation right along with it. Christopher Lynch has spent most of his life around Midway Airport on Chicago's Southwest Side where his family ran Monarch Air Service for over six decades. His research and collection of Midway photos and memorabilia was the basis of a WTTW-Channel 11 documentary on Midway that was broadcast as part of the highly-acclaimed *Chicago Stories* series. Recommended by the *Chicago Sun-Times*.

1-893121-18-6, January 2003, softcover, 10" x 8", 201 pages, 205 historic and contemporary photos, $19.95

The Chicago River: A Natural and Unnatural History
Libby Hill

When French explorers Jolliet and Marquette used the Chicago portage on their return trip from the Mississippi River, the Chicago River was but a humble, even sluggish, stream in the right place at the right time. That's the story of the making of Chicago. This is the *other* story—the story of the making and perpetual re-making of a river by everything from geological forces to the interventions of an emerging and mighty city. Author Libby Hill brings together years of original research and the contributions of dozens of experts to tell the Chicago River's epic tale—and intimate biography—from its conception in prehistoric glaciers to the glorious rejuvenation it's undergoing today, and every exciting episode in between. Winner of an American Regional History Publishing Award: 1st Place— Midwest, 2001; winner of the 2000 Midwest Independent Publishers

Association Award: Merit Award (2nd Place) in History; nominated for the Abel Worman Award: Best New Book in Public Works History.
1-893121-02-X, August 2000, softcover, 302 pages, 78 photos, $16.95

**Near West Side Stories: Struggles For Community
in Chicago's Maxwell Street Neighborhood**
Carolyn Eastwood
An ongoing story of unequal power in Chicago. Four representatives of ethnic groups that have had a distinct territorial presence in the area—one Jewish, one Italian, one African-American, and one Mexican—reminisce fondly on life in the old neighborhood and tell of their struggles to save it and the 120-year-old Maxwell Street Market that was at its core. *Near West Side Stories* brings this saga of community strife up to date, while giving a voice to the everyday people who were routinely discounted or ignored in the big decisions that affected their world. Though "slaying that dragon"—fending off the encroachments of those wielding great power—was nearly impossible, we see in the details of their lives the love for a place that compelled Harold, Florence, Nate, and Hilda to make the quest.
1-893121-09-7, June 2002 , softcover, 368 pages, 113 photos, $17.95

Great Chicago Fires: Historic Blazes That Shaped a City
David Cowan
Acclaimed author (*To Sleep with the Angels*) and veteran firefighter David Cowan tells the story of the other "great" Chicago fires, noting the causes, consequences, and historical context of each—from the burning of Fort Dearborn in 1812 to the Iroquois Theater disaster to the Our Lady of the Angels school fire.
1-893121-07-0, July 2001, softcover, 10" x 8", 167 pages, 86 historic photos, bibliography, index, $19.95

Literary Chicago: A Book Lover's Tour of the Windy City
Greg Holden, foreword by Harry Mark Petrakis
Join Holden as he journeys through the streets, people, ideas, events, and culture of Chicagoland's historic and contemporary literary world. Includes 11 detailed walking/driving tours.
1-893121-01-1, March 2001, softcover, 332 pages, 83 photos, $15.95

Hollywood on Lake Michigan: 100 Years of Chicago and the Movies
Arnie Bernstein, foreword by *Soul Food* writer/director George Tillman, Jr.
Tours, trivia, special articles, historic and contemporary photos, film profiles, anecdotes, and exclusive interviews with dozens of personalities spotlight Chicago and Chicagoans' distinguished role in cinematic history. Winner of an American Regional History Publishing Award: 1st Place—Midwest!
0-9642426-2-1, December 1998, softcover, 364 pages, 80 photos, $15

Guidebooks by Locals

Not a cookbook, but a cook's book!

A Cook's Guide to Chicago
Marilyn Pocius

Chef and food writer Marilyn Pocius's new book takes food lovers and serious home cooks into all corners of Chicagoland in her explorations of local foodways. In addition to providing extensive information on specialty food and equipment shops (including gourmet stores, health food shops, butchers, fishmongers, produce stands, spice shops, ethnic grocers, and restaurant supplies dealers), Pocius directs readers to farmers markets, knife sharpeners, foodie clubs, cooking classes, and culinary publications. Her special emphasis on what to do with the variety of unusual ingredients found in ethnic supermarkets includes "Top 10" lists, simple recipes, and tips on using exotic ingredients. A complete index makes it easy to find what you need: frozen tropical fruit pulp, smoked goat feet, fresh durian, sanding sugar, empanada dough, live crabs, egusi seeds, mugwort flour, kishke, and over two thousand other items you didn't know you couldn't live without!

1-893121-16-X, May 2002, softcover, 288 pages, recipes and walking tours, $15

Ticket to Everywhere: The Best of *Detours* Travel Column
Dave Hoekstra, foreword by Studs Terkel

Join Dave Hoekstra on 66 of his best road trip explorations as he serves up the people, places, events, and history of the greater Midwest and Route 66 byways, dishing them out with his characteristic wit, sense of place, and keen appreciation of overlooked and offbeat America. This book takes readers through the best of Hoekstra's "Detours" column from the *Chicago Sun-Times'* Sunday travel section. A literary favorite of daytrippers, highway adventurers, and armchair travelers alike!

1-893121-11-9, November 2000, softcover, 227 pages, 70 photos, 9 maps, $15.95

A Native's Guide to Chicago, 4th Edition
Lake Claremont Press, ed. by Sharon Woodhouse

Venture into the nooks and crannies of everyday Chicago with this comprehensive budget guide to over hundreds of free, inexpensive, and unusual things to do in the Windy City. Named "Best Guidebook for Locals" in *New City*'s 1999 "Best of Chicago" issue!

1-893131-23-2, Spring 2003, softcover, 400+ pages, maps, $15.95

Order Form

Chicago Haunts _____ @ $15.00 = _____
More Chicago Haunts _____ @ $15.00 = _____
Graveyards of Chicago _____ @ $15.00 = _____
Haunted Michigan _____ @ $12.95 = _____
More Haunted Michigan _____ @ $15.00 = _____
Chicago's Midway Airport _____ @ $19.95 = _____
The Chicago River _____ @ $16.95 = _____
Great Chicago Fires _____ @ $19.95 = _____
Hollywood on Lake Michigan _____ @ $15.00 = _____
A Cook's Guide to Chicago _____ @ $15.00 = _____
_____ _____ @ $_____ = _____
_____ _____ @ $_____ = _____

Subtotal: _____
Less Discount: _____
New Subtotal: _____
8.75% Sales Tax for Illinois Residents: _____
Shipping: _____
TOTAL: _____

Name_____

Address_____

City_____**State**_____**Zip**_____

Please enclose check, money order, or credit card information.

Visa/Mastercard#_____**Exp.** _____

Signature_____

Discounts when you order multiple copies!
2 books—10% off total, 3-4 books—20% off,
5-9 books—25% off, 10+ books—40% off

—Low shipping fees—
$2.50 for the first book and $.50 for each additional book, with a maximum charge of $6.

Order by mail, phone, fax, or e-mail.
All of our books have a no-hassle, 100% money back guarantee.

4650 N. Rockwell St.
Chicago, IL 60625
773/583-7800
773/583-7877 (fax)
lcp@lakeclaremont.com
www.lakeclaremont.com

LAKE CLAREMONT PRESS